BUILDING A CULTURE *of* HOPE

ENRICHING SCHOOLS WITH OPTIMISM AND OPPORTUNITY

ROBERT D. BARR & EMILY L. GIBSON

Solution Tree | Press

a division of
Solution Tree

555 North Morton Street
Bloomington, IN 47404
800.733.6786 (toll free) / 812.336.7700
FAX: 812.336.7790

email: info@solution-tree.com
solution-tree.com

Visit **go.solution-tree.com/schoolimprovement** to download the reproducibles in this book.

Printed in the United States of America

Library of Congress Cataloging-in-Publication Data

Barr, Robert D.

  Building a culture of hope : enriching schools with optimism and opportunity / Robert D. Barr, Emily L. Gibson.

        pages cm.

  Includes bibliographical references and index.

  ISBN 978-1-936764-62-4 (perfect bound) 1. Poor children--Education--United States. 2. Problem youth--Education--United States. 3. Children with social disabilities--Education--United States. 4. Youth with social disabilities--Education--United States. 5. Self-esteem in children--United States. 6. Motivation in education--United States. 7. Achievement motivation--United States. I. Title.

  LC4802.B35 2013

  371.826942--dc23

                                    2013009524

Solution Tree

Jeffrey C. Jones, CEO
Edmund M. Ackerman, President

Solution Tree Press

President: Douglas M. Rife
Publisher: Robert D. Clouse
Editorial Director: Lesley Bolton
Managing Production Editor: Caroline Weiss
Senior Production Editor: Edward Levy
Copy Editor: Rachel Rosolina
Proofreader: Elisabeth Abrams
Text Designer: Rian Anderson
Cover Designer: Jenn Taylor

If you lose hope, somehow you lose the vitality
that keeps life moving, you lose that courage
to be, that quality that helps you go on in spite
of it all. And so today I still have a dream.

—Martin Luther King Jr.

Acknowledgments

In Boise, where I live for part of the year: thanks as always to those at Boise State University—Diana Esbensen, Kelli Burnham, and Bev Moss—for ongoing technical support. Thanks also to Scott Willison for reading and commenting on early editions of the manuscript and for introducing me to Emily Gibson.

In Newport, Oregon, my second home on the Pacific Ocean: thanks for the support and friendship to Dick Schwartz and Beth Mallory, Gus and Veronica Willemin, and Howard Shippey; and to Renae Richmond, Kate Scannell, Scott Paterson, Rick Bartow, and thanks to all the guys who play upstairs in the barn for the therapeutic music.

In schools: there are so many people who have shown me parts of the Culture of Hope in their schools and shared their stories with me, but a few demand special recognition—Karla McCarty and Misty Cox in Johnson County, Kentucky, and Rhonda Caldwell of the Kentucky School Administrators and her daughter, Amanda, who introduced me to the schools in post-Katrina New Orleans. Thanks to my Georgia "brain trust," Tammy Davis and Janet Hamilton. Special thanks to Chris Shade, Director of Federal Programs in Denton, Texas, and all of the principals in the seventeen Title I schools where I worked in 2010, especially Sam Kelley, Missey Chavez, Carlos Ramirez, and Anthony Simms. I will be ever indebted to the remarkable educators of these Title I schools and the many "Denton stories" that found their way into this book. My conscience in matters dealing with race and class in high-poverty schools is, as always, Clemmey and George Jackson of the Ames Iowa Public Schools and Iowa State University. Thanks to School Superintendent Scott Kisner of Virginia for inviting me to work in two school districts where he has provided leadership. And last of all, to Tom Hagley, who is much of the energy behind the successes in the Vancouver Washington Schools, for inviting me to be a small part of the district over the decades.

In the Oregon Department of Education: Donna Bolt, who provides such impressive leadership regarding the homeless kids of the Northwest, and Drew Hinds, who is working so hard to improve alternative school education for the kids of poverty.

Thanks to my former public school students who tracked me down more than forty years after I left Texas: Rob Johnson, Jim Benton, and of course my dear friends Ray and Betty Torres. The principal had sent Ray to my history class because he was "Mexican, couldn't speak English, and was always sleeping in class." Turned out he could speak English quite well and was a musical prodigy, playing drums in local bands until late in the night, which explained the sleeping in class. I asked the smartest kid in the room, Betty Short, to help him with his school work and keep him awake. Of course, they fell in love, got married, and kept tracking me down over the decades. Betty has had a great career in teaching, and Ray went on to music fame, playing with some of the greats, like Ike and Tina Turner. Till the day he died, I was always Mr. Barr the history teacher to Ray Torres.

Thanks to the Solution Tree team, which has been so instrumental in my professional successes: first, the CEO of the "Tree," the remarkable Jeff Jones, plus Jane St. John, Gretchen Knapp, Lesley Bolton, and Claudia Wheatley, and of course the wonderful Douglas Rife, who so loves a good story. And most of all, thanks to Ed Levy, who took our huge, rambling manuscript and did his editorial magic once again, and did it in spite of our constant additions, a family move, and even Hurricane Sandy.

Thanks as ever to my marvelous, patient wife, Beryl Barr, who has once again put up with me barricaded for a couple of years in my study, hunched over a computer, and totally lost in my work. Also, thanks to my wonderful family who live through the distractions of an author always working on the next project when he comes to visit: Brady and Mei Len Barr and their kids, Isabella and Braxton; Bonny Barr and Jerry Williams and the two grandkids, Sam and Sadie.

—Bob Barr

The words in this book bear the fingerprints of the students, colleagues, and significant people in my life. All deserve appreciation and acknowledgment. You are all here; I hope you recognize yourself in the sentences, ideas, and vision of a Culture of Hope.

To my family and friends, who visited me during the two years we spent writing this book, even when I said, "I'm working on the book, so I won't be able to do much visiting." Your company and presence in my life and my home gave me a needed boost and kept me going. Thank you to my parents, for my deep love of words and my belief that I can do anything I set my mind to. And to Dotty, for helping me to really see. My brother Stuart, and my friend Jennifer—I hope you both know how much better the world is because you are in it. Scott, thanks for giving my name to Bob when he was looking for a research assistant. You are a master at connecting the right people at the right time!

The students (and their families) that I've shared classrooms with at Morris, Burnt Ranch, Blue Heron Middle, and Anser Charter—you all contributed to my understanding that the foundation of learning and teaching is relationships.

My colleagues, most specifically Dana Silvernale (thank you for our Saturday PLC partnership), Lisa Cates (we are so on the same page, I wish we could collaborate every day), and the Studebaker Sunday Lunch PLC (we will change things for the better, for our students, one napkin at a time).

The administrators I've worked with who know the importance of building relationships, encouraging the fire in teachers, and trusting educators as professionals, most specifically Dena Magdaleno, Paul Gossard, and Suzanne Gregg.

The Redwood Writing Project, for introducing the power of teachers teaching teachers and for providing my first taste of the potential of coaching.

The teachers, staff, and students of Lower Lake: thank you for opening your classrooms and your school, trusting me to be your coach. This book is most especially for you.

Bob, thanks for taking me on as a writing partner, thanks for the give-and-take of this phenomenal collaboration, and thanks for the memorable writing retreat in Newport. You and Beryl are the rarest of treasures.

Working with Solution Tree has been a hugely positive experience. I'll never forget seeing the cover design for the first time! Ed Levy's encouragement and guidance made the revision review process smooth and delightful, and the input from the editors and reviewers was invaluable.

—Emily Gibson

Solution Tree Press would like to thank the following reviewers:

Leigh Ann Bradshaw
Principal
Oak Ridge High School
Orlando, Florida

Pamela D. Ward
School Counselor
Bertie High School
Windsor, North Carolina

Johnetta D. Wiley
Principal
South High School
Columbus, Ohio

Table of Contents

Reproducible pages are in italics.
Visit **go.solution-tree.com/schoolimprovement** to
download the reproducibles in this book.

Chapter 7
A Sense of Purpose

part three
Implementing a Culture of Hope

Chapter 8
The Power of We

Chapter 9
A Culture of Hope at the High School Level

About the Authors

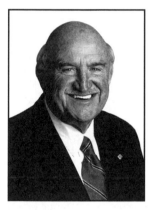

Robert D. Barr, PhD, is recognized as one of the leading experts in the United States on reaching and teaching children of poverty and minority students and helping high-poverty schools become high-performing ones. He is an educator, speaker, author, and emeritus analyst with the Boise State University Center for School Improvement. Bob has keynoted hundreds of state, regional, national, and international conferences and has provided workshops for schools, school districts, and state departments of education in every area of the United States.

Escaping poverty and realizing the American dream are a part of Bob's personal story. His grandparents were sharecroppers and migrant workers, never owning land. The overriding values of his family were hard work, thrift, and the abiding belief that if you kept at it, life would get better. When Bob was in the fifth grade, he cashed in his school banking account so the family could use the $48.00 to buy a mule. Through hard work and sacrifice, his parents saved enough to buy an acre of land, then eight acres, and finally, their dream, a 150-acre ranch in the cedar breaks and rolling hills of Glen Rose, Texas. His parents found their American dream through sacrifice and hard work; Bob found his through education.

Bob has been selected for the National School Boards Association's prestigious Meet the Expert sessions at their national conferences twelve times and has received three national awards for distinguished achievement. He has been a guest on the PBS program *Firing Line*, *ABC World News*, the Fox television show *The O'Reilly Factor*, and has been quoted in the *New York Times*, *USA TODAY*, and the *Wall Street Journal*. In addition, he has provided expert testimony to the U.S. Congress and a number of state legislatures and often serves as an expert trial witness.

Bob is the author or coauthor of over a dozen books on education and has served as professor and director of teacher education at Indiana University, dean of the Oregon State University College of Education, and dean of the Boise State University College of Education.

Emily L. Gibson, EdD, has worked in rural, high-poverty schools since she began teaching in 1992. Her research interests include educating children of poverty, equity and access to quality education, differentiated instruction, school improvement, writing instruction, and classroom and school community. A fellow of the National Writing Project, since 1997 Emily has provided regular professional development in writing instruction for K–12 teachers as a teacher-consultant with the Redwood Writing Project. In 2002, she started Blue Heron Middle School, a charter school learning center for students in grades 6–8 who were struggling to find success in more traditional middle-school settings. Emily currently serves as an instructional coach in high-poverty schools in California.

Raised primarily by a single mom with health issues, Emily grew up on welfare, Aid to Families with Dependent Children (AFDC), and Medi-Cal, yet her childhood home was filled with laughter, creativity, and a passion for learning. But school was not a place where she felt belonging, hope, or safety. Instead, she experienced bullying and the social stigma that came with being a low-income child. She made it through high school with the help of a biology teacher who called her "Dr. Gibson" and her equine friends at a stable down the road, who taught her about hard work, responsibility, and love. During her high school years, she mucked stalls, carried feed, brushed horses, cleaned tack, and rode in the Pacific coast rain. Working two jobs, she put herself through college.

Emily's doctoral work focused on parent perceptions of school improvement and school choice. She has also earned a second BA in psychology and an MA in education with an emphasis on differentiation, brain-based instruction, and parent involvement.

Emily is the co-author of "Graduate School Learning Curves: McNair Scholars' Postbaccalaureate Transitions," with Scott Willison, PhD, published in *Equity & Excellence in Education*, April 2011.

Preface

Almost everywhere, the job of teaching is getting more difficult and demanding. Visit practically any classroom in the United States, and you will find more poverty, more diversity, more languages, more special needs, and less financial support than ever before. Too often, parents seem to be either irrationally demanding or lacking the time or energy to care. In state after state, there have been major budget cuts and, in a few, the elimination of collective bargaining rights. There is also the intense and growing pressure for teachers to be more and more effective. Some of my observations in schools have filled me with despair; others tug at my heart. A few have awakened an anger that has prompted me to do more.

Around the year 2005, as I finished the field research for *The Kids Left Behind* (Barr & Parrett, 2007), I began to notice striking similarities within a group of schools I was observing. All of these successful schools were utilizing most of the strategies identified in the emerging high-poverty, high-performing schools research, but some were doing—and achieving—much, much more. This book, the culmination of almost a decade of working with schools, was born from a desire to describe the value-added efforts of these unusually effective schools and to generate from my observations a manageable concept that others might find useful. The result of these insights is the identification of an approach to school reform that I call the "Culture of Hope"—a way to more effectively teach students with the greatest needs and help them find opportunities to live better lives.

A number of experiences began to change my perspective on high-poverty, high-performing schools:

- Conversations with teachers in high-poverty, high-performing schools and with my friend Rick Stiggins helped convince me that many poverty-level students do not believe that they can learn. Poverty, especially generational poverty, seems to teach students from low-income families that they can do little to influence their environment, and this includes learning effectively.

This learned helplessness may be the most important issue of all when attempting to effectively teach many low-income and minority students.

- In so many school districts, I discovered that poverty-level students who effectively learned the basics and succeeded at the elementary and middle school levels seemed to falter and fail when they reached high school. Far too many students—over 25 percent nationally in 2011—left school prior to graduating (Balfanz, Bridgeland, Bruce, & Fox, 2012). This was true of many school districts considered to be high performing. This tragic loss represents an enormous problem, both for our schools and our society.

- Working with so many schools in a number of states over time, I discovered that educators at the local level were engaged in a new conversation. Teachers, administrators, and even school board members were talking about the growing consensus regarding effective strategies to close the achievement gap and successfully teach poverty-level students. Almost everyone agreed that, with the research now in, the challenge was to effectively *implement* the agreed-on strategies. A review of the work being done by Rick and Rebecca DuFour (DuFour, Eaker, & DuFour, 2005; DuFour, DuFour, Eaker, & Karhanek, 2010), Lawrence Lezotte and Kathleen McKee Snyder (2011), and Robert Marzano (2003), as well as my own work with Bill Parrett (Barr & Parrett, 2007) reveals a research consensus on instructional effectiveness and closing the achievement gap. Yet what I increasingly heard about from teachers and administrators was a lack of direction and support for the social and emotional growth of students from low-income families. Schools that were highly successful in closing the achievement gap and successfully teaching the children of poverty were struggling to find ways to build student pride, reduce the cultural clash that so often occurs when low-income students and families encounter middle-class schools, and help students find a sense of belonging in school. So many high schools were searching for ways to help students find purpose in their lives and find a pathway out of poverty.

All of these discussions seem to grow out of a slow but intense concern about No Child Left Behind's (NCLB) emphasis on assessment. More and more leaders at school and community levels have recognized that students living in poverty need far more than basic skills and good test scores to make it in today's world. A growing number of school educators are urgently looking for direction on these issues and are engaging in what I consider to be bold efforts to try to address their students' social and emotional needs.

In exploring these issues, this book also provides something that rarely gets into print—glimpses into the thoughts of teachers and administrators, and occasionally those of students and their parents. These appear in the form of brief "author journal" entries—dispatches from the front, you might call them. They are notes about the incredible, day-to-day creativity of people who are teaching and learning in the front lines of public education. They also represent my own experiences and thoughts (signed "B.B." throughout the book) and those of my coauthor, Emily Gibson ("E.G."). These dispatches are limited to schools and districts where we have worked, spoken, conducted evaluations or audits, helped to plan improvement strategies, conducted research, or carried out observations. Our journal entries cover high-poverty, high-performing school districts, as well as a number of low-performing and even failing school districts, including one of Kentucky's lowest performing districts. Perhaps most important was an opportunity to work for about twenty days with Title I elementary and middle schools in Denton, Texas, during the 2011–2012 school year. While all of the notes are from real schools, classrooms, and communities, in many cases, to preserve privacy, we have omitted names and places. My hope is that these dispatches build a bit of admiration for our frontline educators and help other teachers, administrators, specialists, and board members envision exciting and effective ways to help their students. I love the bumper sticker that reads, "The Future of America Is in School Today." I believe this is true, and it serves to remind us of the critical nature of the work of education.

Looking back over the notes and experiences collected from over a decade of work, I am always struck by the energy and creativity that teachers and administrators bring to their work in high-poverty schools—surely the most demanding jobs in public education. I am always impressed with their deep and intense commitment, hard, hard work, and dedication. I have seen this dedication in the dozens of teachers I know who pursued National Board status; in a young language arts teacher in Boise who is now teaching more than 160 middle school students each day, thanks to budget cuts; in the struggling, poor, beat-up schools of the back roads of America. I have seen it in Bastrop, Louisiana; Martinsville, Virginia; Mobile, Alabama; Northern Florida; Troup County, Georgia; and Oregon and Idaho's small rural schools.

I am also struck by the tragic, depressed atmosphere in failing schools, especially where teachers and staff seem to have given up on their students.

Reviewing my notes from dozens of schools across the United States at all levels, in urban, suburban, and rural areas, I realized that I had been describing the nature of the Culture of Hope. While these characteristics can be difficult to identify during brief school visits, the cumulative data from my ongoing work caused the features of this concept to emerge dramatically and powerfully.

During 2011, I had the good opportunity to meet and work with Emily Gibson, who was just completing her doctoral studies at Boise State University. Emily has had a rich variety of experiences in public education in California. She has taught at both the elementary and secondary levels, worked as a professional development provider for the Redwood Writing Project, and for six years directed a small middle school charter site in Northern California. While sharing with me some of the background research she had done for her doctoral studies, I was surprised to discover that some of her work focused on the relationship between the concept of hope and education. Emily introduced me to the work of a number of scholars who have discussed in great detail the connection between hope and the academic success of low-income elementary students. This proved to be a remarkable discussion, for it connected what I was learning in schools with new education literature I had yet to encounter.

While I was beginning to identify how schools were using a Culture of Hope as a powerful influence in teaching and learning, Emily was in her classroom and beginning graduate studies exploring the world of research and educational literature. While I was somewhere in a school cafeteria interviewing teachers in some back-roads community, Emily was on her laptop, searching for pertinent research. Though we hadn't yet met, we were on the same page, approaching the same issue from two different perspectives.

This book represents our efforts to bring these two perspectives together. For me, it has been an unusually delightful experience. After more than thirty years studying low-income and minority students and authoring or coauthoring more than a dozen books, and after a professional lifetime consulting in high-poverty schools, I believe that the Culture of Hope represents an essential and largely overlooked component of the research. This partnership between a retired university scholar and a young doctoral graduate has pushed both of us to renew our efforts to document and describe what we consider an important development in effective education for students living in poverty.

—Bob Barr, Newport, Oregon, 2012

Introduction

*In our schools, we have done everything in our power to confront the single great-
est challenge that confronts our poor and minority students: their sense of futility
and helplessness. In the midst of so many family difficulties and negative outlooks,
we are not just focused on teaching and teaching well, we are also cultivating hope.
Come see our schools. We think we have developed a curriculum of hope. We think
we have a Culture of Hope.*

—Karla McCarty and Misty Cox, Johnson County, Kentucky

This book is about schools that are cultivating hope one student at a time, replacing
helplessness with hopefulness. It is about hope for some of public education's most
vulnerable and challenging students: the children of poverty.

It is also about building what we call a Culture of Hope in schools, based on a distinctly different instructional approach being used by a growing number of schools,
an approach that emphasizes social and emotional growth to help children of poverty
succeed in the classroom and ultimately find a pathway to a better life.

This Culture of Hope appears to truly be a grassroots movement, evolving simultaneously in a variety of rural, suburban, and urban school districts. Although a
few federally funded programs, known as the TRIO Programs (U.S. Department
of Education, 2008), provide support for students from low-income families to
successfully transition from middle to high school and then college and both the
Association for Supervision and Curriculum Development's (ASCD) Commission
on the Whole Child (2007) and the National Urban League (2011) have recommendations that emphasize some aspects of the Culture of Hope, no federal policy,
national program, major professional development effort, or published book has yet
championed this approach.

Similarly, while a number of important research reports and scholarly papers in the fields of psychology, educational psychology, and neuroscience have explored the concept of hope and its implication for schools (Commission on the Whole Child, 2007; EdVisions, 2010; Jensen, 2009; Maslow & Lowry, 1973; Newell & Van Ryzin, 2009), for the teachers and administrators experimenting with this model, it is simply a commonsense response to the daily problems and challenges in their schools and classrooms. It may represent some of the best work being done in public education—yet it could be argued that, at least in part, it is what good schools have *always* done.

Over much of the first decade of the 21st century, observations and discussions in high-poverty schools in more than twenty states indicated that high-performing schools went far beyond academic success as measured by achievement tests, and provided a "value-added" education that focused on students' social and emotional growth. In other schools, there was something missing: even though teachers seemed to be applying the standard protocol of effective schools, their students remained disengaged from learning. Interviews with teachers and students revealed that many students from low-income families did not believe they *could* learn; for others, especially those who experience a clash of cultures with the public school, it seemed to be a point of honor to *not* exert effort for some middle-class teacher. These students simply chose not to learn. Even more dramatic was the discovery of the low expectations in failing schools, where no one, it seemed, not teachers, students, or even parents, truly believed the students could be successful. This was particularly evident in low-achieving high schools.

Value-Added Schools

When the authors questioned educators from different districts in different states about the observed value-added strategies (focusing on what educators had traditionally called whole-child education), it became evident that these widely separated schools were wrestling with similar questions:

- How can schools help students overcome the debilitating learned helplessness and hopelessness that so often accompany poverty, especially generational poverty?
- How can schools soften the cultural conflicts that so often characterize the encounters of poor families and their children with middle-class schools?
- How can schools help students reflect on their social and economic situations and develop reasonable long-term goals?
- What can schools do to develop poverty-level students' pride and personal efficacy?

- How can educators help poverty-level students and their families feel a sense of belonging to the students' school?

At the high school level, discussions often focused on these questions:

- In addition to effectively teaching the basics, how can schools provide organization and support that will help students develop talents and interests, succeed in school, graduate, and find success beyond high school?
- Why are so many students who achieved effectively at the elementary and middle school levels struggling, failing, and dropping out of high school?
- How can schools better integrate the world of jobs, careers, and professions into the academic curriculum to make school more relevant?

A central question in nearly all of these conversations is whether schools have a role in helping students find a pathway out of poverty. If so, what is that role?

Culture of Hope Schools

Visiting schools that embrace a Culture of Hope is an energizing experience. Like all public schools, they have difficult problems and challenges, but they seem to approach those challenges from an optimistic, positive perspective. Such schools have an atmosphere of excitement; a can-do spirit is everywhere. High expectations and optimism seem to permeate the building. A powerful expectation of academic success and personal encouragement permeates the building, and visitors feel a welcoming spirit and enthusiasm about teaching and learning. Mutual respect among teachers, students, and parents is evident; the school feels safe and orderly. Charts showing assessment data are displayed in every classroom, as well as in the hallways.

Everyone seems to feel fortunate to be part of such a school. Students exhibit personal pride in their accomplishments and want to talk about and share their successes. They are excited about learning and reflect personal confidence. In high school, they think and talk about the future. Teachers, too, are enthusiastic and involved in ongoing collaboration. The school in turn collaborates with parents to help their children find the way to a better life.

On paper, these descriptors seem embarrassingly Pollyannaish, if not downright corny, like some idealistic writer's view of what public education would be in a perfect world. They seem especially off the mark during, at this writing, a spate of teacher layoffs and budget cuts. Yet, remarkably, these descriptors accurately depict real life across the United States—in high-poverty, high-unemployment Appalachian school districts or at urban or inner-city Title I elementary and middle schools; in the KIPP Academy and Harlem Children's Zone sites, as well as at schools aligned with the Coalition of Essential Schools (2006). All these schools are achieving the essential academic goals of any other high-performing public school, but they are also accomplishing much more: they are building students' personal pride and sense of belonging. These students stay in school, graduate, and find a purpose and plan for their own lives.

Structure of This Book

This book consists of ten chapters divided into three parts. Part One, "An Apartheid of Ignorance," comprising the first three chapters, describes the problem and introduces the solution. Chapter 1, "Poverty Is No Excuse," reviews how changes in the world outside of school affect the lives of students and the schools that serve them. Chapter 2, "The Tragedy of High School Dropouts," illuminates the failure of our public school system, culminating in the dropout crisis. Chapter 3, "A Culture of Hope" introduces the key elements found in Culture of Hope schools and reviews the foundational research.

Part Two, "The Four Seeds of Hope," consists of chapter 4, "A Sense of Optimism"; chapter 5, "A Sense of Belonging"; chapter 6, "A Sense of Pride, Self-Esteem, and Self-Confidence"; and chapter 7, "A Sense of Purpose." Together, these seeds of hope lay the foundation for the transformation of schools as experienced by children coming from high-poverty environments.

Part Three, "Implementing a Culture of Hope," consists of the final three chapters. Chapter 8, "The Power of We," provides a template schools can follow to begin or expand upon a schoolwide Culture of Hope. Chapter 9, "A Culture of Hope at the High School Level," reviews fundamental changes that contribute to success, continued enrollment, and graduation for students from low-income families. And chapter 10, "Hope Fulfilled," outlines a series of academic and social benchmarks that students must meet during childhood and adolescence to set them—and keep them—on course for postsecondary success.

Reproducible surveys found at the end of several chapters may also be found online (at **go.solution-tree.com/schoolimprovement**). The two appendices contain supplemental information about the *Newsweek* and *U.S. News & World Report* surveys, and links to a number of other resources mentioned in the book. Finally, a glossary defines some of the terms and concepts we have employed.

part one

AN APARTHEID
of
IGNORANCE

Chapter 1

Poverty Is No Excuse

How important is education? I will tell you how important it is. For my children, it is the only hope they got. I am telling you it is their only hope. I don't know about your kids, but for my kids, education is a matter of life and death.

—Low-income parent, Denton, Texas

People in the United States who were healthy and willing to work were once able to find good jobs with excellent incomes and benefits. Even without a high school education, they could find jobs to build a life for themselves and their families. They earned enough to buy a home with an FHA loan and own their own car, and maybe even buy a boat or camper. They could afford to send their children to college. Unions in the United States were strong, and they were able to demand good wages and benefits for their members. Even in right-to-work states, there seemed to be ample work and a world of opportunities. Unfortunately, that world is disappearing at a rapid rate, with an ever-growing separation of wealth between the upper 10 and the bottom 25 percent, between the "haves" and the "have-nots," between the very rich and the "other America" of poverty (Domhoff, 2011). In fact, the top 1 percent of households in the United States own 38.3 percent of all privately held stock, 60.6 percent of financial securities, and 62 percent of business stock. The top 10 percent own 80 to 90 percent of stocks, bonds, trust funds, and business equity, and over 75 percent of all non-home real estate (Domhoff, 2011).

Freedom and Justice for Some

This separation between rich and poor is seen in the crumbling inner cities and gated communities of suburbia, the back roads of rural poverty, and the sleek shopping boutiques of the affluent. Today, those with upper incomes seem to grow wealthier, as the number of people living in poverty continues to increase. After poverty rates had dropped to 11.3 percent in 2000, the "U.S. poverty rate grew to 15.1 percent in 2010" (Fletcher, 2011, p. 6). This means that currently one in six Americans is living in poverty. For minorities, the situation is even worse: "The [poverty] rate for black children climbed to nearly 40 percent and more than a third of Hispanic children lived in poverty" (Fletcher, 2011, p. 6). The economic recession that started in 2007 and sent out ripple effects that continued into 2012 has only served to exacerbate the problems of the poor, with more than a million new children falling into poverty between 2009 and 2010 (University of New Hampshire, 2011).

The National Urban League points out that only one in five blacks over twenty-five years of age has a bachelor's degree, compared to one in three whites. No wonder the league maintains that "education is the civil rights issue of our time" (National Urban League, 2011). While the term *apartheid* specifically denotes formal policies of racial segregation once practiced in South Africa, it is increasingly being used to describe segregation in schools (see Barr & Parrett, 1995; Kozol, 2005a, 2005b; Orfield, Kucsera, & Siegel-Hawley, 2012; Street, 2005). Segregation along race, ethnicity, spoken language, and socioeconomic status has been exacerbated by the end of formal desegregation policies (Orfield, Kucsera, & Siegel-Hawley, 2012). However, the term *apartheid* has also been used to describe broad social and economic divisions in American society based in part on the lack of high-quality education—an apartheid of ignorance (Barr & Parrett, 1995). Education is no longer just important; in the technological world of today it has become an essential prerequisite to economic success. Increasingly, education has become the only door of opportunity to the good life in the United States, if not the world.

Education as a Civil Right

Education divides the world in a most extraordinary way. It is the borderline between the haves and the have-nots. As a result, a high-quality education has emerged as a civil right that must be guaranteed for all children. John Jackson, of the Schott Foundation, has called the right to learn "an inalienable human right" (2011). In the classrooms of our nation's schools, students will struggle over various pathways to the future—pathways either to poverty or greater prosperity. The civil rights battles of the past have moved out of the bus stations and lunch counters, streets and neighborhoods; the battleground has moved into our schools.

Job opportunities with a decent wage and benefits have all but disappeared for those without specialized education or training. Technology, the movement of manufacturing outside the United States, and international competition have eliminated millions of jobs: the jobs of secretaries, bank tellers, retail clerks, postal workers, bookstore workers, autoworkers and mechanics, steelworkers, lumberjacks, telephone operators, film developers, airline support personnel, stockbrokers, and with the growing use of virtual courses and programs, even teachers. Computers, the Internet, ATMs, online banking and reservations, and marketing have transformed the world of work—especially for the uneducated.

Perhaps one of the most dramatic examples of the changes wrought by technology can be found in the United States military, which has been transformed into a high-tech, cutting-edge organization. The military now uses everything from unmanned drone aircraft to robotic "soldiers," from heat-seeking imagery to instant worldwide communication. Once a reliable pathway out of poverty for poor and minority students, the military no longer considers high school dropouts as recruits, and some branches will not even consider those with general equivalency degrees (GEDs) (Powers, n.d.). Rather than being an available career path for dropouts and marginally educated youth, the military seeks the best and brightest of our high school graduates. In this regard, it is no different than private sector employers.

Increasingly, good jobs demand a minimum of an associate degree or participation in specialized certificate or vocational training programs. According to Daniel Hecker (2005), 80 percent of the thirty fastest growing jobs will require education beyond a high school diploma, and 36 percent of new jobs will require a bachelor's degree. Check out any current classified job listings, and Hecker's predictions from 2005 can be found to be remarkably accurate: very few jobs are available for those with only a high school diploma. In order to find good jobs that include living wages and benefits, most high school graduates must continue with their education.

New York Times columnist Thomas Friedman (2012) claims that "average" is over: "In the past, workers with average skills, doing an average job, could earn an average lifestyle. But that possibility no longer exists. Being average just won't earn you what it used to" (p. A29). The reason, Friedman says, is that today there is so much more "above average cheap foreign labor, cheap robotics, cheap software, cheap automation and cheap genius" (p. A29). To find a good job, even to maintain an average lifestyle, demands something that makes a worker above average—and that something, he maintains, is education. He cites the unemployment rates for Americans over twenty-five years old:

- Less than a high school diploma, 13.8 percent
- With a high school diploma but no college, 8.7 percent
- With some college or associate degree, 7.7 percent
- With a college degree or higher, 4.1 percent

The message is loud and clear: education beyond high school has become an essential requirement for the good life in the United States. While education has always been a door of opportunity in our country, technological changes in the world have increasingly made it the *only* door of opportunity—and the ticket for the good life in the United States, if not the world. It confers economic rewards that those without education can only dream of obtaining.

Journal

A few years ago, while keynoting the national conference of a group that focuses on the education of the homeless, I had the good fortune to be seated by a very engaging and well-informed woman. It took me a few minutes to figure out that she was the first lady of Arkansas, Janet Huckabee, wife of then-governor Mike Huckabee. While waiting for the session to start, she explained to me that the organization hosting the conference had asked her if she would be willing to familiarize herself with the homeless issue and say a few words to the conference participants.

As a response to this invitation, she arranged to spend the night under the city bridge in downtown Little Rock with the large number of homeless who made that location their home. Mrs. Huckabee refused to have a police escort, because she knew it would frighten and intimidate the homeless. She went down by herself, introduced herself to the people living there, and asked if she could spend the night with them and ask them a few questions. They offered her some coffee, and they settled down for a long and provocative conversation. While she said she never really slept much, she learned more about homelessness, more about Arkansas . . . in fact more about America than she had learned in her entire life. She came away with new and important insights into the relationship between poverty and economic opportunity. She came away convinced that the only hope for addressing the needs of poverty was a high-quality public education.

Before she stood up to make her presentation to the group, she turned to me and said, "You know, spending an evening with a group of the homeless would be a really good way for everyone to learn a little bit more about their community. It probably would be a good idea for all the experts on homelessness in America." She welcomed me to Arkansas, and said she hoped I had a real good stay in her state.

That afternoon, I left the Peabody hotel and took my daily jog. I ended my exercise and walked up under the bridge in downtown Little Rock to ask the homeless gathered there around a fire if any of them had ever met the Arkansas governor's wife.

There was a round of laughter, and one man said, "Sure. Come on over. Would you like some coffee?"

We talked deep into the night. Three women with five kids were bundled up near the fire. The kids, ages three to six, were working and coloring in notebooks.

> One of the women told me, "Our life is hard, and we live without much hope,
> but we couldn't make it without all of the help from the schools and the agen-
> cies. Somehow, our kids are going to get a good education and not end up like
> us. I guess education is our only hope." —B.B.

Unfortunately, millions of American youth have not gotten this message. For, as
we shall see in chapter 2, the dropout problem has reached staggering proportions
in the United States.

As a result of these social transformations, millions of Americans have become
unemployed, underemployed, or unemployable, and the percentage of citizens
living in poverty has escalated in the most dramatic manner (University of New
Hampshire, 2011).

Journal

The headline of the newspaper the day I arrived for a state conference in
Tucson, Arizona, warned "Gutter Punks Take Over Downtown." The gutter
punks were homeless teenagers. When my host asked me what I wanted to do
while in town, I replied that I would like to interview some of the homeless teenagers. Even though my host was not really excited about the idea, he drove me
down. It didn't take long to find us a "gutter punk." He was fourteen years old,
and he had a brother who was twelve. He said their mother went for cigarettes
one night and never came home. After they were evicted from their apartment,
they lived on the streets. They had been homeless for three years.

"How on earth are you able to survive?" I asked.

The young man said they could not have survived had it not been for their school,
which fed them every day and even gave them warm clothes in the winter. They
took a shower each day at the school.

He concluded by saying, "Our school is our lifeline. It is really all that we have. I
don't know what we would do without the school. We work hard to keep our
grades up, and with the school's help, we are going to make it." —B.B.

Some worry that focusing on the problems and needs of poverty-level students
encourages schools to have low expectations for learning or provides excuses for
their failure to teach all students effectively. But without a careful understanding
of these issues, schools will not be able to design the programs and strategies that
address them (Rothstein, 2008). In fact, Richard Rothstein and others argue that
school-based responses are not enough; schools must help poor families access the
supportive services available in their community. That is because the conditions in
poverty-level homes can cause children to arrive at school unprepared to learn (Barr

& Parrett, 2007; Rothstein, 2008). Low-income families may not have health insurance, and children may have medical checkups less frequently. Illness, poor nutrition, and a lack of dental and vision health can interfere with school attendance and learning. Moreover, children who grow up in poverty often have few or no adult role models with professional careers or successful experiences with education. Instead, the adults in their families typically have low-paying jobs and experience frequent layoffs. Because of these uncertainties, families living in poverty may be extremely mobile and suffer more stress than middle-class families (Moore & Vandivere, 2000). High mobility can result in a lack of continuity in learning and the associated need for extensive remediation and re-teaching (Jensen, 2009).

Journal

The school's Healthy Start coordinator had been trying to get Ronald glasses. For a variety of reasons, including family mobility, incarceration of Ronald's significant adults, and high absenteeism, it had taken almost two years. But the day Ronald came to school with his new glasses, he beamed. He thought he'd been given the ticket to reading. I overheard him say to his reading tutor, "Watch this. I can read now!" This was not a child who had to be reminded to wear his glasses. Without the concerted efforts of Healthy Start, classroom teachers, and his reading tutor, it wouldn't have happened. Not because the adults in Ronald's life didn't care about him, but because they simply couldn't muster the resources. —E.G.

Students living in poverty may come from homes that have cell phones, televisions, and electronic games, but they are less likely to have computers with an Internet connection. Children who live in homes with household incomes under $50,000 are less likely to have access to computers (68 percent) or handheld devices (11 percent) than children who live in homes with incomes over $50,000 (92–97 percent for computers, and 25–50 percent for handheld devices) (U.S. Census, 2010). A significant "digital divide," or "digital differentiation" related to income, exists between those who consume information on the Internet and those who create information (Modarres, 2011). There are still families in the United States who are outside the digital network:

> In 2003 (the most recent data available), children's access to computers at home and their home Internet use rose with household income. At that time, 43 percent of children in households with incomes of less than $15,000 had access to a computer at home, compared with 96 percent of children in households with incomes of over $75,000. Children's Internet use at home followed a similar pattern, ranging from 17 to 63 percent. (Child Trends, 2012)

See chapter 5 for more discussion of technology and social networking.

Low-income children are read to with less frequency and are exposed to less complex language and vocabulary (Rothstein, 2008); they have few books and little print material; some may not even have pencil and paper in their homes. As a result, many enter school with more limited vocabularies and are not "reading ready."

In response, many effective schools have supplemented their extensive instructional improvements by becoming "full-service schools" that offer families one-stop coordination of essential community supports and services (Comer, Joyner, & Ben-Avie, 2004; Dryfoos, 2010; Jensen, 2009).

Journal

This morning, I noticed in the news that there were 1.6 million children in the United States who were homeless in 2010 (Bassuk, Murphy, Coupe, Kenney, & Beach, 2010). I went back to make sure I read correctly—that this was the number of homeless children, not an overall number of homeless people. That means that one in every forty-five children in our country is homeless—not just living in poverty, but homeless. The report indicated that this was a 38 percent increase since the U.S. recession started in 2007. That number, 1.6 million, is almost the same as the entire population of Idaho. And even in Idaho and Oregon, the two states where I now reside, the numbers of homeless children are equally remarkable: Idaho has 7,500 homeless children, Oregon more than 10,000. What a monster problem this presents for schools and teachers. What I am so impressed by, and so optimistic about, are the school districts I have visited that have determined to keep the children of poverty learning effectively and staying in school until they graduate. They are determined to help these youth find a pathway out of homelessness . . . a pathway out of poverty. —B.B.

Learned Helplessness

Most debilitating of all is the attitude of helplessness and despair of many who live in poverty (Beaumont, 2009; Jensen, 2009; Rothstein, 2008; Rotter, 1975). They may believe they have little power to change their lives and futures. Some researchers describe this as learned helplessness, an attitude that can cause one to assume one's life is completely subject to an external locus of control (Beaumont, 2009; Jensen, 2009; Rotter, 1975). The theory of learned helplessness provides an intriguing explanation for so many of the difficulties teachers face when working with poverty-level students: lack of motivation and effort, inattentiveness, failure on standardized tests, absenteeism, and even some classroom disruptions (Ingrum, 2006).

Rather than personal efficacy, children of poverty feel their lives and destinies are controlled by luck, chance, or other powerful external influences and that personal effort is futile (Conrath, 2001). According to Eric Jensen (2009), "Many kids with learned helplessness become fatalistic about their lives, and they are more likely to drop out of school or become pregnant while in their teens" (p. 113). The other danger associated with learned helplessness and external locus of control is that, through working with students from low-income families over time, teachers may come to accept or expect this type of defeatist behavior (Rotter, 1975). When teachers believe that students have deficits, students perform more poorly (Jensen, 2009). In one study, 49 percent of teachers surveyed thought higher-order thinking was inappropriate for poor and low-achieving students (Zohar, Degani, & Vaaknin, 2001). Learned helplessness thus seems to be self-fulfilling for students from low-income families; too many teachers "expect less, get less" (Jensen, 2009, p. 13), and the cycle continues. The teachers themselves fall into feelings of helplessness, which can, over time, sink an entire school into despair.

Journal

I'd watched Jessica react numerous times in class. When presented with something she viewed as new or difficult, she would reject it loudly: "This is stupid. Why do we have to do this? I don't care." Or she might start shouting out and being difficult, and reacting explosively when corrected by her teacher, which eventually would get her removed from the class. When I looked at Jessica, I didn't see a behavior problem. I saw a child who was so used to being wrong, so used to being stupid, that she was protecting her dignity and self-worth in the only way she knew how. One day I saw her in detention and invited her to my room to work and talk. We talked about different kinds of learners, and how kids who were really good at sports and at doing things with their hands often struggled in school. Jessica said she'd had one teacher in fourth grade who made learning fun and made it make sense. That teacher had given her hope, but two years later she was ready to give up again. She shared how overwhelmed she was by spelling and by how fast her teacher read the words for the test. So we made plans for her to come to my room to take the weekly spelling test. The first test we worked on together, she got four out of twenty words correct. But on twelve of the words missed, she was only off by one letter, and they were all vowels. Jessica delighted in writing all the missed words correctly and had this hint of positive energy. We planned to work together every Monday for fifteen minutes to go over the lists and break them into syllables and discuss the vowels. I found that this girl who was so resistant and defensive really wanted to learn, she just needed to know that she could. She needed help to change her learned helplessness into learned hopefulness. My personal goal was to not just help this student learn reading and spelling, it was to help her experience hope in her life and to know that she could realize her dreams. I work on this every day in every way I can, with every student I see. —E.G.

Boredom, Apathy, and Cultural Anger

The learned helplessness of far too many poor and minority students tends to show up in classrooms as a lack of motivation, particularly at the high school level. Even though many students from low-income families are arriving at high school better prepared than ever (Education Trust, 2005, 2009), they often become disconnected and bored with their studies in secondary school. Robert Samuelson (2010), a columnist who writes about economics for *TIME* magazine, asked what difference it makes when students make great gains earlier in their schooling if those gains are erased by their high school experiences. And while Samuelson (2010) reviews the common explanations for this reality—"too few effective teachers, no transformative changes in curriculum and pedagogy—his conclusion is that the larger cause of failure [at the high school level] is almost unmentionable: shrunken student motivation." This sounds surprisingly like what one hears from teachers and administrators almost everywhere.

For some teenagers, the content of the traditional comprehensive high school curriculum is so far removed from the everyday circumstances of their lives that their personal motivation simply dries up and disappears. Although students may have understood the importance of reading and math in the lower grades, many simply give up when faced with the realities of high school English, history, science, and advanced mathematics. As Daniel Pink (2009) suggests, the old external rewards of good grades and academic awards are no longer sufficient. What is needed instead is the inner motivation that comes from autonomy, mastery, and purpose—characteristics too often missing from the curriculum.

For many students from low-income families, it may even be a point of honor, driven by cultural anger, not to learn. These students have no other way of legitimately protesting schooling that does not work for them (Kohl, 1994). Minority and low-income students may choose not to meet the expectations of white middle-class teachers; to do so risks separating them from their friends and is seen as disloyalty, if not outright betrayal. Thus, it is essential that teachers overcome their own racial and class prejudices and work to help students understand the connection between learning and their futures. Cultural conflicts between teachers and students represent a major obstacle to effective teaching and learning. While this issue has rarely shown up in research, it is often evident in urban classrooms (Delpit, 1995; Kohl, 1994; Jensen, 2009).

The clash of cultures, learned helplessness, disengagement, and lack of motivation all lead to what researchers describe as *lost talent*: these are students who could, in fact, succeed in school, graduate, and be effective in postsecondary education (Snyder et al., 2002), but instead fail and drop out, attempting to enter the job market at a great disadvantage. This lost talent is due less to intelligence or ability than it is to social and emotional issues and to the lack of such essential motivational supports as self-esteem, attitudes of optimism, and goal orientation (Snyder et al., 2002).

Journal

An alternative high school teacher in Georgia told me, "If students do well on a test, they do not see that it was a result of their work. They will say the test was easy or they were lucky. If they do poorly, they will say the test was not fair or the teacher sucks. If they did not do their homework, it was their baby sister's fault or their parents' fault. They just don't get it. They don't understand that if they do their homework and study for tests they will excel. We have to take them one step at a time, helping them achieve success again and again with small lessons, constantly showing them that they can do the work, constantly pointing out the relationship between their work and their success, constantly telling them, 'You can do this!'" —B.B.

If the children of poverty are to learn effectively and keep working hard for a better future, teachers must not surrender to student helplessness, apathy, anger, or lack of motivation. Putting it bluntly, Herbert Kohl (1994) states, "I have never known a child, no matter how superficially unmotivated she or he might seem, whose indifference, hopelessness, or rage did not mask a lively imagination and dreams of challenging work, lasting love, and fullness of being" (p. 73).

Autonomy and Resilience

Studies show that teachers may be able to override learned helplessness through careful instruction and high expectations. In the first research on resilient students, Bonnie Benard (1996) found that successful students from low-income families had an attitude of "autonomy" rather than dependence. Resilient students from low-income families had an ability to "act independently and to exert some control over [their] . . . environment" as well as a "sense of task mastery, internal locus of control, self-agency, and self-efficacy" (Benard, 1996, p. 99). Students from low-income families need this type of internal personal strength to resist the negative messages about themselves and their culture that are so often instilled by low-performing and failing schools—schools where teachers may have low expectations for student achievement and behavior, and high expectations for student failure, a combination that can inadvertently teach students that they cannot learn (Benard, 1996).

Joel Brown, Marianne D'Emidio-Caston, and Bonnie Benard (2001), along with many educators in high-poverty, high-performing schools, believe that resiliency skills can be taught, and data from a decade of research seem to support that conclusion

(Jensen, 2009). But teaching them is a complex and demanding task, one that is made even more difficult by the interplay of diverse cultures in a classroom setting (Payne, 2003).

Teachers' sensitivity to cultural differences, language issues, and behavioral expectations can help students find a sense of belonging, safety, and respect that is a prerequisite to effective learning (see chapter 4, page 48). Helping poverty-level students come to believe that they can learn effectively, that they belong in school, and that they will succeed is one of the greatest challenges facing schools. Feeling a personal connection with teachers and other staff members is essential for fostering these beliefs.

Journal

An alternative school teacher, in Portland, Oregon, said, "Our students just drive us crazy. They seem to believe that they have little or no influence over their own lives. If you talk to them, you come to learn that the only hope that they seem to have is to get lucky. They talk about winning the lottery or being picked for a reality show. One student told me his family won a million-dollar prize. When I questioned him, I learned it was one of those Publisher's Clearing House sweepstakes junk-mail advertisements. He told me his father had already quit his job and they planned to now buy a new doublewide trailer. Just crazy. Our teenage girls talk about some guy with money coming along and sweeping them off their feet and then living happily ever after. I have a photo in my office that just breaks my heart. It is of the wedding of one of my female students. She and her bridesmaids are all wearing dresses that they bought from secondhand stores and they look so elegant, in spite of the fact that the bride is seven months' pregnant. But the guys, they have on jeans and T-shirts and sneakers, all untied, looking like they just crawled out from under their cars. Our young women watch TV constantly; they often have romantic ideas associated with becoming pregnant and being loved and cared for. But too often the guy disappears. Our young women are preyed upon by older teenage boys, men over twenty-one years of age, and even their mothers' boyfriends. Unless our school is very successful in keeping these young women in school in a supervised environment, our experience has been that they will have another baby by the time they are twenty-one and will live out their lives in poverty. Our young men talk about 'getting lucky' with a girl; they talk about maybe winning the lottery or being picked to play NBA basketball by a recruiter. And while young men and women of poverty may have different perceptions of their roles in society, both share this tragic belief that they are all but helpless to do much of anything to improve their lives. They wait for some external force to make things better, but usually just the opposite happens. The primary hope of my students is to be lucky." —B.B.

Conclusion

The good news is that there *are* schools scattered around the United States where students are being engaged and learning effectively.

Elementary and middle schools have demonstrated that poverty-level students can be taught effectively and that the achievement gap between poor and affluent students can be closed or at least significantly reduced by building what has come to be called a Culture of Hope. But while many elementary and some middle schools have made great improvements in their effectiveness with students who are growing up in poverty, high schools stand in stark contrast. High schools in the United States have not closed the achievement gap for lower socioeconomic groups; in fact, the gap is larger today than since 1970 (Reardon, 2011). Thus, even those students who have had successful educational experiences prior to secondary school too often stumble, falter, and begin to fail in high school; ultimately, large numbers simply drop out and fail to graduate. This represents a problem of staggering proportions and contributes to almost all of the United States' most pressing social and economic problems. The next chapter describes the difficulties and frustrations of the search for effective education for all students at the high school level.

Chapter 2

The Tragedy of High School Dropouts

The sad fact is that so many high school teachers simply do not feel any responsibility for the huge number of struggling students who slowly disappear during the ninth and tenth grades. Often, the counselors are worse, telling low-income students that they can't go to college, not encouraging them— actually slamming shut the door to their future. So many core subject teachers believe that if they don't fail about 7 to 9 percent of their students, they are not being rigorous. When kids drop out, teachers are relieved and say, 'They didn't belong here.'

—High school at-risk program coordinator, Iowa

All levels of public education are in need of continued improvement, and all schools, K–12, bear responsibility for the high dropout rate in the United States, but high schools represent a special tragedy of enormous proportions. Designed as the capstone of public education, the high school was to have served as the ticket to the American dream. Offering something for everyone, it was to prepare students for citizenship, college, and even a vocation. Sadly, this cultural icon has served almost no one well. The American high school does not teach even our best and brightest students adequately. In terms of international competition, our students lack essential knowledge and skills in science, math, and technology; our best students tend to be less than competitive with students from other parts of the world. Approximately 75 percent of students who go on to college must repeat high school courses or take remedial courses (Monahan, 2011), and only 40 percent of students who enroll in college graduate by the age of twenty-seven (Education Projects in Education Research Center, 2011).

While national statistics show a slight decrease in the number of school dropouts, the numbers of those who fail to persist through high school remain disturbingly high (Balfanz et al., 2012). Data for the 2011 school year placed the national dropout rate at 25 percent of U.S. students and even higher for poverty-level and minority students (Balfanz et al., 2012). This is a slight reduction from the 28.3 percent reported in 2011 (Editorial Projects in Education Research Center, 2011), but this still represents an enormous failure of our entire public school system.

It is especially distressing in light of an analysis by the Brookings Institution (2011) that concluded students who fail to earn a high school diploma and do not pursue postsecondary studies have a less than 44 percent chance of achieving middle-class status in their lifetimes, while for those who do graduate from high school and complete a postsecondary degree, the chance of achieving middle-class status increases to 85 percent. In other words, students can double their chances of achieving middle-class economic status during their lifetimes by completing a thorough education.

We also know there is a sad relationship between dropping out of high school and unemployment, welfare, teen pregnancy, drug and alcohol abuse, and incarceration. In all, 54 percent of dropouts are unemployed, compared to 32 percent of high school graduates (Dillon, 2009). Ongoing studies since the start of NCLB not only show the relationship between a failure to graduate from high school and a variety of social and economic problems, including drugs, alcohol, and unemployment; even more alarming, they connect the dropout phenomenon to the growth of the U.S. prison population (Editors of Rethinking Schools, 2012). When students leave school with inadequate education, they find themselves trapped without the prerequisites for employment. Unable to find a way to support themselves economically, too many dropouts turn to drugs, alcohol, and antisocial behavior. Far too many end up in the criminal justice system.

Calling the relationship between school dropouts and incarceration a "pipeline to prison," educators and researchers are concerned that NCLB may have become a "perverse incentive to allow or even encourage students to leave [school]" (Editors of Rethinking Schools, 2012, p. 6). A review of 2005 prison data reveals that close to 79 percent of the men and women in U.S. state prisons and 59 percent of inmates in federal prison were high school dropouts, many with serious literacy problems (Brudevold-Newman, 2006).

Journal

Statistics show that more and more of our country's resources are managed by the wealthiest 10 percent of our population (Domhoff, 2011). But until you have driven the back roads of the "other America" and seen the nature and the tragedies of poverty, I don't think you can really imagine the stark differences between the "haves" and the "have-nots." Drive through rural Louisiana, Arkansas, Mississippi, Alabama, South Carolina, Northern Florida, the South Side of Chicago, or East St. Louis. Drive through the Appalachian portion of Kentucky, the Mississippi Delta region, or even Southern Virginia, where communities have never recovered from the closing of the textile mills decades ago. What is so striking about these areas is how little the poorest of poor seem to have and how drug and alcohol addiction and the crime so often associated with poverty seem to have all but overwhelmed the hard work and determination of many communities. The use of crack cocaine, methamphetamine, and alcohol abuse has transformed neighborhoods, and the offspring of addicts have brought immense needs to the already tapped out schools and classrooms of our poorest communities. So much of this seems to reflect a deep and enduring hopelessness. In the richest nation on earth, there are millions of Americans living in a third world environment of generational poverty, homelessness, and hunger. The only hope for the immediate needs of children in these communities tends to be the local churches and, of course, the public schools.

No matter the sad realities of these students' lives, there are kind and caring teachers doing everything possible to help these challenging kids learn effectively. Even in the forgotten back roads of poverty, there are dedicated teachers at work in their classrooms, their churches, and their communities, helping kids and their families reach out for a better life. —B.B.

Middle School Roots of the U.S. Dropout Crisis

For many students, the transition from the self-contained classes of elementary school to the large, complex world of middle school simply proves too much, and they never recover. Going from one classroom with one teacher to as many as seven or eight different teachers with a mix of students they do not know leads them to feel isolated and alone. This is why U.S. Secretary of Education Arne Duncan (2011) described middle school as the "Bermuda Triangle" of K–12 education.

To address this issue, research has increasingly documented the importance of an early warning system during the middle grades, where an estimated 75 percent of dropouts can be identified (Balfanz, 2009). After reviewing this research, former First Lady Laura Bush concluded that "a lot of the kids who drop out in high school really drop out of middle school—they just *leave* in high school" (Duncan, 2011). When asked about their high school experiences, high school students will typically focus on the lack of challenging curriculum, the impersonality, the boredom and lack of relevance, and the feelings of personal disengagement. They speak about being lost in the maze of hallways jammed with students they do not know, of being too frightened to go into restrooms, of no one caring whether they come to school or not. They mention the social cliques, hazing, and even worse, the brutality of bullying. For many, particularly for children of poverty, large American middle and high schools are frightening, intimidating places.

Research has identified three specific middle school predictors of dropping out of high school—poor attendance, misbehavior and suspensions, and failure in courses in English language arts or mathematics (Duncan, 2011). The first two of these warning indicators specifically reflect social and emotional issues, while the third is often an outgrowth of these same issues. All three, as we shall see, can be addressed effectively by building a Culture of Hope.

The Search for Effective High Schools

The dropout problem, involving more than a million new students each and every year—one every twenty-six seconds (Aud et al., 2010)—represents a massive cost to society in terms of unemployment, food stamps, emergency housing, police, and prisons, as well as lost tax revenue and drained social services (Alliance for Excellent Education, 2011; Bruce, Bridgeland, Fox, & Balfanz, 2011).

While efforts to reform high school education during the past hundred years have come and gone (Ravitch, 2010; Tyack & Cuban, 1995), few have led to anything more than superficial or organizational changes, with scattered, isolated successes that often fade as the visionary leaders or motivated teachers move on to new opportunities. (Leaders who help transform schools are in high demand as authors and consultants and are sought out for higher-level administrative positions.)

In 2007, Karin Chenoweth stated that "all the resources of the Education Trust—and they are considerable—had been spent trying to find high schools that were successful in educating poor kids and kids of color, and they were coming up empty" (p. 47). This remains true. A careful review of education literature regarding high-poverty, high-performing schools finds literally tens of thousands of high-performing elementary and middle schools, but it remains difficult to find any mention of more than a dozen or so successful, large, high-performing high schools that enroll significant numbers of poverty-level students. Most successful high schools are unusually small, serving two to three hundred students. In fact, their success is often attributed to their small size, and these same small schools appear repeatedly in different educational sources (Chenoweth, 2007, 2009; Commission on the Whole Child, 2007; LeBlanc-Esparza & Roulston, 2012). This focus on only small high schools inspired the authors to search for larger, more "traditional" high schools that were successfully educating high-poverty students.

Within the United States, only a handful of large, comprehensive high schools that have had success with poverty-level and minority students have been documented, and the literature has identified even fewer districts where the achievement gap has been closed and the dropout rate reduced (see appendix A, page 229). Among them are Cinco Ranch High School in Texas, with over 3,000 students; Whittier Union

High School District in California, with five high schools serving 14,000 students; and Washington County School District, Maryland, with nine high schools serving over 6,500 students (DuFour et al., 2010; Layton, 2012; *U.S. News & World Report*, 2012).

The search for high-poverty, high-performing schools is further hampered by the fact that there are often insufficient data on graduation rates or enrollment policies (Chenoweth, 2007). Some reports of effective high schools have outdated information, without verification of the schools' current levels of success. For example, Granger High School in Washington State, which is used often as an example of a high-poverty, high-performing high school, experienced a massive turnaround under the guidance of Ricardo LeBlanc-Esparza. Under the new leadership of Paul Chartrand, Granger High's extended graduation rate (98 percent), postsecondary success (80 percent enrollment in college or training programs), and high attendance and parent involvement have continued (von Zastrow, 2009). However, as of this writing, Granger's test scores remain below Washington State averages, with 55 percent testing proficient or above in reading and 16 percent testing proficient or above in mathematics (*U.S. News & World Report*, 2012).

Criteria for Study

Our efforts to identify high-poverty, high-performing high schools quickly led to frustration. An extensive search of the literature led to one dead end after another and a surprising number of misrepresentations, if not outright deceptions. As a result, the authors identified six criteria that could be used to sort out and select effective high schools as well as criteria that ensured the schools would represent typical high schools with current data. To be selected for our study, we wanted the schools to have:

1. Data from 2010–2011 (reflecting current school performance)

2. Enrollment of over eight hundred students

3. Open enrollment (any student could attend, without an application or lottery)

4. A diverse student body with a large segment of low-income students (50 percent or more of the student population are eligible for subsidized lunches)

5. On-time graduation rates of over 85 percent (the target percentage for AYP is 90 percent by 2019)

6. Documented academic success of low-income students when calculated for this subpopulation, as compared to the total school population

Mining the *Newsweek* and *U.S. News & World Report* Lists

Two major magazines publish lists of outstanding high schools, *Newsweek* and *U.S. News & World Report (U.S. News)*. *Newsweek*'s list utilized all our criteria as variables of analysis, so we began our search among the one thousand schools in *Newsweek*'s database, America's Best High Schools 2012 (Daily Beast, 2012). We found only nine with enrollments above eight hundred. Perhaps even more shocking, when the criterion of size was removed, there were only thirteen schools out of 1,000 that met our criteria for a high-performing, high-poverty school (table 2.1). So we kept those thirteen on the list, to allow readers perspective on the scope of high-poverty, high-performing open-enrollment schools from *Newsweek*.

We then examined the *U.S. News* (2012) database and found eight from our list of thirteen high schools. Thus, eight high schools—six with enrollments above eight hundred—appeared on both magazines' lists of outstanding schools. (See appendix A, page 229, for information about both databases, the search process, and the specific criteria that disqualified the five schools from the *U.S. News* list). While there may be more schools on the *U.S. News* list that met our criteria for high-performing, high-poverty, open enrollment neighborhood schools, the *U.S. News* list does not allow for sorting by criteria.

Every one of these thirteen schools embodies components of the Culture of Hope. All are reported to have college and career readiness programs, high academic rigor for all students, strong social support systems, and extensive co-curricular and extra-curricular activities. Most have some form of service-learning or community projects. All serve high-poverty, high-minority populations. Most important, each of the schools has been successful in teaching low-income students as well as having a high graduation rate. What is striking is how few of *Newsweek*'s one thousand outstanding schools are high poverty. This finding matches what a 2001 study in Illinois (Illinois State Board of Education, 2001) found: low-poverty, high-performing schools are quite common. The only type of school harder to find than a high-poverty, high-performing one is a low-poverty, low-performing school.

It must be kept in mind, however, that both the *Newsweek* and *U.S. News* data have methodological or statistical flaws. Specifically, *U.S. News* does not include data on school dropouts or demographics of student bodies, so their ranking of outstanding schools is suspect. *Newsweek*'s lists fail to include a majority of the high schools in the United States, because schools had to complete a self-survey in order to participate. As a result, many schools were left out of their list. (For a complete discussion of both *Newsweek*'s and *U.S. News*'s methodologies, as well as our methods for finding schools, see appendix A, page 229.) For the complete database of the thirteen schools on both lists, and some further comments on our research process, see page 230.

Table 2.1: High-Poverty, High-Performing High Schools Based on *Newsweek* and *U.S. News* Data

The shaded rows denote schools in both the *Newsweek* and *U.S. News* reports that met all our criteria.

School Name	City, State	Enrollment	*Newsweek* Rank (Among 1,000 schools)	*U.S. News* Rank (Among 4,877 schools)
Coast Union	Cambria, CA	230 (too small)	785	844
Penn-Griffin School for the Arts	High Point, NC	557 (too small)	298	None
Carpinteria	Carpinteria, CA	721 (near 800)	989	1842
Medgar Evers College Prep	Brooklyn, NY	802	491	None
Hidalgo Early College	Hidalgo, TX	979	833	None
Yonkers	Yonkers, NY	1024	409	24
Eastside	Gainesville, FL	1500	259	None
Glen A. Wilson	Hacienda Heights, CA	1690	690	556
University City	San Diego, CA	1800	783	371
Woodside	Woodside, CA	1835	983	None
La Quinta	Westminster, CA	2038	866	196
Mark Keppel	Alhambra, CA	2408	592	795
Valencia	Placentia, CA	2500	447	156

The end result of our analysis was to conclude that in the entire United States, there are only a handful of large comprehensive high schools serving poor students that can be verified as being effective—a tragic conclusion given the high stakes in the lives of students. Sadly, there seem to be more large comprehensive high schools that are "failure factories" than there are truly effective schools (Balfanz et al., 2011).

But there is a small glimmer of hope in all of this. The number of high-poverty, high-performing high schools may be growing, with more models available for how to make high schools work for all students. In addition, the number of high-poverty, high-performing high schools of choice—charter, magnet, and preparatory academies—is impressive (on the *Newsweek* and *U.S. News* lists, the majority of highly ranked schools serving high-poverty/high-minority populations are schools of choice) and shows what is possible. Using the lessons learned from public schools of choice to transform neighborhood high schools is explored in more detail in chapter 10 (page 205).

Journal

At a National Youth-at-Risk Conference (March 2012), in Savannah, Georgia, in a session featuring award-winning schools, one high school reported a graduation rate of 94 percent. They later reported that 60 percent of their high school's 1,500 students were in the ninth grade. When asked what happened to all those students prior to graduation, the presenter replied, "We really don't know. Since many of our students are Spanish speaking, we think they go back to Mexico." Who knows what their actual graduation rate might be, but it is probably far lower than the 94 percent reported by this "award-winning" school. Perhaps even worse, the representative from this school seemed to truly believe that they were an outstanding school; somehow they were able to ignore or misinterpret the data staring them in the face. —B.B.

A Failed Institution

The difficulty in finding and documenting effective high schools dramatizes a staggering challenge to educational reformers, because the issue is not simply improving an institution with a few specific, documented problems. The real issue appears to be that the keystone, culminating institution of our K–12 public education system is simply not working. Hundreds of failed high schools destroy the lives of a new generation of teenagers each year. Although the number of these failing high schools declined by 457 in the eight years since 2002, more than 1,500 "failure factories" remain in operation in the United States. If the same rate of reduction continues into the future, there will still be more than a thousand of these tragic schools in 2020 (Balfanz, Bridgeland, Fox, & Moore, 2011).

Research has identified and described the following specific problems at the high school level, which we explore in the next section:

- Failure to close the achievement gap
- High dropout rates
- Reporting of faulty dropout data
- School bullying and violence
- Students not prepared for college
- Low math and science scores

Failure to Close the Achievement Gap

The No Child Left Behind (NCLB) reforms powerfully demonstrated that the achievement gap between poor and affluent students could be closed at the elementary and middle school levels. Unfortunately, the NCLB reforms were flawed (Ravitch, 2010) and the income-achievement gap at the high school level was higher in 2012 than at any time since the 1970s (Reardon, 2011). NCLB tended to narrow the school curriculum and focus attention on reading and math to the exclusion of other curricular areas and to emphasize standardized basic skills assessments and test results, causing some schools to resort to cheating. If the goal of public education is to prepare students to be economically and personally successful, we now know teaching students from low-income families to read and do math is not enough; achieving success at the elementary and middle school levels is not enough; in fact, even graduating from high school is no longer enough. Low-income students have been arriving from middle schools academically better prepared than ever before; due to the increasing effectiveness of K–8 schools, the Education Trust has regularly reported significant closure of the achievement gap at the elementary and middle school levels (Education Trust, 2005, 2009). And as described in chapter 3, the successes of high-poverty, high-performing K–8 schools have been well documented in research since 2000.

But high schools have not been as successful. According to the Education Trust (2009), the gaps between African-American and Latino twelfth-graders and their white peers are bigger than they were in the late 1980s. As a result of this failure to address the academic needs of low-income and minority students, a significant proportion of these students struggle during their high school years and ultimately drop out of school.

High Dropout Rates

As noted earlier, the U.S. dropout rate for the 2011 school year was 25 percent (Balfanz et al., 2012). For poor and minority students, the rate is even larger: nationwide, 35–40 percent of minority students leave school before graduating. Considering this issue from the side of those who receive diplomas helps further dramatize the problem: in the first decade of the 21st century, the graduation rate for students in high-poverty schools *dropped* 18 percentage points, from 86 percent to 68 percent, while there was no measurable change in students' graduation rates at low-poverty schools (Aud et al., 2010).

The dropout rate is an even more serious problem in urban schools. For example, the Portland Oregon Public Schools, serving a medium-size American city, reported an increase of 5 percent in graduation rates after a major initiative to track down and provide advice and counseling to high school students who did not return to school. Despite this improvement, the district's graduation rate still measured 59 percent, similar to other large urban districts (Goodall, 2012). Data associated with No Child Left Behind in Chicago and New York City—both urban districts with extensive reform efforts—illustrate the severity of the problem. On average, in the city of Chicago, 40 percent of all students drop out of high school before graduating (Rammohan & Ponce, 2011). New York's rates are similar, with 35 percent of all students dropping out of school before graduation (Bloomberg, 2011).

While these data describe an enormous set of problems for students after they leave school (unemployment and underemployment, to name just two), they also present the United States with huge increases in the cost of social services, drug rehabilitation, law enforcement, prisons, and so on (see chapter 2, pages 20–21, for a discussion of these issues).

Reporting of Faulty Dropout Data

Many school districts may obscure accurate data on the number of students who fail to graduate. As a result, the dropout rate for a school or school district has become highly politicized. In the past, if low-performing students dropped out of school or did not participate in high school assessments, the school could often report higher levels of success for those who did. This became a potential incentive for high schools and districts to overlook and ignore the huge number of students who were leaving school.

Since there was no universally accepted or required formula for determining dropouts, school districts and states computed their dropout or graduation rates in a wide variety of ways, with many simply reporting the number of students passing graduation exit exams. This ignores the numbers of students who were present in the ninth grade who have long since left school and thus are not available to take the exit exams. Changes in national educational requirements have resulted in a common definition and formula for determining graduation rates (the four-year adjusted cohort formula divides the number of students who graduate in four years by the number of first-time ninth graders who entered the cohort four years earlier), as well as the inclusion of reading and mathematics achievement data to determine the success or failure of a school or district (Balfanz et al., 2012).

School Bullying and Violence

High schools in the United States have been the scene of a number of horrific episodes of violence. In addition to the Columbine and Newtown tragedies, there have been multiple high school shootings since 2000. As a result, many high schools utilize security systems with metal detectors similar to an airport's, require see-through backpacks, and have adopted a "lockdown" mentality complete with security guards or police officers patrolling the buildings and grounds.

Bullying continues to be a major national concern in both public schools and colleges. In the United States, high school students regularly experience intimidation, scapegoating, racism, and violence. The age of instant handheld communication creates a new and sometimes even deadly venue for these forms of aggression (Hinduja & Patchin, 2012). Among surveyed students twelve to seventeen years old, 90 percent reported witnessing what they considered to be cruelty on social networking sites (Lenhart et al., 2011).

Students Not Prepared for College

Another failure of our schools involves students who graduate and go on to college. Increasingly, colleges and universities must provide students with remedial courses in English and mathematics; almost all institutions of higher education also provide "basic skills centers" where students with marginal skills can get remediation in reading, writing, and basic math. In the United States, 75 percent of high school graduates who enrolled in college in the fall of 2010 needed to take remedial courses (Monahan, 2011). Taxpayers and legislators alike object to the use of millions of tax dollars to provide free public K–12 education, only to have the graduates of this system take the same courses again for remediation as college freshmen (Balfanz et al., 2012).

Of the students who do graduate from high school, on average 70 percent continue on to college. However, postsecondary education has its own unfortunate dropout rate: only 40 percent of those who enroll have earned a baccalaureate degree by the age of twenty-seven (Editorial Projects in Education Research Center, 2011). The real competitive success of American education occurs at the collegiate and graduate level, where U.S. students compete for classroom seats with international students from around the world. Sadly, few of these successful students come from poverty-level families, as low-income students have often dropped from the attendance sheets well before college.

Low Math and Science Scores

Low math and science scores earned by U.S. high school students on international assessments, such as the *Trends in International Mathematics and Science Study* (TIMSS) based on the National Assessment of Educational Progress (NAEP) scores, are alarmingly low enough to attract the attention of political, economic, and educational leaders. There are a number of often used (and equally often discredited) arguments as to why U.S. students compete so poorly with international students. For example, one such argument goes, public schools in the United States educate and test students of all academic levels, while other nations only test high-achieving students who are educated in college-prep academic programs. But, again, the reality is that by the time these tests are given, large numbers of low-income students have long since dropped out of U.S. schools. The fact therefore remains that the test scores of the best and the brightest of our high school graduates fall far below the achievement levels of many other nations' students.

According to the 1999 TIMSS scores, the United States comes in at an average level in elementary school but settles near the bottom at high school, with the physical sciences and higher mathematics being the worst areas (National Center for Education Statistics, 1999). The 2007 TIMSS (Gonzales et al., 2009), which did not report scores for high schools, showed no real improvement over 1999 scores for fourth and eighth graders. At the high school level in mathematics, the United States ranked only above Cypress and South Africa, and in science, only above Italy, Hungary, Lithuania, Cypress, and South Africa (National Center for Education Statistics, 1999). Nearly every industrialized nation in the world ranks above the United States.

Why We Are Failing

If these are the problems and failures of high schools, what are the reasons? What is happening at the high school level that leads to such failure? Is it societal? Changes in technology? Drug use? Moral failure of students and teachers alike? Is it, as many in education have said, the families that are failing, not the schools? Research has helped answer these questions, and for good or bad, the failure can be largely explained as problems with the institution of the American high school.

Since NCLB was enacted in 2001, there has been a growing consensus around three key characteristics needing change: (1) large school size, (2) departmentalization and the normal-curve mentality, and (3) tracking and segregation of students by ability. These characteristics are, notably, the exact opposite of what learners find in a Culture of Hope.

Large School Size

Comprehensive high schools in the United States tend to be large institutions, commonly serving over fifteen hundred students, with some urban schools topping four thousand. We know that large school size correlates with increased student discipline problems, student isolation, and troubled students being overlooked, dropping "through the cracks," and leaving school without anyone seeming to notice or care (Leithwood & Jantzi, 2009; Public Schools of North Carolina, 2000). Researchers recommend school sizes of under 600 for secondary schools serving high-poverty student populations (Leithwood & Jantzi, 2009). All other demographics and school characteristics being equal, an increase of four hundred additional students to the total number of students in a school leads to an approximately 1 percent increase in dropouts (Public Schools of North Carolina, 2000).

Journal

Conversations with low-income and minority students in many high schools over the years revealed a consistent set of issues. Poverty-level students talk about being the kids "on the back row" who teachers tend to overlook. The students talk about raising their hands to contribute in class or to ask a question, only to find that teachers tend to ignore them. They talk about being lost in the huge crowd of other students, of being nameless and invisible. A dropout in Oakland, California, told me that none of his teachers even knew his name and would never call on him in class.

He told me, "Since I felt invisible, I decided to just disappear. One day I just pushed back my chair, got up, and walked out of school and never went back. I'm sure no one even knew I was gone."

In another interview, published some time ago, I wrote about a young student who left a large middle school for a small alternative school program with a surrogate family atmosphere. He talked about changing from "an invisible man" to a "family man." —B.B.

Large high schools are also associated with greater problems of truancy and disorderliness. Principals of high schools with over one thousand students report moderate or serious problems with discipline, issues of tardiness, absenteeism, physical conflicts, robbery, vandalism, and drug and alcohol problems (Public Schools of North Carolina, 2000). Increased positive behavior and academic outcomes are associated with smaller schools (Leithwood & Jantzi, 2009; Public Schools of North Carolina, 2000). For high schools, the optimal size is between four and eight hundred students; unfortunately, the school size traditionally associated with economic efficiency and economy of scale is eight to twelve hundred (Public Schools of North Carolina, 2000). However, the perceived cost effectiveness of larger schools has been countered by more recent research (Leithwood & Jantzi, 2009). In a meta-analysis of research on school size since 1990, when student graduation rates were factored into cost effectiveness, smaller secondary schools graduate a significantly larger proportion of their students than larger secondary schools. Additionally, the higher academic performance of larger schools, as measured on SAT/ACT tests, may be an illusion created by lower-performing students dropping out before testing as juniors and seniors, thus skewing a larger school's data (Leithwood & Jantzi, 2009). When the currency of a school is measured in diplomas, smaller schools have a higher profit margin.

Departmentalization and the Normal-Curve Mentality

Discussions with high school teachers and administrators suggest that using academic content areas, rather than student needs, as the organizational structure for high school creates problems for low-income and minority students. Many middle schools recruit and hire teachers with elementary certification to combat this very issue and foster student-centered learning. Departmental organization can also lead to teachers adopting a normal-curve mentality, because they feel pressure to show academic rigor by failing a percentage of students. In conversations with high school teachers from 2002–2012, the authors found many who described their primary job as cultivating the top 20 to 30 percent of their classrooms, leaving struggling students to fend for themselves.

Tracking and Segregation of Students by Ability

Far too many American high schools continue to "select and sort" students, identifying those who they think have the ability to succeed and continue with their education and those who need less demanding courses and curricula. Though an avalanche of research has documented the disastrous effects of tracking, the concept is still widely practiced. While the course names may have changed from Remedial English, Basic Math, and "Bonehead" Science, to Consumer or Opportunity Math, Everyday English, and Backyard Science, the concept is the same: segregate low-performing students into "slow learning" courses and educational tracks where they are not expected to learn, which keeps them out of more rigorous classrooms, allowing teachers to focus on students with "more potential."

Journal

I worked with a school district in Iowa for a number of years. During my first visit to this school district, I was surprised and saddened by what I found. Everyone told me, "This is one of the United States' premier school districts." The district had five school board members with PhDs. And when it came to advanced placement courses completed and percentage of students going on to college, the high school was among the best in the country. Then I learned the rest of the story.

First I discovered that the funds to support at-risk students had been used to hire two new faculty members, but both were athletic coaches with no experience in working with struggling students. When I visited their two special at-risk student classrooms, both teachers were showing films unrelated to the subject of the course. Most of the students were asleep in the darkened room, anyway. Then, when the principal took me on a tour of the school to see all of the advanced placement classes, I stopped him and asked, "Wait a minute. What's going on in that classroom?" The teacher in the room was reading a newspaper at the front of the room, and most of the kids had their heads down on their desks. He explained that it was a class in Opportunity Math—"a course for kids who can't learn algebra." By this time I was in a steamy mood and in a fairly loud voice said, "The reason these kids are not learning algebra is not because they cannot learn it, but because you're not teaching it to them."

When we got back to the principal's office, I asked for dropout data for the school. He seemed puzzled about this request. "You know," he responded, "I don't really know if we keep that kind of data. I don't think that we have very many students who drop out." It took the school counselors two days to come up with names of fifty students who counselors thought might have dropped out of school. No one had any idea how many dropouts there were at the school or even any idea how to find out how many. Even worse, no one seemed to care. —B.B.

Prior to the revolution in practices that transformed Adlai E. Stevenson High School into the successful, high-performing school it is today, the school provided an example of the negative effects of tracking. In the school's earlier days, students were organized into five different ability groups for their entire high school career (DuFour et al., 2010). Students who did not put forth sufficient effort to be successful in a course were reassigned to a less demanding one. A student who failed algebra could drop down into a modified algebra course; continued failure would lead to a step down into a general math course (DuFour et al., 2010). Richard DuFour, Rebecca DuFour, Robert Eaker, and Gayle Karhanek note that "from the student's perspective, there was always an easy way out of class, because the school would inevitably offer a less-challenging program. The less a student did, the less he or she was required to do" (DuFour et al., 2010, p. 58). This type of tracking encourages what some educators call "intentional non-learning" (DuFour et al., 2010, p. 103).

Conclusion

The sad truth regarding high schools in the United States is that the data document a long history of chronic failure with students most in need of support. The characteristics of high schools that have led to this failure have likewise been carefully documented since the late 1960s. The three cornerstones of failure for high schools are large school size, departmentalization and the normal-curve mentality, and tracking and segregation of students by ability. Yet, after fifty years of pressure to reform this failed institution, U.S. high schools remain largely unchanged. Conversations with high school leadership in several states revealed a resigned complacency that, regardless of the criticism, things are not likely to change much in the future. As we have stressed in this chapter, the future of our country in no small way depends on the revitalization of this battered institution.

The next chapter explores the components of a Culture of Hope.

Chapter 3

A Culture of Hope

I love my school. I feel so safe here, so cared for and supported. I feel like this school is the only place in my life where I feel that I really belong. I know that these teachers will do almost anything for me. . . . . I know it sounds silly, but this school has changed my life. It is a big happy family, where everyone cares for one another.

—High school student, Washington

School culture has been a frequent topic of educational research over the years. In his book *The Culture of the School and the Problem of Change*, Seymour Sarason (1971) explains that all institutions, public entities, and corporations have what he calls an "institutional culture" that has considerable effect on the people in that environment. Sarason (1971) defines institutional culture, whether in a school or a corporation, as "patterns of behavioral regularities" (p. 27) and concludes that such a culture is a powerful "conforming force" (p. 29) leading to uniform behavior and attitudes. The result is that when people come to work at a school, especially new teachers, they do not change the institution or culture; instead, the school tends to change the new people. Studies done in the 1990s of new and fifth-year teachers found that, over time, teachers tended to adjust more and more to the behavioral norms of their school (Sanders & Rivers, 1996).

Later studies (Deal & Peterson, 1999) of corporate and school culture define institutional culture more simply: "This is the way we do things here, or, this is not the way we do things here" (Lezotte & Snyder, 2011, p. 102). Others define school culture as the "hidden curriculum," or the unseen factors in a school that influence behaviors (see, for example, Apple, 1971; the concept of school culture and change is also detailed in *The "Grammar" of Schooling* [Tyack & Tobin, 1994]).

School culture can have a powerful positive or negative impact on students. If a school's staff share agreed-on beliefs that all students can learn and achieve high levels of academic success, there will be a significant student benefit (DuFour et al., 2010).

If, on the other hand, a school is characterized by conflict, class and racial prejudice, and teachers who question whether or not all students can learn effectively, a negative or toxic school culture results, one that seriously impairs not only learning but also students' personal perceptions of themselves and their abilities (Cromwell, 2002).

According to Sarason (1971), the conforming power of schools all but overwhelms educators' efforts to change instructional programs, which explains why educational reform is often described as just one pendulum swing after another. He concluded that it would be easier to start a new school than to change an existing one—a belief underlying the early alternative school and charter school movements. Starting a new optional program enables a group of like-minded educators to quickly join together and create an educational program with strongly unified core beliefs.

Better understanding of school reform and school cultures has led to more effective change models and more success at improving schools (Barr & Parrett, 2007). Research on high-poverty, high-performing schools has documented that, while it is not easy, school improvement comes only with attention to the attitudes, values, visions, and expectations of the entire school culture (Lezotte & Snyder, 2011). One vital indicator is the level of hope.

Journal

An elementary teacher-leader in Arkansas said, "It took us about three years before we finally were able to have a teaching and administrative staff that shared a consensus philosophy. We knew that was important at the start, but we had no idea how important it really was. To work in a school where everybody believes that each student can learn effectively is just incredible. We all believe in building student pride and self-esteem and respecting and welcoming parents as partners. It has changed our school, and it is now just an incredible place to work, but it was not easy. We had to really work at hiring, and we all worked at developing our school as a professional learning community where we shared a common belief about our kids. It was hard work, but oh my, was it worth it. And of course, the students benefit so much from the uniform message that we send in each and every classroom." —B.B.

Hope Theory

A growing amount of research exists on the concept of hope; psychologists have, in fact, developed a motivational construct that they refer to as Hope Theory (Newell & Van Ryzin, 2007). To these scholars, hope is not an emotion but "the process of thinking about one's goals, along with the motivation to move toward those goals, and ways to achieve those goals" (Snyder et al., 2002, p. 820).

Ronald Newell and Mark Van Ryzin (2007, 2009) pointed out some of the benefits of a school culture based on hope:

- School cultures that promote hope affect students' in-school as well as out-of-school lives.

- More hopeful students go on to perform better in college.

- Higher-hope students are more likely to stay in school and graduate.

- Individuals with higher levels of hope report more optimism about life, better physical health, greater levels of happiness, and less anxiety and depression.

Because of the unusually positive findings of hope research, there is ample justification to use it as a filter for evaluating school environments. The Hope Survey, a research-based online instrument available to all schools, provides just such a means of evaluation (EdVisions, 2010). Designed to measure students' perceptions of their school environment, the survey draws together reliable, valid measurement instruments from different sources and has been used with a variety of demographics. The survey measures students' perceptions of "autonomy, belongingness and goal orientations, as well as their resulting engagement in learning and disposition toward achievement" (EdVisions, 2010). Educators can go to www.hopesurvey.org to learn more about the survey.

Resilience Factors

We have already mentioned resilience as a factor in the success of high-poverty schools. Nan Henderson and Mike Milstein (1996; as cited in Tileston & Darling, 2008) identify twelve factors that characterized the "resilient" poverty-level student, and Henderson and Milstein (1996), as well as Benard (2003), report examples of schools where these attributes are being taught successfully. These twelve factors are:

1. A good, strong sense of selflessness, or giving of one's self

2. Possession of life skills, such as good decision-making, self-control, and assertiveness

3. An ability to be sociable

4. A sense of humor

5. An internal locus of control

6. Autonomy

7. Orientation toward a positive future

8. Adaptability and flexibility

9. An interest in and connection to learning

10. Self-motivation

11. Personal competence in one or multiple areas

12. Some elements of self-worth or self-efficacy (Tileston & Darling, 2008, p. 164)

Journal

A pre-service teacher in Boise, Idaho, told me, "I always envisioned myself in a well-ordered classroom where the children are quietly and happily learning and where everyone loves me. But what if that doesn't happen? I have this fear that the children won't respond—fear of discipline problems and fear of simply being a bad teacher. I wonder what will happen if I am not received with enthusiasm or if my class leans towards chaos. Though my intentions are good, I may fall back on what many perceive as the 'role of teacher,' that is to maintain control at all costs and keep the children clean and quiet. I must not be guided by that fear to maintain a class where everyone must always work or pretend to work. I must be willing to take risks, allow myself to make mistakes and learn from them. I must try out new things and discard those that don't work, even if they may seem to work for everyone else. Most importantly, I must listen and respond to the children and their needs. I chose this career to teach children, not just 'play teacher.'" —E.G.

Established Research

While much of the documentation underlying this book comes from direct observations in dozens of public schools in more than twenty states, the concept of a Culture of Hope can also be found in the established school-reform research base, which has identified a number of consensus points regarding effective strategies for improving high-poverty schools. While each of these strategies relate to a culture of hope, a few of them relate directly to the social and emotional growth of students and have been highlighted. These clusters of strategies almost always include the following (Barr & Parrett, 2007; Chenoweth, 2009; Lezotte & Snyder, 2011):

- Provide a safe and orderly environment.
- Engage parents, communities, and schools.
- Have a clear and focused mission.
- Ensure effective district and school leadership.
- Understand and hold high expectations for poor and culturally diverse students.
- Target low-performing students and schools, starting with reading.
- Promote teacher collaboration.

- Support personal relationship building.
- Align, monitor, and manage the curriculum.
- Create a culture of data and assessment literacy.
- Build and sustain instructional capacity.
- Reorganize time, space, and transitions.

Maslow's Hierarchy of Needs

The concept of a Culture of Hope is also supported from the field of psychology, where it rests on Abraham Maslow's (Maslow & Lowry, 1973) hierarchy of needs (figure 3.1, page 40). A celebrated psychologist and academic, Maslow conceptualized the basic needs of human beings in five ascending levels: (1) physiological needs, (2) the need for safety, (3) the need for love and belonging, (4) the need for esteem, and (5) the need for self-actualization. This model was used in ASCD's 2007 report, *The Learning Compact Redefined: A Call for Action, A Report of the Commission on the Whole Child*. Although the needs are organized in a hierarchy, as Maslow and others point out, one does not move up this hierarchy in a linear process; human beings may focus on the satisfaction of various needs simultaneously. Later in his career, Maslow further refined his ideas and created new levels, the aesthetic and cognitive needs, and the need for self-transcendence—a stage at which an individual connects to something greater than the personal ego through helping and serving others (Maslow & Lowry, 1998). Other models of human motivation have been proposed, but Maslow's continues to be one of the most popular and often cited (Huitt, 2007).

Unfortunately, Maslow provided no empirical evidence to support his theory, and some researchers have been unable to substantiate his claims (Korman, Greenhaus, & Badin, 1979; Lawler & Suttle, 1972). Nevertheless, the construct has proven useful in helping educators understand the importance of needs in regard to teaching and learning, and research has documented the strong relationship between human needs and effective learning (Commission on the Whole Child, 2007). When certain basic human needs are satisfied, students are more likely to become engaged in school and achieve academic success, as well as to develop a variety of important social skills (Commission on the Whole Child, 2007).

The Culture of Hope

Based on research on high-poverty, high-performing schools, education and psychology research, Maslow's theory of human needs, and observations in dozens of schools, it is possible to conceptualize a new understanding of effective schools: schools with a Culture of Hope. This culture is built upon four major components, which have come to be referred to as the seeds of hope:

- A sense of optimism
- A sense of belonging
- A sense of pride
- A sense of purpose

Research described throughout this book and especially in chapter 10 provides compelling support for concluding that the social and emotional development of children and youth are important to, if not inseparable from, success in school and in later life. The seeds of hope form the foundation of these social and emotional developments.

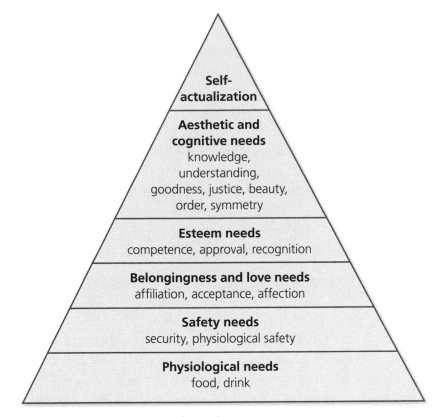

Figure 3.1: Maslow's hierarchy of needs.

Figure 3.2 summarizes the pathway from poverty to a Culture of Hope. Our focus in the next four chapters will be on the four major components, or seeds, of a Culture of Hope—a sense of optimism; a sense of belonging; a sense of pride, self-esteem, and self-confidence; and a sense of purpose. While these major characteristics of a Culture of Hope do not map exactly onto Maslow's hierarchy, the strong correspondence between them is obvious.

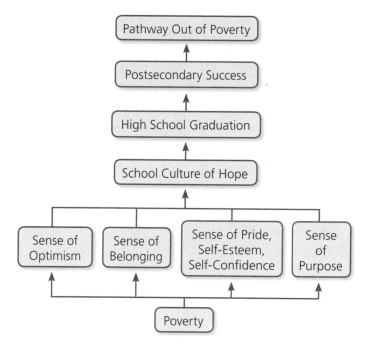

Figure 3.2: Culture of Hope flow chart.

Conclusion

Chapter 1 reviewed the tragic characteristics of poverty as well as their impact on student achievement in school. Care has been taken to explain the devastating impact that the learned helplessness and hopelessness associated with poverty has upon student learning. Chapter 2 described the tragic failure of public education to adequately educate all students and keep students in school and graduating. Specific failings of the middle and high school levels were identified and discussed. In the final chapter of part one, the Culture of Hope was introduced and related to research in the field of education on high-poverty, high-performing schools.

While based on a number of rather simple concepts, a Culture of Hope involves a complex, long-term commitment to excellence. Ensuring a Culture of Hope demands a schoolwide, even districtwide, agreement to develop and maintain positive school atmospheres, an emphasis on the development of personal assets, a commitment to the difficult transformation of the high school, and support for a variety of K–12 activities including improved transitions between school levels, career exploration, and postsecondary advising during the middle and high school years. The transformation of the high school represents a major challenge to and primary goal of school improvement due to the scarcity of exemplary models. The Culture of Hope represents a focus that may well provide the emphasis needed to help high schools make this transition possible. The Culture of Hope holds the promise of providing students from low-income families the necessary foundation to succeed in school, graduate from high school, and find purpose and direction in their lives. Developed across the entire K–12 experience, it can provide students with the necessary support that may, one day, help break the vicious cycle of generational poverty.

Part Two, The Four Seeds of Hope, describes the four main components of a Culture of Hope, beginning with a sense of optimism.

part two

THE FOUR SEEDS *of* HOPE

Chapter 4

A Sense of Optimism

How much hope and optimism your kids feel at school is more important for boosting achievement than IQ. . . . Without it, all other strategies will fail.

—Eric Jensen, neuroscientist, 2011

Developing learned optimism and hope is crucial to turning students with a lower socioeconomic status into high achievers (Jensen, 2009; Seligman, 2007). While these most basic foundational needs are most fully met at the home and community level, schools have huge and essential roles in addressing them. And for so many children and youth, the school may in fact be the most important factor in not just instilling basic human hope and optimism, but in overcoming negative influences of far too many poverty-level homes and communities. And if current brain research is correct (Sharot, 2011), the development of human hope and a sense of optimism may well be among what Maslow described as essential physiological needs.

Instilling optimism in students from low-income families cannot be random or occasional; it demands a unified, sustained, schoolwide effort. Moreover, schools' efforts in this regard are related to intriguing new research on the human brain. Scientific evidence suggests that a so-called "optimism bias"—a belief that the future "will be better than the past and present" may be "hardwired" into the human brain (Sharot, 2011, p. 40). Researchers now believe that to make progress, it must be possible for individuals to imagine alternative futures and to believe that they can be attained. The opposite appears also to be true: pessimistic expectations seem to "shape outcomes in a negative way" (Sharot, 2011, p. 44).

For poverty-level students, who tend to arrive at school with a feeling of learned helplessness and often experience a clash of cultures with middle-class schools, the possibilities offered by developing a sense of optimism seem especially promising (Seligman, 2007). A school with a strong atmosphere of optimism and classrooms filled with high expectations and positive reinforcement not only teaches students effectively, it also transforms students' brains, IQs, and lives (Jensen, 2009).

Observations of high-poverty, high-performing schools suggest that a sense of optimism is created through:

- A welcoming environment
- An atmosphere of respect and safety
- An emphasis on success
- Communitywide celebrations
- An emphasis on the positive
- High expectations
- Coordination of community services

A Welcoming Environment

Walk into a school where a Culture of Hope has developed, and you experience a welcoming atmosphere. These schools want students and families to feel at home, to think of the school as *their* school. They have high energy and excitement for learning. There are numerous highly visible signs and posters with positive messages, and the halls are enhanced with student-designed murals and displays of student artwork and school assignments. Often, the building signage is in both English and Spanish, and the message board outside the school may use multiple languages. In one elementary school in Denton, Texas, visited by the authors, the entire staff met in the front hall each morning to welcome students to school. Each was greeted by name and usually received about half a dozen hugs by his or her first few steps into the building. At many of the effective secondary schools the authors visited, the teachers stood at the door to their classrooms before each period and greeted students by name as they welcomed them to class.

At many schools where there is a Culture of Hope, kindergarten and first-grade teachers visit the homes of new students and their families during the summer to be sure everyone feels ready and welcome and is aware of the high expectations teachers have for their child's learning.

Journal

At a Denton, Texas, elementary school serving over 60 percent Latino students, the halls were filled with framed prints of world-class Latino artists, including Diego Rivera, turning their school into an art gallery of pride and beauty. Every day, students and parents would pause in the entrance hallway of the school to admire these great paintings. You could see the cultural pride on all the faces. One mother said to me, "I never knew there was a Mexican artist like this. In fact, I don't think I ever even saw a work of art until I came to this school. Just look at these paintings! It makes me so proud."

At another elementary school in Texas, the principal told me, "It is such a delight to walk through the building and see the signs in English and Spanish and listen to the rich diversity of children speaking in two languages. We were never approved as a dual-language school, but as more and more Latino students moved into our area and the demographics of our school changed, it just seemed to happen. I think we used to feel bilingual education was a kind of remediation program, something that you worked to get out of. Over time, we have come to understand that to be bilingual is a wondrous gift, and that we should share that gift with everyone, students and teachers alike. Walk through our schools and see students helping one another with language development. What is even more wonderful is to see students helping their teachers pronounce Spanish words, just as teachers were helping students learn English. Our dual-language program is now our school's greatest pride." —B.B.

Here are some ways schools can create a welcoming environment—the "front door" of building a schoolwide sense of optimism:

- Welcome each student, every day, at the door to the classroom.
- Greet students by name and offer a handshake, pat on the back, or hug, depending on school norms.
- Ask questions as students transition to your classroom ("How was the ball game?" "How did you do on that test you were worried about?" "How are you feeling today?"). Ask about their families and homework ("Did you have any problems with your assignment?"), and so on.
- Have staff greet students each day as they enter the school. Some schools gather on the steps to welcome students each day.
- Assemble the whole school in the morning for rituals that connect students and adults into a family.
- Cover the school with student artwork, signs, posters, and information.
- Have students conduct school surveys, and post the results.
- Conduct whole-school surveys and display the results in giant graphs that allow students to see themselves in the data, while also getting a sense of the size of the school.
- Show student photos and lists of student achievements in sports, arts, and academics throughout the school to make for a welcoming atmosphere.
- Regularly call and write home to tell parents and families about wonderful things their children are doing, every day. Call two or three parents every day to communicate something positive.

An Atmosphere of Respect and Safety

In this age of high-profile bullying and school violence, there is nothing as important as a safe and orderly school. On Maslow's hierarchy of needs (figure 3.1, page 40) the need for safety is positioned just above our physiological needs. The hallmark of such a school atmosphere is respect between and among students, teachers, and parents—an essential requirement for effective learning.

Compounding the problem is the language of teenagers today. Whether in a shopping mall, in city parks, or in schools, teenage language too often reflects the vulgar "trash-talking" bravado and bullying that fill modern-day media, electronic games, and television footage of many professional athletes. Modern-day media may have greater influence on contemporary youth than school or even family. Nielsen surveys indicate that, by the time students reach school age, they have already spent more hours watching TV than they will spend in school for the next twelve years (Barr & Parrett, 2008; McDonough, 2009). They will have seen thousands of murders and over a hundred thousand acts of violence (Barr & Parrett, 2008). The most effective way for schools to counter these forces is to have schoolwide agreement on acceptable behavior and language, to be consistent regarding school rules and enforcement, and to surround students with caring and supportive adults who model respectful behavior.

Journal

A middle school student in California told me, "Since I came to this school, my life has completely changed. In the school where I came from, I was afraid to go to the restroom, so all day I would squirm around and be uncomfortable. All I could think about was getting home and going to the bathroom. At this school everything is different. Now my mind is on learning, not the restroom. For the first time in my life I feel that people really care about me. I feel like I fit in here in ways I have never felt before. I feel safe. Everyone seems to like one another, and everybody tries to help everyone else. I never dreamed a school could feel like this. It is like a family." —B.B.

The definition of a safe and orderly school has "moved beyond rules and disciplinary practices . . . to creating a cooperative, nurturing environment with a strong academic focus" (Lezotte & Snyder, 2011, p. 103). In addition, it is now almost universally accepted that a small number of school rules, uniformly enforced, is better than many rules only sporadically or randomly enforced (Lezotte & Snyder, 2011). And while it is viewed as rather unusual, some scholars and school faculty feel it is important that students and parents be actively involved in the creation of school rules. This approach, called judicious discipline, reflects the democratic way of life of the broader culture in which we live, and shows students that their ideas are respected (Gathercoal, 2006). Data suggest that judicious discipline seems to lead to a safer, more orderly school environment and to a significant reduction in school disruptions (Barr & Parrett, 2001). Some schools go even further, and rather than teach students good behavior actually teach students skills they need to become actively involved in resolving their own disputes and disagreements, or reducing their number. Many schools now teach students the techniques of peer mediation and conflict resolution and provide time and organization for students to participate in the use of these effective skills. Other schools have students serving on discipline panels that review student misbehavior, and student representatives join with adults in determining penalties or punishments. (For a review of schoolwide approaches to student conflict, teaching social skills, and schoolwide positive behavior supports implemented throughout the United States, see Crawford & Bodine, 1996; Crawford & Bodine, 2001; and Positive Behavioral Interventions and Supports [PBIS]: www.pbis.org).

Journal

I first heard about one of the most interesting school experiences I've ever come across, the "Student for a Day" program, in a small alternative school outside Louisville, Kentucky. On that day, the teacher dresses like a kid and goes out somewhere and rides the bus to school and then returns on the bus at the end of the day. During the day, he or she attends a complete set of classes, sitting through each class period, just like a student. He or she has to eat with the students in the lunchroom and take the usual teasing of any new student.

Schools who use the Student for a Day program report that every teacher returns from the experience talking about how bone-crushingly boring it is to sit through all of the classes each day, and teachers talk about how to make the school day a more engaging experience. There is another reason that the program is so important: school faculties have been surprised by how much their students respect the teachers for doing this. The program becomes a huge signal to students that teachers care about them and want to ensure that their school experience is constantly improving. In some schools, they report that students now want to be teachers for a day. —B.B.

An atmosphere of respect and safety should permeate individual classrooms and the entire school campus. Strategies for building this include the following:

- Ensure that all adults on campus speak to all students with respect.
- Expect respectful communication among students.
- Have a schoolwide plan for teaching social skills and communication.
- Implement a conflict management program in which students are trained to help peers solve problems.

- Train the office staff in standard procedures to ensure that the office runs smoothly and that anyone who comes into the school is greeted warmly.

- Make sure that schoolwide procedures are clear and explicit to everyone, so students and adults both know what is expected and can do the right thing.

- Treat students with the care and consideration given to family members.

- Respect each student's ideas, interests, and decisions by providing time for students to share, plan, and suggest. Create suggestion boxes for the school, for individual classrooms, and for community places like the library.

- Promote the reasonable use of video games and television viewing, especially violent games and shows, through parent education and class discussions.

- Have a zero-tolerance policy for bullying and violence, while also having structures in place to teach students how to deal with conflict and differences.

An Emphasis on Success

A Culture of Hope school makes an intense effort to encourage students and their families to believe that they can learn and succeed. Some schools use positive chants and songs, with entire classrooms—and occasionally the entire school—chanting, "We can do it. We can do it! We can learn. We can learn!" At one middle school, students were awarded T-shirts emblazoned with the words "I Am Smart" when they experienced an academic success. How great to stand in a classroom with all these beaming faces smiling over their "I Am Smart" shirts. Schools building a Culture of Hope involve students in monitoring their progress toward instructional goals. You will often find students plotting their own assessments on a personal graph of their learning progress.

The Johnson County, Kentucky, school district illustrates what can happen when there is a districtwide commitment to success, as Bob Barr learned during interviews he did in the district in 2009. Educators and parents in this Appalachian community, with 68 percent of students on free or reduced lunch, are in widespread agreement that they have the "best schools in Kentucky," and the Johnson Central High School earned a bronze ranking in *U.S. News*'s list of America's best high schools in 2007. The leaders of this district refer to the school atmosphere as the "gold standard." The gold standard means having the highest expectations possible for student learning; it means working with each and every student to ensure that he or she succeeds; and it means finding and hiring teachers and administrators who will carry on this expectation of excellence. All prospective new teachers are interviewed by both a site-based elected parent group and an educator group, with both groups striving to ensure that every new hire has the right abilities and attitudes. Many teachers absorbed this understanding from a young age, when they themselves were elementary students in the local schools, and were told that they were attending the best school in Kentucky. The county's many state and national awards for excellence are a tribute to their success, but in the district, it's second nature—the district accepts it, the community expects it, and the students believe it (personal communication between Bob Barr and administrators in the Johnson County, Kentucky, School District, during the 2009 school year). This statement, which everyone seemed to know, had become the informal slogan for the community and the district.

Johnson County Central High School's 2009 cohort graduation rate of 76.7 percent is higher than both the state average of 70.5 percent and the national average of 73.4 percent (Balfanz et al., 2012). Though the high school's graduation rate is still far below where they would like it to be, they have shown steady progress, much like other Culture of Hope schools and school districts throughout the United States.

Journal

An elementary principal from Florida described her classroom evaluation of one of her most effective teachers, who was working with one of the school's most demanding groups of students.

"How can I describe this teacher?" the principal asked. "It was like watching a sixteen-wheel Mack truck grinding up a long hill. And when some students continued to struggle, the teacher did not slow down or stop; it was like she just kept downshifting and pushing forward and upward with more and more energy. She has such high expectations for her students. You just knew that all of the students were going to make it to the top academically." —B.B.

To encourage a sense of optimism, here are ways teachers can place more emphasis on success in the classroom and across campus:

- Communicate a unanimous, belief that all kids can and will learn. Every person who comes in contact with students should be saturated in this belief.

- Ensure that students hear positive messages everywhere: "You can learn." "You can excel." "You can succeed." "You can accomplish great things."

- Hold poster contests in which students create posters for different messages.

- Have high expectations. Students will live up to or down to the expectations of the adults in their lives. If students understand that their teachers believe in them and expect them to do great things, they will tend to exert greater effort.

- Plan short lessons that students can complete quickly in order to gain the confidence of repeated successes. Success breeds success.

- Focus on what students have done well, instead of what they have missed. Share three things they did well, and one thing to work on.

- See the suggestions in chapter six (pages 96–98) for more ways to support academic success.

Communitywide Celebrations

Culture of Hope schools enrich their welcoming atmosphere with celebrations that honor the cultural heritages of their students and the surrounding communities. Celebrations tend to encompass the entire community and provide a vehicle for school, family, and community members to join together. Calendar events—like Black History Month, Martin Luther King Jr. Day, Cinco de Mayo, and La Raza—as well as unique, locally based events, showcase different cultures' music, art, and food and help everyone participate in a learning experience. In the West it might include Rodeo Day or Future Farmers of America (FFA) Day at the county fair. Such celebrations send a loud message to all cultural groups that they are welcome at and important to their school.

To celebrate student successes, many schools establish a Wall of Honor in the front hall with the name of every student who has achieved academic proficiency. Other schools give large numbers of classroom and school awards and recognitions to ensure that students are honored for their achievements. Schools will often arrange for students to make presentations at local professional clubs' meetings, giving the community a chance to meet students and hear about their accomplishments.

Celebrations are important to the overall atmosphere of a school, but they must be authentic events reflecting the positive feelings of the school staff. We have visited schools where a positive, celebratory atmosphere with food and music helped ease tensions as schools' demographics changed dramatically due to shifting residential patterns and immigration.

Journal

The K–8 School on the Arapaho Reservation outside Lander, Wyoming, hosts a family night once a month. The entire community is invited to participate. The school opens the gym and encourages families to play basketball with their children. They open the computer lab, where older students help families learn to use the Internet. They open the Culture Center, located on school grounds, where they offer a variety of cultural classes on language and Arapaho culture. They serve dinner, and there are always nurses on hand to answer questions and to talk to parents about childhood diabetes. On the evening of my visit, the entire community made jack-o'-lanterns from a load of pumpkins that had been donated. Family night was an evening filled with songs, laughter, and family fun. It was a great celebration of the Arapaho life and culture. —B.B.

Specific ways that teachers and school staffs can incorporate more communitywide celebrations to foster optimism include the following:

- Meet with community members to learn what is important to different community groups.

- Plan for regular schoolwide celebrations during the year. Make a master calendar of what will be done each month to ensure there is at least one schoolwide celebration each month.

- Provide monthly celebrations of student success.

- Arrange for multiple ways that students can gain recognition in academics, arts, social skills, and athletics.

- Hold music and other performance events, including talent shows and stand-up nights, for students to share what they are working on.

- Have competitions between classes, across grade levels, and for the whole school. Post progress and results in public places.

- Hold a monthly potluck for the school community so people have an opportunity to meet and mingle.

- Conduct a survey of families to find out what they can share with the school community. There are amazing talents in every school's extended network.

An Emphasis on the Positive

Schools with a sense of optimism emphasize the positive. In one school in Hutchinson, Kansas, the teachers began sending students to the office when they had done something good—for example, when they had a significant learning experience or had done a good deed. Notes went home to parents emphasizing the positive achievements of their students. In every classroom, there was positive reinforcement of the idea that all students can learn and be successful. Students seemed to be levitating out of their desks with this powerful support. This emphasis on the positive transformed the school, almost eliminating student disruptions and discipline problems. The assistant principal said, "My job has changed completely. Rather than meeting with disruptive students and working with them, now I spend most of my day talking with students about what they have done well. I get to add my praise and reinforcement. This simple program has transformed our school" (personal communication between Bob Barr and administrators in Hutchinson, Kansas, during the 2007 school year).

Journal

A principal from an Oklahoma alternative school told me, "In our little school, which serves kids who have had such a tough time and have often been in trouble, our greatest emphasis is on respect. Kids arrive at our school with their hats on backward, a Raiders jacket, and chains around their necks; they look like thugs. In a few weeks, the hats come off, the Raiders jackets are left at home, and they become kids again. I am sure we do our part, but a big reason for the change is the other students. They just love our school and have this wonderful positive attitude about it. You will often hear them say to new students, 'Hey, don't screw up our school. We don't wear that kind of stuff here. You need to look around and see what it takes to make it here. If you don't, you won't be here very long. This school just about saved our life, and you are not going to do anything to ruin it.'"

An elementary school teacher in Ohio said, "At our school, they were trying to replace the 'self messages' that students too often used about themselves (I am ugly, I am dumb, I can't do this work) with positive messages of pride (I am so smart! I can do this work! I am proud of myself and proud of my family)." The teacher laughed and said, "In a very real way, we are in the messaging business." —B.B.

Here are methods teachers and counselors can use to increase the emphasis on the positive:

- Work to ensure consensus belief among school staff of positive, high expectations for all students.

- Select students to be the target of positive attention from a group of adults (or the entire staff). For two weeks, the adults make a concerted effort to check in with these students and to show genuine care and concern.

- Use positive reinforcement. This can be a powerful tool in the classroom over time and has proven to be far superior to threats and punishment. Focus on students who are doing what is expected instead of those who are not following directions. What receives attention will grow.

- Meet regularly with parents to talk about students' academic, social, and emotional learning.

- Meet regularly with parents to discuss long-range plans, career and college readiness, high school expectations, and so on.

- Help parents, especially those who are low-income, elevate their expectations for their children and seriously consider future opportunities for them.

- Look underneath negative behavior for its cause, and use it to connect with the child. A student who throws a paper to the floor may find the assignment overwhelming, irrelevant, or boring, or the child may have just had an argument with a parent, or learned that his uncle is in the hospital. A simple question or two ("You seem upset. Want to talk about it?") opens the door for communication.

- Teach students a variety of positive class and school cheers, and use them regularly.

- Encourage mutual greetings between students and adults when they cross paths on campus: "Hello, Mary!" "Hello, Mrs. Wright!"

High Expectations

The power of a single teacher's high expectations on student achievement is well documented (Barr & Parrett, 2007). Imagine the impact of an entire school's staff and faculty surrounding students with expectations for high achievement (Barr & Parrett, 2008). In her study of high-poverty, high-performing schools, Chenoweth (2007) concluded that high expectations were a key characteristic. Teachers, administrators, and counselors in these schools, even at the elementary level, "talk with their students about going to college or into high-level technical training" (p. 217).

Journal

A fourth-grade student in Oregon once told me, "How did I learn that I was smart? Well, my teacher just kept telling me that I could do this schoolwork, and how smart I was, over and over. Until one day it just came to me: 'Girl, you can do this work! You are smart!' I guess my teacher made me learn I am smart." —B.B.

In 2009, as Rayzor Elementary School in Denton, Texas, was trying to gain approval as a feeder school for the International Baccalaureate (IB) program, teachers had students learning highly sophisticated concepts like integrity (see the journal entry on page 57).

At Hodge Elementary, also in Denton, Texas, to counter the cripplingly low vocabulary levels of their poverty-level students, the school celebrated a new "Word for the Day" every day. All teachers wore the word on their lapels, and if a student used the word correctly in a sentence, he or she received a small recognition or reward. At the end of the day, the word was added to the growing "Word Wall" in the front hallway of the school. A visit to the school impressed us with the sophistication of these vocabulary words (the word for the day was *credible*), and we were surprised at how well students could use them in sentences. The school principal, Sam Kelley, explained that the best part of the program was seeing the kids stop at the Word Wall each day to review all the words they had learned. The principal said, "Our little Word for the Day program is transforming the vocabulary of our students and building a strong foundation for reading. And it happens every time one of our kids walks into the school and down the front hall."

Journal

At an elementary school in California, the bus driver walked into the school and told a teacher that one of his first-grade students was reading to a group of kindergarten students on the ride home from school each day. The little girl would sit among a group of younger children and read across the page using her finger. She would encourage her "students" to follow the words with their eyes, teaching them how to segment the words using hand chops on her forearm, the way her teacher was showing the first-grade class. She kept telling the kindergartners, "You can do it! You can learn to read!" —E.G.

In a school district in Bloomington, Indiana, an elementary school developed a partnership with the Indiana University School of Music, in which the university purchased small violins for the low-income first graders and provided tutors to teach them to play. To everyone's amazement, in a few months the first graders were planning concerts for the entire school.

Journal

At a Georgia elementary school, where families had been encouraged to read to their children in the evenings, one little girl told me, "My mother can't read, so each evening I read to my mother! And you know what? She loves the stories! She wants me to keep reading to her. I tell her, 'Mom, I just know that you can learn to read! It's easy. I will help you.'" The parent reading program was clearly working, just not exactly the way it had been originally envisioned. —B.B.

High expectations reinforce optimism for learners. Teachers can raise the expectations they have for learners in the following ways:

- Use and teach vocabulary. Instead of using the term *verb* in primary grades, and then introducing *predicate* in the upper grades, use *predicate* from the beginning.
- Communicate the expectation that every learner can succeed; some learners just have different ways of getting there.
- Share stories of people who overcame obstacles to find success; read books, watch films, do research reports, and invite people to speak to the class.
- Define success both as a class and as a school. Make sure students have many models of different kinds of success—family, educational, career, financial, creative, and so on.

- Use random selection strategies to ensure that all students, not just those who volunteer, are called on regularly. Random selection communicates that every student has a valid and meaningful role.

- Have students explain directions, teach the class, share solutions, and so on.

- Select one student a day, randomly, to be a "focus" student. During each lesson that day, focus in on exactly how that student is doing, what he or she is learning, and how he or she is responding. Call on that student more often, and seek his or her input into what is happening. You might make this public and call the student the "class ambassador" for the day, that is, the student who is providing a window into how the class is going.

Journal

The staff of Rayzor Elementary School, which serves a broad range of students, impressed me with its efforts to be formally recognized as an International Baccalaureate feeder school. After five years, the intellectual level of instruction in the school had dramatically improved.

On one of my visits, after reviewing the personal traits emphasized as essential learning goals for every student in the school, I was skeptical that elementary students, especially low-income and English as a Second Language students, could master these extremely complex goals. The school counselor smiled and encouraged me to go out into the hall, select a few students at random, and see if they had learned any of them. I quickly picked three different students representing different ages and ethnic groups. When the counselor told them what we were doing, they all looked at one another, smiling, and one exclaimed, "Try us out!"

Feeling a little embarrassed, I asked, "Okay, can any of you give me an example of living a principled life?" All three students raised their hands and cried out, "I can! I can." One said, "It's like if you find money in the hallway, you don't just keep it, you try and find the owner." I then asked about the meaning of *integrity*, and while two of the students were puzzled, the third said, "It is being good, even when you are alone and there are no teachers around."

The counselor explained that integrity was the new concept teachers had been working on, and some of the students had not yet mastered it. "Try another," she said. I selected "balanced life" from the list of traits. Once again, all three students eagerly gave fine examples. One said, "It's when you don't do school work all of the time, but you leave some time to play." Another responded, "Don't just eat junk food; be sure and eat some healthy food . . . but some junk food is all right."

One of the oldest principles of effective, individualized instruction has always been to treat all students as if they were gifted. At Rayzor Elementary School, I saw this principle in action—and what a wonder it was to behold. —B.B.

Coordination of Community Services

Schools that are truly committed to transforming the learned helplessness of poverty-level families and their children recognize that they have a wide range of responsibilities that go far beyond academic instruction.

Often referred to as full-service schools (Dryfoos, 2010) or community schools (Comer et al., 2004), many provide before- and after-school, Saturday, and summer programs. Some also provide nutrition during weekends and summers or provide or help families find available health services in the community. Some schools purchase washers and dryers to ensure that students have clean clothes. Full-service and community schools provide a sense of belonging and purpose (Comer et al., 2004; Jensen, 2009). These schools:

> …integrate social and health supports with educational enrichment. They teach low-income parents how to help their children do better in school and connect families to the resources they need, such as welfare, help with income taxes, the citizenship processes, and even assistance in creating small businesses. Through this process, the school becomes a hub, improving the safety and stability of the neighborhood. (Dryfoos, 2010, p. 220)

Given the great challenges of living in poverty, few programs or activities are as helpful and powerful in building and conveying a sense of optimism, respect, and success as providing family services at the local school.

To build optimism through the coordination of community services on site, schools can do the following:

- Be alert to problems in or frequent moves by the family—excessive absences, lack of winter coats, medical or dental needs, and so on—and serve as an early alert system to inform counselors or social workers about perceived needs.

- Recognize that if students are hungry, cold, or sick, they will not learn effectively. Schools must have a system of helping families find necessary services.

- Create a snack cupboard where staff and community members can bring pre-packaged food that can be given to students in need.

- Encourage students and staff to bring unwanted books, toys, and school items to a school "swap meet." Students can earn dollars for the swap meet in class, which they can redeem once a week.

- Use a parent survey to find out what needs families have, in order to plan ways to meet the most critical needs.

- Offer parent education nights, with dinner and childcare.

Next Steps

For educators who are interested in developing or enriching their school's sense of optimism, the following process has been provided.

The staff and educator teams should complete the reproducible Staff and Team Questionnaire: A Sense of Optimism on page 61 (and at **go.solution-tree.com /schoolimprovement**). Their responses should be summarized and compared in small groups. Where there are significant differences in perceptions, the groups should discuss why individuals perceive their school in such different ways. To gain maximum school effectiveness, there should be strong consensus on the basic beliefs of the school staff.

The reproducible Student Questionnaire: A Sense of Optimism (page 63 and online) can gauge students' feelings about school. This questionnaire provides a powerful reality check for staff perceptions about a school, and if administered again later in the school year, it will provide a way to monitor shifts in student attitudes and measure progress.

These starter questions can be used as a part of a larger questionnaire developed by teachers, administrators, or counselors that relates directly to the school and its programs.

Any survey of student perceptions should be anonymous and used only after careful orientation of the students and their families. If parents object to the survey, their children should not be asked to take it.

If there is widespread agreement regarding needed improvements, those areas should become the focus of specific goals, discussions about interventions, and assessments of intervention effectiveness. Use the Discussion Topics: A Sense of Optimism reproducible (page 64 and online) to facilitate these collaborations.

Refer to the section in chapter 8 titled "Assessing the Institutional Culture" (page 154) for detailed information about conducting surveys and arriving at consensus.

Conclusion

In this chapter, the first of the "seeds of hope" was discussed: helping students develop a sense of optimism. Reviewed research suggests the human brain may in fact be "hard wired" for optimism. This reinforces the importance of teaching students, especially poverty-level students, to replace their feelings of helplessness through a program of learned "optimism." The use of school culture to effectively teach students new attitudes and ways of approaching obstacles was also discussed.

This chapter explored seven essential characteristics of school cultures that resonate with optimism: a welcoming environment, an atmosphere of respect and safety, an emphasis on success, communitywide celebrations, an emphasis on the positive, high expectations, and coordination of community services. Taken together, these characteristics combine to surround students and infuse them with attitudes of optimism and hope.

Such a culture is an essential prerequisite to helping students develop the other seeds of hope—a sense of belonging; a sense of pride, self-esteem, and self-confidence; and a sense of purpose, which we explore in depth in the next three chapters.

Staff and Team Questionnaire: A Sense of Optimism

Complete this survey, summarize the responses, and then compare them in small groups. When there are significant differences, the groups should discuss why individuals perceive their school in such different ways and work toward consensus (see chapter 8, page 151).

Rank each statement using the following scale:

Needs Improvement   Effective Practices   Exemplary Practices

1   2   3   4   5   6

1. The school's décor, signs, and greetings create a welcoming atmosphere. _____

2. The people who greet visitors at the school entrance at the start of the school day are warm, friendly, and engaging. _____

3. Students and parents from different cultural and ethnic groups feel welcome when entering the building. _____

4. School staff welcome parents as partners in the school. _____

5. The school staff have a solid understanding of the problems associated with poverty. _____

6. The school staff have a solid understanding of the basic human needs that are so essential to effective learning. _____

7. The school has developed a systematic program to ensure that the basic human needs associated with the school are being provided for each student. _____

8. Students feel safe and respected in the school. _____

9. The school has a strong zero-tolerance policy regarding bullying. _____

10. The school is effective in reducing or eliminating bullying. _____

11. All students in this school are treated with respect. _____

12. All school personnel in this school are treated with respect. _____

13. School personnel respect those from different ethnic or cultural backgrounds. _____

14. All school personnel believe that all students can learn effectively. _____

15. School personnel are well prepared to effectively teach all students, including poverty-level and minority students. _____

1 of 2

16. The school classrooms emphasize a "mastery learning approach" designed to ensure that all students achieve learning goals. _____

17. The school monitors student achievement and behavior in order to identify students who need immediate intervention. _____

18. The school has a system for remediation or intervention for students who have been identified as needing it. _____

19. The classrooms and school as a whole emphasize student success and positive reinforcement. _____

20. The school has discipline policies used consistently throughout the school. _____

21. The school does not use a punitive student discipline system. _____

22. The school and classrooms clearly exhibit high expectations for behavior and learning. _____

23. The school has regularly scheduled events to celebrate academic successes and cultural events. _____

24. The school helps low-income and minority families and their students locate and utilize community services. _____

25. Overall, how would you rank your school as being a welcoming place of safety and respect? _____

Student Questionnaire: A Sense of Optimism

Respond with: 1 = do not agree; 2 = agree; 3 = strongly agree

1. I feel welcome when I come to school. _____

2. I enjoy school and look forward to coming each day. _____

3. I feel safe and respected in my school. _____

4. I have never been bullied in my school. _____

5. My teachers care for me and respect me. _____

6. My teachers always encourage me to do my best work. _____

7. My teachers are helpful when I have a problem. _____

8. My school does not tolerate bullying. _____

9. I feel respected by other students at my school. _____

10. I get immediate help whenever I struggle or have a problem. _____

11. All my teachers have confidence that I can be successful in school. _____

12. At school I feel like I am part of a big, happy family. _____

13. People respect one another in my school. _____

14. There are always people who welcome me when I arrive at school. _____

15. All the different minority groups are respected in our school. _____

16. My school seems really interested in me and provides me with help in so many ways. _____

Discussion Topics: A Sense of Optimism

After filling out individual staff questionnaires and examining the student questionnaires, staff members, teams, book groups, and other adult groups should come together to explore the following topics of discussion.

1. Does our school have a clear vision?

2. How do student perceptions differ from those of the school staff? Why do they differ?

3. Do *all* students and their families feel welcome in our school?

4. How could we make our school atmosphere more welcoming and supportive for students? For parents?

5. Do any students in our school feel intimidated or bullied?

6. How can we make our school safer, and how can we help everyone—teachers, parents, and students—feel more respected and valued?

7. What else can we do to celebrate student successes and family cultures?

8. How can we help poverty-level families find the available services they need in our community?

9. How can our school staff gain a better understanding of the conditions of poverty in our community and how these conditions affect learning for our students?

Chapter 5

A Sense of Belonging

No one leaves the ninth grade, I mean no one, until we help them find a place where they feel they belong.

—School counselor, Corbin High School, Corbin, Kentucky

Finding a sense of place or belonging is important to individuals regardless of age, but for poverty-level students, finding a place of acceptance and belonging is a vital prerequisite to effective learning. For them, it is the second seed of hope. Emphasizing the foundational importance of belonging, Maslow placed belonging just above safety on his hierarchy of needs (figure 3.1, page 40).

There are a few key times in a young person's life when belonging is crucial to emotional health, and a student's first days in school is one of them—particularly for children of poverty who may be having their first experience outside their home and culture. The first encounter with the middle-class values that are so much a part of public education tends to be a dramatic shock that can leave poverty-level students feeling isolated and alone. The need for connectedness and belonging may become intense.

The other times that belonging assumes great importance is during later childhood, when students make the transition to middle school and again when they enter high school. It is during these periods of youth development, when their physical, biological, social, and cognitive transformations fill their lives with such uncertainty, that students rely even more on the stability provided by their schools' environments. Students from impoverished backgrounds are particularly vulnerable during these periods of transition from one school environment to another.

The fact that many low-income and poverty-level families are highly mobile also makes belonging a great and continuing challenge. The need for belonging is so important that effective schools often take on the characteristics of a surrogate family with an atmosphere of caring and support.

While middle-class students tend to spend their time going from one organized group activity to another—clubs, athletics, and other sponsored activities—and stay more connected via Facebook, Twitter, and their handheld mobile devices, children of poverty may lead more isolated lives. Living in poor neighborhoods increases this isolation and may reduce access to resources by constricting one's personal network of close ties (Tigges, Browne, & Green, 1998). Research on African American families living in poverty has found that teenagers from this socioeconomic group are less likely than whites living in poverty and less likely than affluent African Americans to know a person outside their family with whom they feel comfortable discussing important issues, and they are less likely to have a college-educated person in their network of contacts (Tigges et al., 1998). The digital revolution has only exacerbated this distance between poverty-level and middle-class students.

The isolation of teenagers as a group has also increased in an era when students lack the meaningful roles they once had in the time of family farms and shops (Heller, n.d.). As a result, teens tend to connect closer with peers than with adults, increasing the pressure to find a network of close friends. For those who do not have such a network of friends, the pain can be enormous, and in some areas, the need for belonging and affection leads to membership in gangs (Heller, n.d.). In many surveys, even affluent and academically successful students report feeling alone and alienated from parents, teachers, and even peers (Kantrowitz & Wingert, 1999), and research indicates that individuals' perceptions of their social status, rather than their actual social status, influence feelings of isolation (Kliff, 2008). Teens who perceive that they are well liked tend to do better than teens who perceive they are not, regardless of the number of friends they actually have (Kliff, 2008).

Belonging and Learning

Learning is strengthened when students feel a sense of belonging; unfortunately, the inverse is also true, in that students who lack a sense of belonging struggle to learn. Schools may even interfere with students' development of connections with peers and staff. Rather than alleviating isolation, school practices often make it worse. Tracking students into remedial programs and retaining or expelling them, for example, separates students from their peers and promotes a sense of low self-worth. Students without a sense of belonging tend to experience more anxiety, eating disorders, and depression and too often suffer through the negative feelings associated with low achievement (Kazdin, 1993; Newell & Van Ryzin, 2007). As we saw in chapter 1, this trail of failure may even turn into a "pipeline to prison" (Editors of Rethinking Schools, 2012).

On the other hand, research from the fields of sociology, psychology, and education has documented the positive outcomes associated with strong social connections and being part of a group: better grades, better attendance, less bullying and violence, and a decrease in risky behavior (Barr & Parrett, 2001). Research from the Search Institute (Benson, Galbraith, & Espeland, 1998) identified forty factors in schools, communities, and homes that relate to positive and negative student behaviors; in fact, many of these relate directly to feelings of belonging, including healthy relationships with adults, a caring school climate, adult role models, positive peer influence, and youth programs.

Journal

Marilyn struggled every day to control her behavior. She seemed to be in trouble all the time due to impulsivity. Her reading tutor and I decided to do an intervention and invited her to our room for lunch. She would come, eat her lunch, and talk with us the whole time. When I saw her in detention, I'd sit down and work with her on her unfinished work. Some days she'd stop by before school started. After a week of these social calls, Marilyn's teacher commented that she was doing much better in class. She was more settled, less impulsive, and followed directions more easily. Marilyn had found a place where she felt special and felt she belonged in this big school. When she needed a reprieve from the pressures and noise, she had a place to go. —E.G.

The benefits of belonging are summarized by Newell and Van Ryzin (2007):

In school, positive peer relations and teacher/student relationships are vital to maintaining high levels of motivation, engagement, achievement, and positive behavior. . . . Belongingness also has a profound impact on adolescent mental health and wellbeing. Intimate, supportive relationships can enhance adjustment, perceived competence, and self-esteem; they can also reduce emotional distress and suicidal thoughts and lead to lower levels of involvement in high-risk behaviors. (p. 467)

Research on resilient children and youth has likewise identified strong interpersonal relationships as a critical characteristic of successful low-income students (Benard, 1997; Krovetz, 1999). Resilient students' flexibility, sense of humor, and interpersonal skills help them build more positive and stronger relationships with peers and adults. The good news is that the traits of resiliency can be developed in students who have not acquired them before starting school (Krovetz, 1999).

Journal

On the first day of after-school tutoring, I passed through the gathering area where students were eating a snack before heading to the playground to play for a few minutes before meeting their tutoring teachers. A seventh-grade boy sat hunched over a table, the picture of discontent. I kneeled down next to him. "You don't look real thrilled to be here."

"I'm not," he spoke into his knees.

"Oh. This wasn't your choice?"

His head shook.

"Do you know why we wanted you here?" He shook his head again, but then made eye contact with me for the first time. "We want you to be successful, and we want you to have a great life. We want you to be able to read as well as possible before you get to high school. What do you want to do with your life?"

"I'm going to be a mechanic. Everyone in my family is a mechanic. My dad's a mechanic. He's teaching me how."

"That's great! Do you need to read to be a mechanic?"

"Yeah. You have to read manuals. Everyone in my family was boat mechanics, but my dad switched to cars. I'm following him."

We talked about different motors for a minute. I asked him if his dad was a strong reader. He indicated no, his dad struggled like he did.

"You know, it's common that people who are gifted with their hands and mechanical things often struggle with reading. I sure hope that you find the tutoring valuable."

He said thanks and went outside for his break. I hoped that our conversation helped him view his tutoring with a different mindset. At the bare minimum, I hope he knew I cared, and that rather than just being criticized and lectured, someone was interested in listening to him; someone really cared. —E.G.

Research now suggests that students' social networks actually enhance learning: "Social interaction contributes a remarkable amount to the improvement of educational skills, but it also contributes to a child's overall health and well-being" (Marshall, 2012). Students learn easily from one another—and seem to love learning when doing so. The better a student's social network—whether it's at lunch tables, through after-school homework clubs, or via online connections—the better that student's friendships and the more powerful the learning outcomes (November, 2011). Learning effectiveness tends to be enriched by whom you know, and students from low-income families may suffer because of their lack of social connections. The tendency toward isolation of poverty-level students in schools and classrooms may also serve to reinforce negative attitudes and learned helplessness.

A variety of related research involving youth gangs, athletic teams, extracurricular activities (Barr & Parrett, 2008), and even the military (Junger, 2010) has helped identify the powerful positive outcomes of being a member of a group.

Addressing Students' Needs

Students and their families will be drawn to a school or classroom that addresses their basic needs in an effective manner. This type of atmosphere conveys a powerful message: *Here is a place that welcomes you; here is a place that is working to help you.* So often in low-income communities, students can be found arriving long before school opens, in anticipation of safety, a warm and caring welcome, and the thought of a hot breakfast.

Specific ways that schools can help students find a sense of place include the following:

- Building relationships
- Creating a surrogate family at school
- Developing students' interests and talents
- Exploring careers
- Using social networking to enhance belonging

When the atmosphere of the school addresses students' needs, learning increases, emotional health is supported, and attendance improves.

Building Relationships

Chenoweth (2009) identifies relationship building as one of the five essential characteristics of schools where effective education is occurring. While she points out that the culture of an effective school results from rigorous, effective, and engaging instruction that occurs every day in every classroom, "establishing good personal relations is one of the first things tackled in a completely dysfunctional school" (p. 201). In a failing, dysfunctional school, everyone tends to disrespect and blame everyone else: students, parents, teachers, and principals. In contrast, strong, positive relationships seem to come from a genuine caring for students. Chenoweth (2009) quotes a teacher who describes her school this way: "We're a kind school. We really care about each other. The teachers care about the children" (p. 202). When students experience this type of caring, they will often reciprocate. In high-poverty, high-performing schools, it can be difficult to find students or parents who have anything negative to say about their teachers or school.

In Culture of Hope schools, teachers care about students and their families. They care if students do their work, and whether or not they do it well. They make sure students know exactly where they are in their learning and what they need to do to achieve their goals. They care if a student is absent and why. They practice complete honesty with students, never giving them false praise or using trite techniques to improve self-esteem (Chenoweth, 2009). Instead, they build students' self-esteem through genuine recognition and praise of students' hard work and accomplishments.

You hear it often in schools with effective relationships: we treat our students exactly as we want our own children to be treated. Chenoweth (2009) concludes her emphatic support for building strong relationships in this way:

> It takes a great deal of work to establish the right kind of tone and atmosphere in . . . [high-poverty, high-performing] schools. But once it is established, students feel safe and able to learn; teachers feel safe and are able to teach; and not incidentally, administrators are able to turn their attention to other issues, such as improving instruction. (p. 205)

Such schools and classrooms attract students and families, helping them feel safe and cared for and ensuring they have a place where they belong.

Nothing helps students feel a sense of belonging like strong relationships with fellow students. Here are some ways teachers can help encourage and develop student relationships:

- Match students with similar talents and interests in small groups and encourage them to work together using their unique skills or interests.

- Develop a buddy system in the classroom, so that students help one another and work together on projects. It is also a great way to quickly "check roll." This kind of partner work benefits all learners, but especially low-income and English learners.

- Know students well enough that you can encourage them to participate in extracurricular activities they may like. Schools with few co- and extracurricular activities can brainstorm ways to creatively increase their offerings. Such activities not only build relationships and a sense of belonging, but also improve attendance and academic performance (Jensen, 2009).

- Use class and morning meetings (Kreite, 2002; Nelsen, Lott, & Glenn, 2002) to foster relationships, understanding, compassion, and connection between students.

- Use workshop models, such as writing workshops and reading workshops, which help students get to know and rely on each other to accomplish real learning (Atwell, 1998; Graves, 1994).

To build relationships, Donna Walker Tileston and Sandra K. Darling (2008) suggest the following learning experience:

> Provide a variety of ways in which students can learn together and strengthen acceptance of differences (through collaborative groups, circle sharing, four corners, group study, partner groups, think, pair, share, cooperative learning, peer evaluations and so on). (p. 170)

The more students know each other, the more they care and can have compassion for each other, just as in families.

Creating a Surrogate Family at School

We have already seen that some schools attempt to meet the basic needs of poverty-level students for food and safety and health care—needs that may not be met at home. At the academic level, some schools, especially at the middle and high school levels, design instructional programs in small groups of minischools, alternative schools, or career clusters. This permits a small group of teachers to work almost exclusively with a small group of students. In such educational settings, everyone comes to know everyone else. The students attend class with students they know, rotating through a series of teachers who view themselves as a team. These personal connections make it easier for teachers to personalize learning and address students' specific needs within the instructional program. A program's size can have a powerful impact on learning, due to the increased level of caring and support (Barr & Parrett, 2008; Jackson & Davis, 2000).

Students in these small, personalized programs talk about feeling that they are part of a family. They exhibit a sense of ownership. When developed effectively, such programs have an enormous influence on poverty-level students who may come from family situations that lack structure or are dysfunctional. A surrogate family atmosphere may well serve as an antidote to the disruptions often associated with life in poverty.

Much of the research on the surrogate family atmosphere comes from the alternative school movement. Research on alternative, magnet, and charter schools documents the power of the school environment as a surrogate family (Barr & Parrett, 1997). A school or classroom with a surrogate family atmosphere can transform students' attitudes and lead to improved learning (Barr & Parrett, 2001). Barr and Parrett (2001) summarize the research in this way:

> For . . . children who may not have had or do not have a supportive, caring family, or who have had school experiences that may have been brutally negative, the "surrogate family atmosphere" can have an immediate positive impact . . . [such schools] create an "all for one, one for all" community of camaraderie among teachers,

parents and students similar to that found in elite military organizations, superior athletic teams, cohesive private schools and successful companies. (p. 73)

At the elementary level, this classroom atmosphere is encouraged through two-way communication between teachers and families, home visits, and partnerships with parents. At the secondary level, it is developed when large, impersonal comprehensive schools are reorganized into the small, personalized educational programs associated with learning communities, minischools, career clusters, or alternative schools. It is also developed by surrounding students with caring and demanding teachers with high expectations and by emphasizing respect among teachers, administrators, parents, and students.

Another powerful contributor to a surrogate family atmosphere is choice. When families and students have the opportunity to participate voluntarily in a school program, their feelings of connectedness are enriched. The opportunity to freely choose to participate or not to participate represents a powerful motivation for learning as well as a powerful influence in feeling that they belong. Choice is also essential for teachers. It is imperative that the teachers of students from low-income families not only believe that they can have a positive impact on student learning but also that they choose to work with these students.

Journal

I will never forget the student I met in Portland, Oregon, who had left Jefferson High School, a large comprehensive high school in the city, to attend the Metropolitan Learning Center, a small grades 3–12 alternative program. The student was striking. She had bright blue hair, lots of body art, and enough earrings hanging from her ears to sound like wind chimes when she walked down the hall.

When I asked her why she left Jefferson High School, she laughed and said, "They thought I was totally weird."

After sharing a laugh with her, I asked, "Well, how have you found it here at MLC?"

She thought about that for a few seconds, and in a serious tone, she said, "You know, I am not weird anymore. I was totally accepted; I feel like an orphan who has been adopted into this big happy family." —B.B.

Teachers can help students to feel a part of a surrogate family in a number of ways:

- Teachers must know each and every student by name, and know about the students and their families.
- Aspects of learning must be personalized according to each student's needs and interests.

- An atmosphere of respect must exist in the classroom and across the school.

- A surrogate family atmosphere works best in small groups of teachers and students working together for much of the school day, to foster relationships.

- When students and teachers voluntarily choose to participate in an educational program, their commitment to learning increases.

- Attitudes of caring and respect are essential for both teachers and students.

- A family atmosphere demands that parents be involved as full partners in teaching and learning decisions as well as school rules.

Developing Students' Interests and Talents

Schools can do much to help students find and develop their unique talents and interests through participation in school activities, clubs, and extracurricular activities. Nothing can match the effect of involvement in programs related to interests and talents on students' personal pride, positive attitudes, sense of belonging, and even school attendance (Damon, 2008).

Effective schools have learned that offering a large array of activities provides huge payoffs for students in so many ways. Examples include, but are not limited to, the chess club; choir, band, or orchestra; Future Farmers of America (FFA) and Future Homemakers of America (FHA) programs; the drama club; and the yearbook club. To ensure that *all* students are able to participate in clubs and activities, many schools schedule extracurricular activities during the school day.

The development of talents and interests can also provide the foundation for students discovering purpose in their lives and a lifelong connection with others who share the same or similar talents and interests.

Teachers can help students to develop their talents and interests in the following ways:

- Talk with students and explore what they are excited about; listen to what they talk about.

- Know two to three things that each child is good at or attracted to, and help children connect to activities that are related to their interests.

- For poverty-level students, do much more than provide students with a list of clubs and activities. Teachers and counselors must develop programs that permit students to experience a large number of possible activities in which they might never consider participating.

- Encourage students who are participating in clubs and activities to invite other students to join for a session or two to help students get a sample of what various experiences might be like.

- Bring in many guest speakers who have varied interests, experiences, and backgrounds. The more voices students hear, the greater the chance they will find a connection to a passion.

Journal

A high school band director in Covington, Kentucky, told me, "Don't ever forget the power of music in the lives of many African American kids. They connect with music. I go all over town scrounging up beat-up used musical instruments just so we can have a band." He said, "It doesn't take me long to find something a kid can play, and before you know it, they're hooked. Every morning before school my room is packed with kids who are not just coming to school, but coming to school early to practice. I also help these kids understand that if they work hard and sacrifice for their music, they just might find a way to continue their band work at the college level. They hear that. They understand that. They get it that their music might provide a way to a better future. Once kids find music, find their place in our school band, they are hooked. After that, they are a better student and there are no more attendance problems."

Navo Middle School, located at about a twenty-minute drive outside of downtown Denton, Texas, is surrounded by very affluent homes, but it also serves a large group of students from low-income families bussed out to the school. I stayed after school to see a practice session of a step team. This group of predominately minority students was just exploding with energy and talent, stomping their feet and clapping their hands in a rapid-pace rhythmic dance. Incredible! Although they were definitely outsiders in this affluent community, they had found a place of belonging. The pride and self-confidence they were gaining through this program was so obvious. I do not think I have ever seen students work so hard and so enthusiastically as these steppers. —B.B.

Exploring Careers

An important tool for developing student interest and talent is career education, especially at the secondary school level. For middle and high school students, finding a connection between school and possible careers can have a tremendous positive impact on motivation. Secondary students, especially students from low-income families, may become bored and disinterested with a school curriculum that seems far removed from their daily lives. For that reason, effective schools begin early to connect students to the world of jobs, careers, and professions, helping them bridge the gap between their interests and talents and the world of work.

Once students find a particular career choice, whether it is cosmetologist, X-ray technician, or lawyer, they can plan how to get from where they are to where they want to go. If the school program uses career themes to organize learning, students benefit from working with peers who have similar interests. Through career-themed courses, job shadowing, and community service in their interest areas, students make friends and find mutual support and connection with like-minded adults. All of this leads to students finding a sense of belonging, not only in school, but after graduation as well.

Teachers can help students consider career opportunities in a number of ways. For example:

- Ask students to work in small groups to conduct a simulated job search. They use current classified ads in newspapers or online to look at a large selection of possible jobs. Working together, they select a particular job or job category and try to learn as much about it as they can, possibly even interviewing people who work in that job or profession. They learn about salaries and educational and training requirements. Finally, students complete a mock job application and mock interview.

- Hold a career fair at the school. While it takes considerable organization, most communities seem excited about participating, especially if there is a community college or college in the area. Students get to walk around and talk with people who are professionals in the widest possible array of careers and jobs.

- Present a survey of students' career interests as a graph in a whole-school community area. The graph can serve as a springboard for conversations with students about career options. Students who selected similar career pathways can work together to collect information and make presentations.

- Invite community and family members in to talk about their jobs or careers.

- Have a "career of the week" at school, when a hot job or career prospect is highlighted and discussed throughout the school.

Using Social Networking to Enhance Belonging

Few things define modern teenagers more than their social networks. Twitter, Facebook, YouTube, iPhones, texting, tablets, friending, and all of the other electronic games and tools have created an enormous, all-consuming social world for affluent preteens and teenagers. Research suggests that this is not so for the children of poverty (Richardson & Mancabelli, 2011). Even worse, there is surprisingly little research on the ways that technology can be employed to help low-income students find a greater sense of belonging. Part of the problem stems from the significant differences in availability and use of technology in the different socioeconomic classes (Coley, Cradler, & Engel, 1997; Davis et al., 2007). In chapter 1, we described how the "digital divide" of haves and have-nots has transformed rapidly into a "digital differentiation," where more and more students have access to some type of computer technology and an Internet connection. Yet a review of research on this topic suggests the scope of a very large issue still separating poor and affluent students (Richardson & Mancabelli, 2011).

Journal

A friend who teaches in Newport, Oregon, told me about one of her middle school students who did not have a computer or even a cell phone. Somehow the student got a used, broken cell phone, which she pretended to use when she was around her more affluent peers. Of course, some of the other students figured out her charade and began teasing her. It was just heartbreaking, but the incident gave the teacher an opportunity to talk about respect for one another. Technology, the teacher explained, "makes such a divide between affluent and poor students. I think there is an important role for schools in all of this. I hear of schools that are providing computers to all of their students, requiring all students to complete online courses for graduation, and providing digital textbooks. Who knows what the future holds." —B.B.

In affluent schools, access to technology inside and outside of school supports learners in being creators and intelligent consumers of digital information and technology. However, for students growing up in poverty, a lack of access to technology at home as well as at school may lead to a more passive consumption of these new tools. Recognizing the huge potential of social media and electronic technology for fostering "belonging" among poverty-level students, educators may need to assume the long view of emerging potential. Alan November (2012), easily one of the most creative of contemporary educators, has proposed a solution that utilizes technology, social networking, and purposeful student work. While this suggestion represents a conceptual and material leap well beyond what many schools and teachers would consider realistic or possible, his ideas paint a picture of where we could go, perhaps where we are headed, in regards to utilizing technology as a tool for learning and a tool for connecting learners (November, 2012).

Journal

I was surprised when the teacher of a middle school social studies class near Boise, Idaho, told his students at the beginning of class to make sure that they were all turned on. Turned on? I thought he surely had misspoken. Boy was I wrong. This middle school provides all students with iPhones.

When I asked the teacher about this experiment, he smiled and said, "We use the phones every day for learning." He thought a minute and then said to his students, "Yesterday we were talking about the Olympics in London. I wonder who the current prime minister of Great Britain is. I would like this half of the room to use your world history books and this side of the room to use your iPhones and see who can find the name of the current prime minister of the United Kingdom."

Well, the iPhoners had an immediate and correct answer. The students using their textbooks took a while longer to get the answer "Tony Blair," which was incorrect. And there was a wonderful teachable moment when students were asked to explain the reasons for the two different answers. By providing all students with technology, this school had also leveled the playing field. —B.B.

Technology in schools has transformed from the early days of computers in computer labs, or a few classroom computers for centers, to schools with entire classrooms that are networked with handheld devices. Virtual learning is becoming a requirement in some college and high school programs. This expanding world of online learning, both official learning and learning just for its own sake, is transforming the world of education. Tens of thousands of students, from children to graduate students are now taking a physics class composed of randomly developed, short individual video lessons and online exchanges and chat rooms. Even assessment is evolving with technology, as testing companies develop innovative, computer-based standardized tests for the Common Core State Standards.

Technology has now moved learning beyond the educational establishment. November (2012) envisions an entire new world of classroom learning that has the potential to "connect" and engage all children and youth via electronic learning. He is describing an entirely new way of "belonging" and learning.

According to November (2012), in the earlier era of family farming "children were responsible for performing meaningful jobs that were vital to each family's success….Children were essential to the very survival of the family" (p. 1). In more recent times, children's responsibilities have evolved into more passive roles centering primarily on their completion of schoolwork. To restore children and youth as vital contributors to their communities, especially their school communities, November (2012) calls intriguingly for the creation of "digital farms" that contain "jobs" integrating technology, social networking, and the learning tasks of the classroom. These ideas represent a huge break with the traditional, teacher- and textbook-centered classrooms that describe most public schools and dramatize the classroom of the very near future, where, as shown in the following examples (November, 2012), every student has a technological responsibility:

- Some students are responsible for making tutorials to help other students. For example, a student learning how to upload video files to YouTube might make a video of the process and then develop a tutorial for others wanting to learn the same skill.

- Certain students assume the responsibilities of being the class scribes of the day, responsible for taking notes and diagrams for the class's online notebook, to which all students have access.

- Some students assume the role of researchers responsible for finding answers to questions the class identifies during the day (for example, who invented the teapot? What was the Teapot Dome scandal? What is the Tea Party?).

- Students also assume the responsibilities of coordinating collaboration, establishing and maintaining working relationships with classrooms around the world via the Internet.

- Some students might help the class raise money for their community projects or monitor class investments, like an investment banker. The class might raise money and then decide what worthy causes the class will invest in, and the investment banker would provide performance reports for the class's investments. November (2012) calls this "contributing to society."

- Students may assume the role of curriculum developers or reviewers who create podcasts of visual and audio media covering the work students are doing in class and in their "jobs." Students download these podcasts to their mp3 players or iPods to take learning home.

While this description may sound like science fiction to many traditional educators, it bears a great resemblance to the Foxfire Project, where students published a national magazine and actually owned a bank (see pages 125–126). Imagine the Foxfire learning activities in the new technology world and suddenly you have a "digital farm."

Traditional views of technology as tools used to enhance individuals' learning, like glorified textbooks and tutors, are being turned topsy-turvy as innovative educators explore the outer limits of students' learning. The notion of "digital farms" that replace traditional farms, and provide meaningful ways for students to contribute to and even become a vital, essential component of the learning being done in their classrooms and around the world clearly supports a sense of belonging. And finally, these ideas provide a meaningful way to engage low-income students. The challenge of course is to find funding to ensure that all students have access to the tools of technology. With the emergence of computerized standardized assessments, districts will be under more pressure, and will hopefully receive more funding to administer the tests as well as prepare students adequately to take these tests. The end goal, of course, is to ensure that poverty-level students have equal opportunities to grow and develop via the virtual world.

Journal

Look in our library on any given recess and you will see a flock of students clustered around computers. Some are reading for Accelerated Reader, racking up points for the schoolwide contest. Others are working on projects for class. And still others are working on their own projects. All are working with their friends in collaboration or comfortable companionship. You'll see kids writing stories that their teachers will never see, others are creating new languages and writing alphabets and pronunciation guides. Some are researching the *Titanic*, because they are hooked on learning everything they can, while others are trying to find the lyrics to a song they want to sing for graduation.

What makes this so different from other schools is that most of these students do not have access to computers at home. They may have the Internet on their cell phones, and most of them have their own Facebook page, but they do not have access to the content-generating capacities of technology at home. And for many, their classrooms have one computer and their class has one sixty-minute session in the computer lab each week. If they are lucky, they can get in an extra thirty minutes every day by using their recesses. Teachers in high-poverty schools, from the inner-city to the rural backwoods, express a unified plea: "We need technology for our students to use for learning!" —E.G.

Teachers can use technology in the following ways to increase students' sense of belonging:

- Ensure that every student has access to computer technology, at least at school.

- Integrate the use of technology into classrooms and student projects and use technology across the curriculum.

- Use technology to enhance two-way conversations between home and school.

- Build technology skills of low-income students so that they can be active participants in technological learning.

Regardless of the vehicle, children crave a sense of belonging. They wish to belong to a group, tribe, club, or family. Schools have the opportunity, and perhaps responsibility, to provide as many ways as possible for children to find ways of belonging. A sense of belonging is a basic human need, and a prerequisite for learning.

Next Steps

District leadership, school leadership, and learning community teams should complete the reproducible Staff and Team Questionnaire: A Sense of Belonging on page 81 (and online at **go.solution-tree.com/schoolimprovement**) after reading this chapter. Following individual completion of the questionnaire, small groups should compare their responses. Individuals can also share their personal responses in small groups. When there are significant differences in perceptions, the groups should discuss the various points of view and why individuals perceive their school in such different ways.

The reproducible Student Questionnaire: A Sense of Belonging (page 83 and online) can be used as a part of a larger questionnaire for students—to be developed by a small group of teachers, administrators, and counselors—that relates directly to their school and culture.

If there is widespread agreement regarding needed improvements, those areas should become the focus of specific goals, discussions about interventions, and assessments of intervention effectiveness. Use the reproducible Discussion Topics: A Sense of Belonging (page 84 and online) to facilitate these collaborations.

Refer to the section in chapter 8 titled "Assessing the Institutional Culture" (page 154) for detailed information about conducting surveys and arriving at consensus.

Conclusion

In this chapter, we've discussed the importance of addressing the basic human need for a sense of belonging, with a special emphasis on the needs of students from low-income families. A sense of belonging is one of the crucial needs identified by Maslow in his hierarchy of needs, coming directly after physiological needs and the need for safety.

Schools cannot be expected to address all of the human needs of families and their children living in poverty, but they can address the basic needs of their students for feeling connected to the culture of school through a variety of means, including building relationships, creating a surrogate family at school, developing students' interests and talents, exploring careers, and using social networking to enhance learning.

In the next chapter, we look at the third seed of hope—a sense of pride, self-esteem, and self-confidence.

Staff and Team Questionnaire: A Sense of Belonging

Complete this survey, summarize the responses, and then compare responses in small groups. When there are significant differences, the groups should discuss why individuals perceive their school in such different ways and work toward consensus (see chapter 8, page 151).

Rank each statement using the following scale:

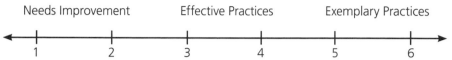

Needs Improvement   Effective Practices   Exemplary Practices

1   2   3   4   5   6

1. In terms of student success in school, the school staff believe that positive interrelationships are as important as effective instructional strategies. _____

2. The school is a place where everyone cares about one another—teachers, administrators, families, and students. _____

3. Positive personal relationships characterize the school. _____

4. In the school, teachers care if a student is absent and why he or she was absent. _____

5. In the school, teachers care if students do their work and whether they do it well or not. _____

6. Students and their families know exactly where the students are in their learning, what they have achieved, and what needs to be learned, and the school helps them understand how to achieve their learning goals. _____

7. The school staff treat students and their families exactly like they want to be treated. _____

8. The teachers in our school participate in two-way communication with parents. _____

9. The school encourages parental partnerships. _____

10. The school encourages home visits. _____

11. The school and classrooms have established a family-like atmosphere of caring and respect. _____

12. Students and their families feel that they have a sense of belonging in the school and classrooms. _____

1 of 2

13. In large schools, a family atmosphere has been encouraged through the organization of small minischools or career clusters. _____

14. The school provides students and families with learning options and opportunities based on choice. _____

15. The school staff believe that every single student should be involved in extracurricular or cocurricular activities. _____

16. The school works to develop each student's interests and talents. _____

17. The school sponsors large numbers of student clubs and activities. _____

18. The school is committed to helping each student explore career options and job opportunities. _____

19. The school is part of a K–12 effort to encourage students and families to attend postsecondary training or education. _____

20. The school has a program to help low-income students access computers and mobile phones. _____

21. The school actively works to help students use social media networks, mobile phones, and computers in constructive ways that aid learning and social development.
_____

22. The school not only provides opportunities for clubs and activities, but actively encourages students to become involved. _____

23. All students participate in some form of extracurricular club or activity in which they can develop their talents and interests. _____

24. Overall, I believe that our students from low-income families feel a real sense of belonging in our school. _____

25. Overall, I believe that our minority students and their families feel a real sense of belonging in our school. _____

Student Questionnaire: A Sense of Belonging

Respond with: 1 = do not agree; 2 = agree; 3 = strongly agree

1. My school is a place where people care about one another. _____

2. I feel that I really belong in my school and classrooms. _____

3. My teachers really care about me and are concerned when I am absent. _____

4. My teachers help me understand what I need to learn and how to be successful in my studies. _____

5. My school feels like a big happy family. _____

6. My classrooms feel like happy families. _____

7. I feel like I am an important part of my classrooms. _____

8. I feel like I am an important part of my school. _____

9. My teachers encourage me to join clubs and activities in the school and community. _____

10. My teachers encourage me to develop my interests and talents. _____

11. Our school has a large number of clubs and activities that I can participate in. _____

12. My school encourages me to explore all sorts of career opportunities for after I finish school. _____

13. I feel like I have a lot of choices in what and how I learn. _____

14. I feel like everyone at my school encourages me to stay in school, graduate, and go on to college or training. _____

15. I feel supported and respected in my school and classrooms. _____

Discussion Topics: A Sense of Belonging

After filling out individual questionnaires and examining the student questionnaires, staff members, teams, book groups, and other groups should come together to explore these topics of discussion.

1. Do the basic needs of students play an important role in decision making in our school?

2. How can we help our students feel a stronger sense of belonging in their classrooms and the school?

3. Do student perceptions differ from those of the school staff? If so, why?

4. How can we help poverty-level students and their families feel cared for and supported?

5. Do we do enough as a school to communicate and connect with parents?

6. Do we help parents know what they can do to help support school learning?

7. Do poverty-level parents feel like partners with the school?

8. How can we help poverty-level students develop strong relationships with one another as well as with more affluent students?

9. Do our students feel that our classrooms reflect a surrogate-family atmosphere?

10. How can we create a stronger surrogate-family atmosphere in our school?

11. Does the school have ample clubs, activities, and extracurriculars so that each student can find a place that relates to his or her needs, interests, and talents?

12. Do we do enough in our school to help students discover or enrich their interests and talents?

13. Do we have ample ways for students to think about and explore career opportunities?

14. Do we have ways for students and their families to begin considering specific career pathways?

15. How could we use social media and networking in a more effective manner in our school?

Chapter 6

A Sense of Pride, Self-Esteem, and Self-Confidence

It's not that students from low-income families cannot learn. It's that they have such low self-esteem that they feel they cannot learn. They have had so few experiences that help them build their self-confidence. So we start our instructional program with a concerted effort to build the personal pride and self-esteem of each of our students. We have found that if we can build pride and self-esteem, the learning will all but take care of itself.

—Elementary school principal, Ohio

Given the characteristics of poverty and its impact on children, the systematic development of pride, self-esteem, and self-confidence is essential for educating students from low-income families. This corresponds to the fourth and next level of Maslow's hierarchy, esteem needs (figure 3.1, page 40). As we have said, the seeds of hope do not necessarily unfold in a linear progression, just as Maslow's human needs do not unfold sequentially. The pyramid of needs simply provides a visual model for seeing the interrelationships that are involved in human growth and development. What we do know is that when the human needs of children and youth are addressed, student attitudes and achievement improve. This third seed of hope both builds upon and contributes to the sense of belonging, just as it builds upon and contributes to a student's sense of optimism and well being.

When speaking of pride and self-esteem, Culture of Hope schools emphasize building a student's pride in his or her family, culture, community, or school. But the primary goal is and must be the development of each student's sense of *personal* pride and self-esteem. Self-esteem is not developed by using hollow self-esteem building strategies (Chenoweth, 2009). Developing a deep, meaningful, personal pride does not come from pep rallies, "touchy-feely" interpersonal team building activities, and the wide variety of school promotions using slogans, stickers, and buttons. Rather, the quality of personal pride arises through personal satisfaction of a task well done and is the result of genuine effort and real achievement.

Building Pride, Self-Esteem, and Self-Confidence

Adults in Culture of Hope schools have developed a variety of ways to build students' personal pride, self-esteem, and self-confidence, including:

- High expectations and positive reinforcement
- Positive personal connection with an adult
- Assumption of responsibility
- Service learning
- Self-monitoring of learning
- Academic success
- Student-directed conferences

High Expectations and Positive Reinforcement

The most effective approach to helping students from low-income families develop a sense of pride, self-esteem, and self-confidence is to surround them with high expectations and positive reinforcement coupled with a continual set of learning successes. Students tend to live up to or down to the expectations of those around them and to develop attitudes that they see reflected in the adults who interact with them (Jensen, 2009).

Expectations and reinforcement are like invisible forces that can work for good or bad—they can make the difference in student success or lead to student failure. Few aspects of teaching and learning are as powerful as this dynamic duo.

High teacher expectations have been the focus of research over the years. In one classic study (Rosenthal & Jacobson, 1968), a group of teachers was told that researchers had identified a group of students in their school who were considered to be "late bloomers" who would have significant learning boosts of high achievement within a few months. The researchers then handed out the names of the students who were supposedly the late bloomers. In fact, the students' names were randomly selected, and none of them had been identified as potential high achievers. Yet the study found that within a few months, the students did in fact experience a boost in high achievement. With no new curriculum, no new involvement with parents, no new homework expectations, no extended time for teaching and learning, and no new afterschool activities, these particular students showed distinctive learning gains. The only variable was the "teacher deception" and the impact the teachers' new expectations had on student achievement.

Similar studies through the years seem to verify the incredible power of teachers' expectations and positive reinforcement. One reason for the success of so many alternative and magnet schools designed for high-risk students is that these students moved from an atmosphere where they had encountered low expectations to a school where they are surrounded by teachers with high positive expectations. We know the power that just one teacher with high expectations can have on a student; an entire staff can have an even more dramatic effect.

Journal

An Ohio middle school teacher told me, "In one of our faculty meetings, we identified a dozen students who represented some of our greatest challenges: high absenteeism, class disruptions, bad attitudes, missed homework assignments, poor performance on tests, and so on. We talked to the principal, the assistant principal, the counselor, all of these students' teachers, and even the bus drivers. We got everyone to agree: for two weeks, we would do everything possible to convey high expectations and provide positive reinforcement to each of these twelve students. Every time we would see one of these students, we would call them by name and say something like, 'How are you? It is so good to see you. We missed you yesterday; I hope everything is all right at home. I will get one of the other students to show you what we did yesterday, and after class, I will help you catch up. It is just so nice to have you in class today.' These messages were repeated all day at the school, on the bus, in the hall, in the lunchroom, and in the students' classrooms. If the student was absent, we called them at home in the evening to see how they were and tell them we missed them at school. Well, the effect was just amazing. Attendance improved, attitudes improved, and the students began to do better academically. The students even began to dress better." —B.B.

Teachers can foster high expectations and positive reinforcement for learners, which fuels pride and self-esteem, in a number of ways:

- Speak to children intelligently and use higher-level vocabulary, but explain it as you use it, with context clues, synonyms, and examples.

- Use a vocabulary word of the day, and expect students to use it as often as they can.

- Use and teach college words—for example, teach *product* and *quotient* when those operations are first encountered in school; teach students to use prefixes and suffixes to understand words.

- Use the Common Core State Standards to promote the use of language through thinking out loud, reasoning, arguing, and explaining.

- Tell students what they have done well and why their thinking is especially strong and unique, whenever possible.

- Use random selection strategies to ensure all students are called on regularly, not just those who volunteer; random selection communicates that every student has a valid and meaningful role.

- Use examples from students' work to illustrate creative, unique, and strong thinking.

- Select one student a day, randomly, to be the teaching and learning assistant, who will model, lead, support, and push the learning objectives of the day.

Positive Personal Connection With an Adult

Research documents the importance of personal connections between students and the adults in their schools. Talk to successful students, and you are likely to hear similar reasons for their success: some teacher or counselor or coach or band director or principal cared about, supported, and challenged them. Nothing seems to build students' personal pride like having valued adults believe in them. However, it seems easier to create positive personal connections at the elementary and middle school levels, where there is more direct person-to-person contact with a few adults, than it does at the high school level. At large, comprehensive high schools, personal connections must be fostered between students and school staff through adviser and mentor programs and by downsizing schools into smaller programs with lower student-adult ratios. An easy way to promote positive and consistent personal connections is through secondary-level advisory groups (see chapter 9, pages 182–183), which are organized for the explicit purpose of providing frequently scheduled time for students, teachers, administrators, and specialists to focus on students' lives and problems. Advisory groups evolve into support groups in which students come to know and help one another under the guidance of an adult in the school who serves as an advocate. This personal advocacy can pay powerful dividends in terms of building trust and positive relationships with students. There are also academic payoffs. The advisory leaders not only get to know students and learn about their problems, strengths, and needs, they can share this information with other adults who work with students and can serve as advocates for their students with other adults in the school. This teacher-to-teacher advocacy and support can lead to significant help for struggling students. Creating opportunities for one-to-one connections between students and significant adults has lasting, reverberating benefits.

Journal

While attending a conference on the education of the homeless, I participated in an event at which sixteen homeless teenagers were acknowledged.
These students had recently graduated from high school and were enrolled in
college. Each talked about the overwhelming challenges they had to overcome:
constant family mobility, the embarrassment of poverty, the stigma of homelessness, and the day-to-day efforts of just keeping body and mind together. Their
talks had one common, uplifting theme: what made all of the difference in their
lives was an adult—a teacher, counselor, coach, or principal—who believed in
and challenged and helped them hang on, stay in school, and graduate. It was
this personal caring and support that made all of the difference.

A community college student in Seattle, Washington, told me, "My brother was
in the military, my father had left home, and my mother was unemployed and
on the way to alcoholism. We were homeless and living with my aunt for much
of the time. Everything we owned was in a rented storage shed, and when we
couldn't make the rent of the shed, we lost everything. But my history teacher
believed in me. I really don't know why. He kept talking to me and encouraging
me and talking about college. It was his belief in me that often kept me going,
kept me doing my homework and coming to school each day, often just to get
to talk to him. He actually took me to the community college and helped me fill
out the registration paper. He took me to financial aid and explained what that
was and how it worked and how I could repay it after I graduated and got a job.
You might say he just about single-handedly transformed my life." —B.B.

Schools can help students develop self-confidence and self-esteem through positive personal connections with adults on campus in a variety of ways. Teachers and
staff can:

- Be on the alert for students who seem to have few friends, seem lonely, or
keep to themselves

- Reach out to students and connect them with other school staff, counselors,
and social workers

- Provide regular opportunities for students to help others (for example, peers,
younger students, other teachers, custodians, and cafeteria workers)

- Learn every child's name quickly, and use it often

- Create a "brag board" in a public place where teachers can write down
wonderful things students do

- Share positive accomplishments with other adults on campus using "pride
notes" that students can take to the secretary, a former teacher, the principal,
or another adult; the adult reads the note and shares in the student's pride of
accomplishment

- Follow up with questions following events in students' lives, so students know they are thought of: "How's your arm?" "Did you get to see your dad?"

- Write personal notes and leave them on students' desks. Teachers can do two or three a day until they've gone through the whole class, and then start again

- Work to ensure that every student in a school is connected with an adult who cares about and is interested in him or her (for example, mentorships, tutors, high school buddies, big brothers and big sisters programs, career contacts)

Assumption of Responsibility

The value of student responsibilities has long been related to the growth of self-esteem, respect, pride, and independence (Barr & Parrett, 2008). So often, schools confine students to passive roles in which they are supposed to be like sponges soaking up information, while isolating them from adults other than parents and teachers. Yet in many effective schools, students take on important roles throughout the building and in the community.

At Corbin High School in Corbin, Kentucky, students broadcast each morning's news and announcements via a student-run, closed-circuit television station. During the night, other students prepare a daily newspaper that is delivered early in the morning to all of the restaurants and businesses in the community. Some schools have identified a wide range of school jobs that students can fill. Students at Meridian Academy in Meridian, Idaho, are involved as members of their school's hiring and student discipline committees. In many elementary schools, students serve on safety patrols that help students cross busy intersections and board buses. Many schools have student "greeters," who welcome people when they enter the building and serve as guides to help visitors find their way around the campus.

Allowing students to assume responsibilities provides them with opportunities to experience the satisfaction that comes with doing a job well. There is the added benefit of receiving the praise and respect of adults other than teachers or family members. Coming into contact with a variety of adults, organizations, and agencies also offers educational opportunities (Barr & Parrett, 2008; see also Educators for Social Responsibility, www.esrnational.org, and the Center for Civic Education, www.civiced.org).

Another worthwhile area of school responsibility is cross-age tutoring. Even students who may be struggling in their own schoolwork can be helpful as peer tutors for younger students; students struggling to read or do math at their own grade level find great value in helping younger students learn to read or work with numbers. Both tutor and tutee benefit from this experience.

An even more ambitious effort involves students in significant instructional roles. For example, some teachers use high school students as teacher aides. Just as university professors may have graduate assistants who assume instructional roles, high school teachers may use students to conduct investigations into a particular area and actually provide in-class instruction.

In one class in Fort Worth, Texas, a history teacher invited students in study hall to work on upcoming historical topics at the back of her classroom or in the library. Over time, the students came to be called teacher assistants, a designation that included students with all types of abilities. The students contributed to the teacher's knowledge base and expanded instructional content by providing interesting and important presentations that enriched instruction. During one presentation, about life in the trenches during World War I, the room was darkened and the class heard selections of music from the period, as well as poetry and excerpts from great literature. The teacher admitted that by himself he could never have taken the time to find, organize, and present this topic in such a powerful and moving manner. Over time, the teacher assistant program took on a life of its own, with students competing among themselves to find the best information and make the most riveting presentations. These were not just homework reports but were important aspects of classroom instruction (see chapter 7, Legacy Learning, page 123, for more examples).

During the early years of the Meridian Academy, two of its programs—Greenbelt Guides and Science Circus—gained national attention as effective, innovative solutions for motivating high-risk students and building personal pride (Barr & Parrett, 2008). In both instances, the academy's high school students developed instructional programs for third graders. In the guides programs, academy students worked with biologists from the university to learn about the wildlife, botany, and ecology of nearby Boise River. After extensive study, the students received blue windbreakers with the words "Greenbelt Guides" stitched across the back. They then led organized walking tours along the river for classes of third graders.

On the heels of the successful Greenbelt Guides program, Meridian Academy developed the Science Circus, in which academy students worked with their science teacher to create hands-on lessons, again targeting third-grade curriculum. Students presented these lessons to third-grade classes throughout the surrounding schools.

In both programs, the third-grade teachers turned their students over to the academy students and acted as observers. At first, elementary teachers were very concerned about this—the academy's students were some of the most difficult in the district, and it was almost impossible to find teachers and schools willing to participate. But the stunning success and glowing reports soon spread by word of mouth, and before long, there was a waiting list of teachers wanting to participate. While the third-grade students certainly benefited from these two programs, the effect on the academy student leaders, who had long histories of school failure and discipline issues, was transformative.

Another nationally recognized program of student service was developed during the early years of the K–12 St. Paul (Minnesota) Open School. High school students in the school created a completely student-run consumer protection agency for the people who lived in the surrounding neighborhoods. Whenever the agency—called Nathan's Raiders after one of the teachers in the school—received a consumer complaint, students thoroughly investigated the situation. Any documented, certified issues were then passed on to the authorities and occasionally even to local media in an effort to correct the consumer abuse (Barr & Parrett, 2008).

Journal

At Rivera Elementary School in Denton, Texas, they have developed a "Star Program" for student volunteers. School staff submit job descriptions, which are compiled into a handbook that describes the jobs and the responsibilities that go with them. Jobs include library helpers, art teacher assistants, bus helpers, and so on. Students talk with their parents and apply. After interviews, the Star participants are selected and go to work. I met a few of the Star students and was impressed with how serious they were about their responsibilities. As one Star student explained, "This is our school, and we get to help make everything work better!" I could see tangible examples of an outstanding school working hard at building student pride and self-esteem. —B.B.

Teachers can foster students' assumption of responsibility and pride in a number of ways. They can:

- Ask students to create a list of all the jobs that students could do to help out in class

- Have students apply for three class jobs, providing a reason why they are most qualified; the teacher can select from the applicants and explain why a particular student was selected. Rotate jobs every few weeks so students are able to apply for and do many different jobs

- Recruit students for jobs around the school. Make a list of things that need to be done, and post the list in prominent places with the names of those whom students should contact if they are interested

- Create service-learning opportunities; perhaps integrate a service-learning requirement into the school program

- Create lessons that require real responsibility on the part of students. Ask them to interview veterans of World War II or the Vietnam War, or the parents of men and women killed during the Iraq or Afghanistan wars

- Ask students to design lessons, plan field trips, order supplies, run fundraisers, create budgets, and so on
- Provide answer keys and teach students how to grade their own assignments

Service Learning

Service learning—a program that has a powerful, positive effect on developing student pride and self-esteem—has been documented as one of the most effective strategies for the prevention of dropouts (Schargel & Smink, 2001). Service learning "integrates meaningful community service with instruction and reflection to enrich the learning experience, teach civic responsibility, and strengthen communities" (ETR Associates, 2012). In classrooms and other community-based organizations across the United States, students engaged in service learning apply what they learn in school to real-life problems.

Comparing traditional volunteering with service learning can help more clearly define this strategy. A volunteer project, such as picking up trash at the beach, provides an important service to the community. And a teacher might design a service-learning project in which, after students collect the trash, they analyze their findings, reflect on statistics from similar clean-ups over the past ten years, and write a report to share with the local media and university detailing their findings.

The benefits of service learning include (Billig, 2000):

- Development of character
- Growth of citizenship skills and community participation
- An understanding of cultural diversity
- An increase in school attendance

Service-learning projects vary from community to community and may include volunteering in hospitals, retirement centers, and government offices, as well as participation in community beautification projects. Students also serve in research efforts, such as gathering data about forests, rivers, and beaches. Perhaps most important, service learning can be connected to career exploration and career interest. (See chapter 7 for more information about service learning as a concept that supports student purpose.)

A well-designed and organized service-learning program, one that strives to match students with purposeful projects, has a profound, positive impact on students. Service-learning programs give an immense bang for their buck when it comes to turning students around and giving them a positive place where they can contribute and receive praise and positive reinforcement. The outcomes of service learning also cross over into the other seeds of hope, giving students a place outside of school where they belong, as well as a sense of purpose.

Journal

After working in the Vancouver, Washington, school district for several years, I came to know about one of the toughest kids in the entire school. I learned that other students had nicknamed this large, intimidating kid "the Beast." A terrible student, he was often disruptive and disrespectful and frequently absent. The exploits of this student were so well known that, whenever I visited Vancouver, I always asked the superintendent how the Beast was doing. Usually, there was some new outrageous story about the kid's exploits.

One year, the building principal at one of Vancouver's high schools asked me to join him on a short field trip over the bridge into Portland, Oregon. We soon arrived at the world renowned Doernbecher Children's Hospital and took an elevator up to the fourth floor. As the elevator opened, I looked out into a children's ward and was stunned to see the Beast walking toward me down a hallway. I am sure my mouth fell open.

I saw he was wearing a white jacket and a nametag that said "David." I asked him what on earth he was doing in the hospital. His answer stunned me.

David said, "I am the mail guy for the hospital. I deliver the mail to each of the departments in the hospital. It's part of my service-learning program in my health career cluster. I'm supposed to volunteer my time two afternoons each week, but I felt that they needed me more than that, so I come every day."

Later, we talked to one of the hospital administrators and listened to his praise for David: "He has done an incredible job here. The nurses have learned that if there are things that need to be done each day, they say, 'David will be here today. He can help us. He will do it.' He has become 'our man Friday,' but he is helping us every day of the week. He helps out with just about everything, even reading to the kids in his down time. We just couldn't do without David." The director continued, "Oh yes, after so many people at the hospital encouraged him, he has decided to go into a nursing education program at the community college as soon as he graduates from high school. In fact, our head of nursing walked him over to the Portland Community College and got him the application papers and information about financial aid. We have already promised him a part-time job this summer, and there is a good chance that our nurses will find him a scholarship." —B.B.

Schools can enhance service-learning opportunities to foster students' feelings of pride in these ways:

- Start with volunteer opportunities at school, on the weekends, such as beautification, garden, or clean-up days.

- Encourage participation in community volunteer opportunities, such as beach or river clean-up, senior centers, museums, animal shelters, and so on.

- Incorporate service-learning into class assignments. Have students help configure service-learning components for units of study.

- Ask students to make presentations on service learning to the class or school community.

- Have a community space where service-learning opportunities, as well as students' results can be posted.

- Have teachers and staff share how they can contribute to the school and larger community with presentations to students.

- Build a service-learning component into the school's requirements.

Self-Monitoring of Learning

Increasingly, effective schools have begun to transfer responsibility for learning to students. This represents a significant shift in the teaching-learning paradigm. Traditionally, students were the mostly passive recipients of teachers' efforts at instruction. However, a growing number of high-performing schools have significantly involved students in establishing learning goals, monitoring their own progress, and explaining their progress at student-led parent conferences. This shift of responsibility for learning to students is paying huge dividends in terms of attitudes, enhanced student motivation, and academic success. The shift is especially important for students who come to school with learned helplessness, because it helps them see direct connections between their actions and their learning.

Journal

In a primary class that I visited often, the teacher and students were working on goal setting and tracking progress. The walls were dripping with data in the forms of charts, graphs, lists, goals, and averages. On a particular day, the class had just posted their fluency scores for the month. When I walked across the room and caught sight of the graph, with 90 percent of the class meeting or exceeding their goals, I was so impressed with the data that I feigned fainting to the floor. The students were silenced for a moment, and then giggled with glee. "We made Dr. Gibson fall down!" I played it up and staggered to my feet. Then, with great seriousness, we talked about the data, what it meant, and how impressed I was with their progress.

Weeks later, the teacher told me her students wondered if they could get me to "fall down" again, and she noted they had a spark of eagerness to do something great that would be worthy of a faint: "Do you think this will knock her over when she sees it?" I had forgotten all about fainting over the data. This was a class that was living and breathing progress and self-assessment, in a very positive way.—E.G.

In effective schools, you find teachers at all levels working with individual students to help them understand and agree on learning goals and develop a process for regularly recording their assessments, monitoring their progress, and plotting their growth on a personalized chart. Walk into a classroom in such a school, and you will see walls filled with individual charts where students are graphing their learning over time. Inevitably, students can answer questions about where they are learning-wise and where they still need to go. Teachers report that student pride and self-esteem grow right alongside the academic growth charts. Students sharing ownership of knowledge and learning with their teachers has become a powerful incentive for effective education and has become recognized as one of the essential strategies for high-poverty, high-performing schools (Stiggins, 2001). Teachers increase students' self-monitoring of learning primarily through modeling and expectations. Specifically, teachers can:

- Model their own thinking processes using think-alouds while reading, writing, doing math, using technology, and so on; make explicit verbal accountings of what is going on in the mind

- Show self-monitoring while teaching by asking students questions such as "How was that explanation? Do you understand the rules the way I presented them? Could there be a better way?"

- Use student surveys and student responses to inform and improve instruction

- Expect that all students will monitor their own learning (This must be taught from the beginning of the year, and takes a lot of effort and redirection. When things aren't going as expected, teachers should ask the class about it: "Class, I expect it to be much quieter during writing workshop so everyone can concentrate. It seems very loud to me. What's going on?")

- Post learning objectives each day and ask students to self-assess how they have made progress; share that this is feedback for the teacher's improvement, too!

- Regularly have students set their own goals for learning, and plan for revisiting goals to gauge progress

Academic Success

No matter how much self-esteem or how great a sense of belonging Culture of Hope schools help students develop, in the end, schools must aim for high academic achievement. If poverty-level students have any hope of finding their way out of poverty, they must have high levels of success in this area. Academic achievement fuels students' self-esteem as well as encourages their need "to know, to understand and explore" (Maslow & Lowry, 1998; as cited in Huitt, 2007, p. 2).

For the children of poverty, the only reliable possibility of finding a pathway to a better life depends squarely on not just one effective teacher, but dozens of effective teachers over more than a decade of schooling. It has long been recognized by educators that almost anything can be taught to students of any age as long as the content is broken down into small, manageable units. And it is through a continual process of small successes in learning that students seem to slowly come to believe that they can learn and be successful.

In one school in Fort Wayne, Indiana, a group of high school teachers decided to reorganize the teaching of algebra. These teachers felt that so many students from low-income families were simply overwhelmed by the intimidating algebra textbook that they organized the course into over a hundred mini-units. Rather than a large, imposing textbook, the students saw only a single short unit. As soon as a student completed that unit and documented his or her success, that student moved on to the next short unit. Over time, students began to help fellow students who were still working on units they had already mastered.

The greatest challenge for public education is to help students who have built a strong record of academic success at the elementary school level to continue that success into middle school and then make a successful transition to high school. In this regard, a successful eighth-to-ninth-grade experience is absolutely essential for building this record of personal academic success. Nothing surpasses the importance of addressing the failure of middle and high schools to keep poverty-level students in school, learning effectively, and graduating. In order for this to happen, the middle and high school experiences must be personalized. Schools must be able to identify students immediately when they begin to falter or fail and have a schoolwide response in place to address the needs of these students (see chapter 9).

Journal

While speaking at a national conference in London, I was invited to visit a small elementary school in one of the poorest sections of Great Britain, which included large groups of emigrants from all over Eastern Europe, as well as the Middle East and Africa. The school had developed a reading program that was outlined on a huge number of colored cards. Students took the first card, the white card, and worked on the first steps in the school's reading program, which included such basics as learning about books and how to care for them. Once the students demonstrated that they had mastered all of the learning objectives on the white card, they moved on to the light blue card, which included the next small steps in learning to read. Every time a student completed a card and demonstrated mastery to the teacher, the entire class would hear an announcement and all would cheer. Then the teacher would get the next color card for the student. Every student knew which color he or she was working on, and what was next. All of the cards were located on the walls around the room. Frequently, students stood and asked the class, "Can someone help me with the green card?" and other students would offer their help. —B.B.

Schools enhance students' personal pride and self-esteem through genuine academic success. Strategies teachers can implement include the following:

- Posting student work and classwide and individual data. Growth charts, goal setting, "My Best Work" displays, and graphs can be used to show real growth.

- Ensuring that every child is represented on the walls, for real growth and progress.

- Posting learning objectives each day, and asking students to self-assess how they have made progress. Share that this is feedback for the teacher's improvement, too!

- Finding something that each child does well, and having that information posted, like a "go to" directory for the class. Frank is good at catching spelling errors, Sara is strong in math facts, Jake knows the entire school and can help you find your way and draw maps, and Julie is a whiz at using Google to find facts. When students ask for help, refer him or her to the directory first.

- Setting kids up for success by planning differentiated lessons where each child is working to his or her ability and goals.

- Regularly having students set their own goals for learning, and planning for revisiting goals to gauge progress.

- Teaching students specific, targeted strategies for handling particular tasks. Prompt to use the strategies, so students can be more independently successful.

Student-Directed Conferences

Highly effective schools often use student-directed parent conferences to engage students. This provides a remarkable and highly effective enrichment to the traditional teacher-parent conferences and represents a powerful strategy for building student pride and self-esteem. In addition to recording their test scores and plotting their learning progress, students collect work samples over time in a personal portfolio that documents and demonstrates their improvement. On parent conference night, the students are on hand to explain their goals and test scores and to show the portfolio to the adults in their family. The teacher may drop by to add a few comments and perhaps point out a particularly promising piece of work, but it is the students who are in charge. Research has documented the power of student-directed conferences and has shown that one of their benefits is an increase in participation by family members (Cromwell, 2010).

Journal

In our class, when we come to the end of a report card period, students and teacher work together to create a list of all that was learned and accomplished. We order the items by importance and list the assignments that represent the learning. I take that list and create a self-evaluation rubric for students to evaluate and grade their own learning. We pass back all the assignments and projects from the term, and students spend time sorting through the evidence of the semester, organizing their writing portfolios, and evaluating themselves with the rubric. For each of the report card areas, they assign a grade to their work, and explain their reasoning. Separately, I complete a rubric for each student based on my evaluation of their work. We then put the two evaluations together, and if there are any differences, I discuss them with the student, and we come to an agreement. After sharing our evidence for our evaluations, sometimes the student says, "Oh, I see now that I didn't meet that goal. I actually agree with your evaluation." Other times, I say, "Wait, I didn't think about that aspect of your work. I'm changing my score to what you put. I agree with you." With still others, we might come to a consensus on a score that lies in between our different scores. The truth is that differences tend to be rare. Usually the student and teacher are on the same page.

After this week of hard work on self-assessment, students write a narrative of their report card, noting the highlights of the semester that they want to share at conferences. Each student has a twenty-minute conference, and they pretty much run the whole show. It is a marvel to watch fourth-graders present the evidence of their learning, explain their strengths, and detail what they plan to work on in the next semester. It took a few years to get parents used to coming to the conference with their children, because it was so different. Now, we don't ever want to go back to the days when conferences were secret meetings between parents and teachers, the content of which was a mystery to students. Students' self-evaluation and student-led conferences provide a real opportunity for building a sense of pride, self-esteem, and self-confidence. —E.G.

At Granger High School in Washington State, student-led conferences led to 100 percent family attendance at parent conferences (LeBlanc-Esparza & Roulston, 2012). Rather than hold parent conferences in the gymnasium or in a classroom with other parents waiting and listening, the school arranged the conferences by appointment and scheduled meetings during times when families were available, usually in the evenings. When students began leading these important meetings, attendance soared to 100 percent. At Granger, "having students lead the conferences was a small but important shift that reflected the reality of a student's situation: they were in charge of their education; what they did or did not do meant everything" (LeBlanc-Esparza & Roulston, 2012, p. 66).

Changing to student-led conferences can seem like an insurmountable challenge, but their benefit to students' pride and self-confidence makes the effort worthwhile. Here are a few entryways into student-directed conferences:

- Implement student self-assessment in one subject area, or for one assignment, and grow from there.

- Have students help create rubrics for assignments.

- Ask students to be responsible for leading one part of the conference, for example by sharing a portfolio, explaining a single subject area's grade, or outlining two ways he or she wants to improve.

- Schedule "mock" conferences with peers, or in place of writing conferences one week so students can practice what it feels like to talk about their work and progress.

- Start small, perhaps with just a few students who volunteer. As the other students see what happens with this process, they will want to join in.

- Encourage students to do work for learning, rather than for the teacher's eyes. Legacy learning, service learning, and other hands-on or minds-on strategies help teachers create learning opportunities that have bountiful intrinsic, as well as extrinsic, rewards.

- Ask students to create assignments, test items, and study guides.

- Regularly display student work and data, so that looking at work and discussing it are regular parts of the school week.

Programs That Build Pride, Self-Esteem, and Self-Confidence

School programs can have a dramatic effect on students' pride, self-esteem, and self-confidence and provide ways for students to participate and excel in something they enjoy. Programs like the following can lead students to find purpose in their life and learning:

- **The Arts**—Citing Gazzaniga et al. (2008), Jensen (2009) writes that, "theater, drama, and other performing arts foster participants' emotional intelligence, timing, reflection, and respect for diversity; build memorization and processing skills; help students win social status and friends" (p. 118).

- **Athletics**—Participation in athletics has a wide variety of benefits. It improves attendance, reduces behavioral problems, and improves student achievement. Athletics also build personal pride and, through activities and exercise, build healthy bodies and physical fitness (Jensen, 2009).

- **Advanced Placement Courses**—Jensen (2009) writes, "An advanced placement curriculum builds hope for a better future, challenges rather than bores, exposes academic gaps to be remediated, and develops pride, self-concept and self-esteem" (p. 122). Even one advanced placement course will introduce a student to college-level work and show him or her that it is possible to accomplish that level of work. Advanced placement introduces students to a new and achievable future. It may be the first step toward a pathway out of poverty. Through a concerted effort, the Vancouver Public Schools in Washington State were able to increase the number of Hispanic students taking advanced placement courses by 38 percent, 2.5 times the rates of improvement at the state and national levels (Webb, 2010).

- **Leadership**—Placing students in leadership roles not only provides opportunities for building pride, self-esteem, and self-confidence, it also fosters belonging and purpose. Serving as conflict managers, providing tutoring to younger students, being on student council, and representing the students' interests on hiring committees are a few ways that schools can provide leadership roles for students.

Next Steps

District and school leadership teams or learning community teams should complete the reproducible Staff and Team Questionnaire: A Sense of Pride, Self-Esteem, and Self-Confidence (page 103 and online at **go.solution-tree.com/school improvement**) after reading this chapter. Following individual completion of the questionnaire, summarize the responses and compare them in small groups. Where there are significant differences, discuss why individuals perceive their school in such different ways. To gain maximum school effectiveness, there should be strong consensus on the basic beliefs of the school staff. Areas of disagreement should be the focus of extended discussions.

The reproducible Student Questionnaire: A Sense of Pride, Self-Esteem, and Self-Confidence (page 105 and online) can be used as the basis for a larger questionnaire by teachers and counselors for a specific school. Any survey of student perceptions should be anonymous and used only after careful orientation of the students and their families. If parents object to the survey, their children should not be asked to take it.

If there is widespread agreement regarding needed improvements, those areas should become the focus of specific goals, discussions about interventions, and assessments of intervention effectiveness. Use the reproducible Discussion Topics: A Sense of Pride, Self-Esteem, and Self-Confidence (page 106 and online) to facilitate these collaborations.

Refer to the section in chapter 8 titled "Assessing the Institutional Culture" (page 154) for detailed information about conducting surveys and arriving at consensus.

Conclusion

In this chapter, we have discussed the third seed of hope, building a sense of pride, self-esteem, and self-confidence. The importance of personal pride, self-esteem, and self-confidence relates to the fourth level of Maslow's hierarchy of needs—esteem needs—as well as the satisfaction of physiological needs and the needs for safety and belonging. The interrelationship between pride and self-esteem, as well as ways to address the human need for esteem were also discussed.

Students must not be deceived with high expectations and positive reinforcement. School programs must use every opportunity to ensure that students learn the crucial lesson that success follows hard work and perseverance. This process builds personal pride as a result of students knowing exactly where they are in their learning, where they need to go, and what they need to do. At every opportunity, teachers should emphasize that students must give it their best, put in the time, work hard, and persevere.

For children in poverty who may arrive at school with the learned helplessness of an external locus of control, it is absolutely essential that they learn and learn well that success is up to them. No matter how effective a teacher or how high the expectations for learning, students must come to understand that a pathway out of poverty is built on hard work and perseverance. What is crucial is not how smart a student is, but how hard a student is willing to work and how much that student is willing to invest in his or her future.

The good news is that the more students find a sense of belonging, develop personal pride and self-esteem, and begin to focus on a purpose or passion for their lives, the more motivation they will have for learning. The more students clearly define a sense of direction and purpose for their lives, the more capable they become of hard work and sacrifice.

The next chapter describes the fourth seed of hope: a sense of purpose.

Staff and Team Questionnaire: A Sense of Pride, Self-Esteem, and Self-Confidence

Complete this survey, summarize the responses, and compare them in small groups. When there are significant differences, the groups should discuss why individuals perceive their school in such different ways and work toward consensus (see chapter 8, page 151).

Rank each statement using the following scale:

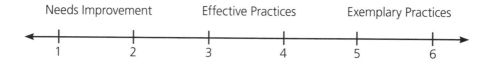

1. One of our school's major goals is to develop pride, self-esteem, and self-confidence in all students. _____

2. All of the teachers and administrators agree that all students can and will learn and achieve high levels of excellence. _____

3. Our school attempts to develop a personal connection between each student and a teacher or another professional staff member. _____

4. Our school encourages every student to work hard and put in the necessary time every day to be successful. _____

5. Our school provides a number of ways a student can assume personal responsibilities in the school and community. _____

6. Our school uses student-directed parent conferences. _____

7. Our teachers and administrators hold high expectations for all of our students' behavior and academic learning. _____

8. Our teachers and administrators use positive reinforcement to help build pride and self-esteem. _____

9. Our school has a system to help students have a positive connection with an adult in the school. _____

10. Our district's high schools are organized into small learning communities. _____

11. Our district's high schools use student advisory groups in which students are together for the four years of high school. _____

12. Our school uses cross-age tutoring. _____

13. Our school has a program so that every student participates in service learning or volunteer experiences outside the school. _____

14. Our school uses a systematic process that monitors the learning of every student. _____

15. Our school uses a student watch program to identify any student as soon as he or she begins to falter academically or have family or behavior issues. _____

16. Our school has an organized system in place to respond immediately when any student is identified as beginning to show family, behavior, or academic problems. _____

17. Our school has a system of interventions/remediation in place to help students who begin to struggle academically. _____

18. Our school involves our students in setting learning goals, monitoring their own progress, and maintaining work samples to document their progress. _____

19. Our school uses parent conferences as a reason for students to prepare portfolios documenting their learning progress. _____

20. Our school emphasizes that success in learning is not about personal ability but about hard work and persistence. _____

21. Our students believe they can be successful in their schoolwork and can achieve a high level of excellence in school. _____

22. Our students believe that they can graduate from high school and be successful in postsecondary education or training. _____

23. Families and community members believe our students can graduate from high school and be successful in postsecondary education or training. _____

24. Overall, I believe our school is successful in working with parents to help them understand their children's potential for success in school. _____

25. Overall, I believe our students know they can learn effectively and achieve high levels of academic success in school. _____

26. Overall, I believe our school is successful in helping each student build pride and self-esteem. _____

Student Questionnaire: A Sense of Pride, Self-Esteem, and Self-Confidence

Respond with: 1 = do not agree; 2 = agree; 3 = strongly agree

1. My teachers believe that I learn and achieve high levels of excellence in school. _____

2. My teachers really believe in me. _____

3. My teachers constantly support and encourage me. _____

4. I often feel that I can't do the work that my teachers assign me. _____

5. My teachers help me understand what I might be able to accomplish in my life. _____

6. I feel a positive connection with one or more adults in my school. _____

7. My teachers remind me that success in school does not depend on how smart you are but how hard you are willing to work. _____

8. I have important responsibilities for helping out in my school. _____

9. I have important responsibilities for helping out in my community. _____

10. I have a major responsibility in preparing and presenting a report on my schoolwork during parent conferences. _____

11. My teachers believe I can succeed in school, graduate, and be successful in college, community college, the military, or a job training program. _____

12. My teachers and counselors encourage me to think about what I want to do with my life and help me make plans to accomplish what I would like to do. _____

13. My school has organized students into small groups, which provide the attention and support I need to be successful. _____

14. I feel that I know my fellow students and that we all help one another succeed. _____

15. I feel a sense of pride about my work in school and know that I can do anything I set my mind to. _____

Discussion Topics: A Sense of Pride, Self-Esteem, and Self-Confidence

After filling out individual questionnaires and examining the student questionnaires, staff members, teams, book groups, and other groups should come together to explore these topics of discussion.

1. Do we have a schoolwide consensus that all students can and will learn and assume high levels of excellence? If not, what can we do about it?

2. Do we have a schoolwide consensus that all of our students will succeed in school and graduate from high school? If not, what can we do about it?

3. Do student perceptions differ from those of the school staff? If so, why?

4. How can our school work more closely with parents to help them have high expectations for their children, in both school and life?

5. How can we involve students in more school and community responsibilities where they find satisfaction in service activities?

6. How confident are we that we can quickly identify students who begin to struggle? Are we prepared to immediately provide intervention or remediation?

Chapter 7

A Sense of Purpose

It doesn't really matter where we are and what we are doing until we know where we want to go.

—Old proverb

In a more rural America, youth came of age working closely with their parents on the family farm or boat; in the family store; in logging, mining, or ranching. That connection between generations has all but disappeared (Scheier & Botvin, 1996), and many of today's youth, especially the children of poverty, come to school with little sense of purpose and little guidance or direction regarding how to transition from the dependency of youth to independent adulthood.

Observations in many high-poverty, high-performing schools show a concerted effort to help students find this sense of purpose and direction. It is important for schools to help students *believe* they can achieve their purpose and to help them develop effective strategies toward that end. This is the fourth seed of hope.

For students living in poverty, especially those from families that have experienced generational poverty, the development of a sense of purpose may be especially important for addressing the issues of external locus of control and internalized learned helplessness (pages 13–16).

Journal

A high school teacher in Oregon shared this story: "As nutty as it sounds, we work really hard in our career cluster to help students find their destiny. It has become a big joke with our students, but they can stand up and quote it: 'If you don't know where you are going, you don't know what you need to do today.' The huge payoff is this: if we can get our students to figure out their career aspirations, even in a general way, it creates this really big boost in motivation. They can start marking off the steps that they must take to get to where they want to go. They start focusing on their future. So, we talk a lot about our own private destinies. We keep asking every student, 'What were you meant to be?' I don't think that anyone ever asked our students who live in poverty that question." —B.B.

Maslow placed self-actualization at the top of his hierarchy of needs (figure 3.1, page 40) when it was first articulated, and he described it then as the ultimate need—to know, explore, and understand. But self-actualization could occur only when a person found his or her purpose in life, what he or she was fitted for (Maslow, 1943; Maslow & Lowry, 1973). He wrote that "a musician must make music, an artist must paint, a poet must write if he is to be ultimately happy" (Maslow & Lowry, 1973, p. 162). He believed that all humans need to discover what they are meant to be—their purpose or destiny.

The Research on Purpose

As William Damon (2008) reports in his book *The Path to Purpose: How Young People Find Their Calling in Life*, very few students (only 20 percent) can express a sense of purpose or direction in their lives. Damon's study reveals four categories of students, as shown in figure 7.1:

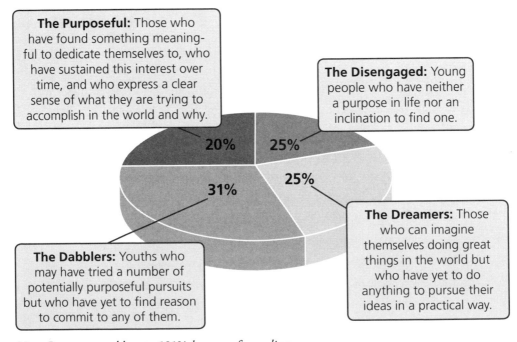

The Purposeful: Those who have found something meaningful to dedicate themselves to, who have sustained this interest over time, and who express a clear sense of what they are trying to accomplish in the world and why.

The Disengaged: Young people who have neither a purpose in life nor an inclination to find one.

The Dabblers: Youths who may have tried a number of potentially purposeful pursuits but who have yet to find reason to commit to any of them.

The Dreamers: Those who can imagine themselves doing great things in the world but who have yet to do anything to pursue their ideas in a practical way.

20%   25%   25%   31%

Note: Percentages add up to 101% because of rounding.
Source: Reprinted with permission of William Damon.

Figure 7.1: Damon's categories of students.

Possible reasons for students' indecisiveness are complex, ranging from rapid technological changes that have transformed the world of communication and work to increased tensions on both local and global fronts. Economic uncertainty and hardship and the lack of assurance that an education will automatically lead to positive employment may all play a role as well (see chapter 10 for a more complete discussion on these issues). These factors may be even more significant for students of poverty, who too often arrive at school without a positive personal vision of the future and with a sense of learned helplessness (Seligman, 1972). Add to these factors the increasing enrollment fees for higher education—even community colleges—that make paying for college more difficult for even middle-income families.

Fortunately, the 25 percent of school youth who are described as dreamers provide a rich opportunity for schools to engage students in systematic consideration and planning for their future. If students are already dreaming, they may well be fertile ground for schools' efforts to help them imagine their future.

Strategies for Building a Sense of Purpose

Researchers have suggested a number of strategies teachers can use to help students find direction and purpose. The following list is based on the work of Damon (2008), Pink (2009), Newell and Van Ryzin (2009), and (summarizing a 2000 study by Seligman and Csikszentmihalyi) Jensen (2009):

- Help students see more relevance in their studies.
- Focus on intrinsic rather than extrinsic motivation.
- Develop community assets that support healthy psychological growth of youth.
- Expand students' horizons.
- Develop their interests and talents through participation in school clubs and activities.
- Foster autonomy.
- Engage students in reflective inquiry.
- Provide learning options.
- Reduce emphasis on standardized tests.
- Continually remind students they can succeed.
- Help students set goals and master the strategies to achieve them.
- Encourage students to dream and dream realistically.
- Encourage hard work and persistence.

This chapter takes a deeper look at five of these strategies—(1) foster autonomy, (2) focus on intrinsic rather than extrinsic motivation, (3) engage students in reflective inquiry, (4) provide learning options, and (5) develop interests and talents.

Foster Autonomy

The power of student purpose must grow out of each student's passions, interests, talents, and aspirations and must reflect *personal* decisions and *personal* goals. This is often difficult in schools where students have little choice in teachers or courses. Schools often presume to know what is best for students and "prescribe" content, assignments, and learning goals. If the concept of purpose is to come alive in the school setting, the role of the school must be to liberate students. Schools must present students with a world of opportunities and help them understand that they are free to pursue any of those opportunities. Unlike students in so many countries in the world, U.S. students' potential options are limited only by their own personal vision, aspiration, determination, and talent. Since poverty-level students have had little experience in making important decisions about school or life, they need careful support and understanding to do so. The only decision that students from low-income families have often had the opportunity to make is whether to attend school or drop out. As a result, students' early decisions about their future may not be particularly thoughtful or productive.

Journal

A school counselor in the Lincoln County School District in Oregon told me, "I often hear that students want to follow in their parents' footsteps and continue the family traditions in fishing and logging, both career areas with declining opportunities. Even after exploring the changes in fishing, declining fish populations, overfishing with nets, the danger of the sea, and increasing government regulation, students may still opt for the freedom of working on the family boat. One fishing family explained it to me this way: 'Well, you don't make much money in fishing, and even that is likely to continue to decline. And it's a dangerous business. But you know, our family doesn't need much money. And out there you are your own boss, and you are totally free. We would much prefer our son to go to the community college and learn a trade, but he loves fishing, and we love him. So we will respect his decision. Who knows, maybe someday he will want to do something else, or maybe he will have to. The community college option will still be there. For now, the kid wants to fish, and we respect that.'" —B.B.

Counselors in Johnson County Schools in Kentucky explain that K–12 students, just like so many college students, change their minds many times. So even though students start out with a focus on a particular profession, over time they may connect their interests with some other career area that can be accessed more quickly. Counselors welcome these changes as evidence of growth and progress. Students may initially talk about becoming a doctor or lawyer, only to learn how lengthy the educational preparation is for these professions. Conversely, other students may start out considering a community college or technical training program only to develop an interest in a more ambitious career choice. Often, schools help students consider futures in large career areas, like health professions, science, technology, or legal professions, which enable students to explore a wide variety of possible careers within a general area of interest.

The role of the school is to help students think about their future, explore the widest possible opportunities available to them, and understand what they need to do to achieve a particular goal. For students from low-income families, it means exposing them to college or community college programs, introducing them to the complex world of college costs and financial aid, facilitating student visits to college campuses, and inviting successful school alumni to talk with high school and middle school students and parents about postsecondary experiences. Regardless of what path students choose, including deciding not to pursue further schooling, it is important for schools to help them and their families—many of whom have never considered postsecondary education—explore the options (see chapter 10, page 205, for more information on pathways out of poverty).

There is one additional, essential point that schools cannot overlook: after surveying the expanse of available options, poverty-level students may select pathways toward the future that do not lead out of poverty or to better economic futures than their parents. Some students may choose to pursue their parents' occupations, even though they are not financially rewarding, because they are personally fulfilling. The important point for schools is to help students explore alternative futures and gain an understanding of the rewards and liabilities of various careers. Ultimately, after discussion and personal reflection, school staff must honor students' decisions.

Journal

I started my first professional job as a U.S. history teacher in a large high school in Fort Worth, Texas, in the early 1960s. While doing graduate historical research at Texas Christian University (TCU), I found a huge collection of original historical sources on local history. The documents had been collected by historians hired by the Works Progress Administration (WPA) during the Depression years of the 1930s and '40s. It was a treasure trove of never-before-published original sources. I presented some of the material I had discovered to the high school's history club and wondered if the students might be interested in not just studying history, but actually writing some original history about the Depression years in their hometown. What happened as a result was remarkable.

The students not only dug through all of the WPA sources but also began reading microfilm copies of the newspapers of the time. They soon focused in on a particular story about the head of the Texas Communist Party, T. E. Barlow, who died in the Fort Worth city jail. The students discovered that after a large rally of unemployed citizens in Burk Burnett Park, money was collected to send a telegram to the governor of the state, who happened to be the state's first female governor. Barlow telegraphed Governor "Ma" Ferguson that Fort Worth was full of unemployed men who were willing and able to go to work and to please come up with some project so that these unemployed men could have a job. The telegram said the men would do anything. When Barlow came out of the telegraph office he and his two companions were arrested by Fort Worth city police for disturbing the peace. That night, Barlow died while in custody.

The students were fascinated to be working on a historical "cold case" murder, because the death proved to be a great controversy at the time. No one seemed to have ever provided a reasonable explanation for how it occurred. The students also discovered that many of the people they had been reading about in the historical documents were still alive and well. So they attempted to arrange interviews with the former chief of police, the doctor who examined Barlow after his death, a former mayor, and others. The students were frustrated that many of these people refused to talk to them, but former Mayor Jack Hammond—who happened to be the chair of the TCU history department—met with the students and became actively involved in their efforts. The students worked night and day, and many used their experiences to later find a career in the field of history. I am sure the students learned more than they ever would have in a classroom with a textbook—but of course, this experience had to be organized as a club activity rather than a classroom activity. A growing number of schools are building in autonomous time for students to experience this kind of learning.

In 2011, some of my former students who worked on the history project came to Boise for the TCU / Boise State University football game and a reunion with their former high school teacher. Over dinner, these students from decades ago talked about the death of T. E. Barlow and still remembered many facts of the case; they talked about how the experiences gave them a completely different view of historical events. They had learned how historians work and the associated frustrations that can accompany historical investigations. Though it was never a question on any test, what they had learned had survived almost fifty years. —B.B.

Pink (2009) describes how the corporate world has used autonomy to stimulate motivation and creativity among employees by giving workers designated time—sometimes one day each quarter, sometimes even 20 percent of their work time—to get away from their assigned duties to think, discuss, dream, and create. He describes one computer software company that schedules a "day off" once a quarter from 2:00 p.m. on Thursday until 4:00 p.m. on Friday. The employees are free to work on anything that they choose to work on, but at 4:00 on Friday, they must report on their work.

The result of these autonomous sessions is impressive. Companies have found that these FedEx Days, so called because ideas "arrive the next day," have led to an incredible array of important new ideas and directions for developments. One company engineer puts it this way: "Over the years, this odd little exercise has produced an array of software fixes that might otherwise never have emerged . . . some of the coolest stuff we have in our product today has come from FedEx Days" (Pink, 2009, p. 92).

This kind of autonomy has rarely been used in schools, but when it has, it has resulted in some remarkable examples of student learning. Schools have scheduled time for students to get together and, through discussion, identify a specific problem that they think needs attention. The students then differentiate work assignments and attempt to address the problem. Often, schools incorporate this concept into a project-based curriculum, which students are actively involved in planning. Examples include adopting a local park to beautify with murals and creatively designed benches; developing an oral history project in which students interview elders, write their stories, and present local schools and libraries with bound copies of the stories; and conducting fund-raisers to purchase toys and blankets for a local animal shelter. A hallmark of these projects is that the students' efforts have a visible impact on their local community. There are wonderful examples of students becoming engaged in projects totally unrelated to their school assignments (see pages 121–126).

Journal

Our school was right on a busy road, just after a sharp, ninety-degree turn. Drivers often whipped around the corner and flung themselves down the road past our school. There were no signs saying "School" because we were a charter school that had just rented the building. As we began our year, we talked about possible service-learning projects. One student talked about the speeding cars and wondered if we could study them to see how fast they really were going. Some students wanted to be able to give drivers tickets. This became our first project of the year, and I could see how it would lead to real learning in mathematics and social studies, as well as purposeful reading and writing.

Two students wrote a letter to the local police department explaining our concern and asking if we could borrow a speed gun. A police officer called them back and made arrangements to stop by to talk to our class. He taught us how to use a speed gun and allowed us to borrow it for three days of testing. For three days, students rotated in pairs, one student holding the gun, one student recording speeds. We charted and graphed and calculated averages, and discussed what the data meant. We compared trucks, cars, motorcycles, and delivery vehicles. We compared male versus female drivers, and we compared times of day. After all our calculations and graphs, students wrote a report to the police station, a report to the local planning department, and letters to the three local news-papers. The local planning department put up new signs before and after our school to help with traffic. —E.G.

Autonomy is an outgrowth of confidence and personalization of learning. Teachers can enhance students' sense of autonomy in the following ways:

- Encourage students to survey and interview family members, create family histories or family trees, and collect family artifacts and stories.

- Hold "museum days" during which students assemble a set of artifacts, perhaps from their early childhood or from family members' military service, or create family timelines with photos.

- Involve students in decision making regarding learning assignments. Students should regularly make choices in what they learn, how they learn it, and why they are learning it.

- Differentiate instructional products, processes, and content that support autonomy.

- Encourage students to take an active role in learning via decision making. This includes allowing students to make mistakes and learn from them. For example, a student might decide to sit on the floor to work on a project but finds that she is uncomfortable or that she gets distracted by others walking past her to get supplies. She might not finish her work and need to take it home, but the experience might be more persuasive than if the teacher had told her she couldn't work on the floor because she would be distracted.

- Allow small groups and partners to work together on assignments. Teach them how to work together and create a climate of high expectations of quality work.

- Talk with students about their interests, talents, and future goals. Students learn to think about their future and the kinds of decisions they need to make to reach their personal goals.

Focus on Intrinsic Rather Than Extrinsic Motivation

Throughout all of the research on human motivation, a common theme is evident: the most powerful, productive motivations seem to occur when a person is able to identify intrinsic high-valued goals and is able to develop effective strategies to achieve them. For example, students may become highly engrossed in music or the school band and devote all of their spare time to perfecting their talents. Other students might be naturally drawn to technology and through self-learned techniques become school experts, even helping teachers. The distinction is this: students are highly motivated to learn without assignments and tests. The research also suggests that extrinsic aspirations—such as good grades on homework or tests and even goals of financial security or achieving recognition—may motivate but be personally unfulfilling (Pink, 2009). A school culture that focuses on extrinsic motivations often leads to student apathy over time, even for academically successful students. Students' engagement in academic challenges, their levels of curiosity, and their interest in attaining mastery decrease, especially during the transition between elementary and middle school (Newell & Van Ryzin, 2009). By high school, many students have become bored and disengaged and have lost interest in school assignments (Newell & Van Ryzin, 2009). This in turn leads to absenteeism, academic failure, widespread cheating, and finally dropping out of school. This trajectory may explain why poverty-level students who have been successful at the elementary and middle school levels so often falter and fail in high school and ultimately drop out.

It may also explain why so many financially successful individuals turn to painting, music, philanthropy, or a new career following retirement (see Hollis, 2005). They may finally be able to focus on something that is personally fulfilling once they have the freedom and financial security to do so. With an aging population and longer life expectancy, more and more people seem freed from extrinsic motivation to find new meaning in their lives. (In later iterations of his hierarchy, Maslow referred to this as the need for self-transcendence—the need to connect with something beyond ego that is often fulfilled through serving or helping others.)

Increasingly, schools are providing students with opportunities to experience service learning, volunteering, cross-age tutoring, and other forms of service. Such programs not only provide a way for students to give something back to their community, but they are also powerful ways for students to find interests, talents, and purpose in their lives.

Journal

I read a story in the local newspaper about an Idaho farming family that wanted their son to go to college. They helped him plan for college, arrange for college tuition and financial aid, and enroll. One September, the young man loaded his car and left to drive up to the University of Idaho. But after driving a while and thinking about his life, he stopped the car, turned around, and drove back. He told his surprised parents that he was not leaving, and he was not going to college. What he really wanted to do was be a farmer. He planned to stay at home and help his parents with the farm. Now three decades later, the young man has expanded the family farm and taken college courses in agribusiness and computer technology, where he learned essential skills to help make farming more productive. He explained how happy he has been as an Idaho farmer and how glad he is that he did not go to college as a teenager. —B.B.

Research is quite clear that the most powerful and fulfilling motivations are intrinsic; strong intrinsic motivation provides students with a sustainable drive to succeed in school as a means to achieving important personal goals (Pink, 2009). Over time, research on human motivation has shown that students with strong intrinsic purpose in their lives tend to experience greater success in both K–12 schools and college than students with more extrinsic motivations (Snyder et al., 2002). Unfortunately, developing intrinsic motivations can prove to be unusually challenging when many poverty-level students suffer from an external locus of control. Only through the systematic development of intrinsic motivation will poverty-level students be able to stay in school, master essential cognitive skills and knowledge, graduate, and pursue postsecondary learning.

Alternative, magnet, and career-themed schools often emphasize student autonomy, mastery, and purpose (Pink, 2009). Other schools, like the EdVisions schools funded originally by the Bill and Melinda Gates Foundation, have strong records of academic success and social and emotional growth, including the development of a sense of purpose (Newell & Van Ryzin, 2007). The EdVisions design was based on Hope Theory research (see page 36). Though much of the progress in and research on schools that develop personal purpose among students tends to occur in special, independent, alternative, and charter schools, more and more traditional public schools are providing examples. And while much of the discussion centers on motivation related to current studies, teachers and administrators increasingly emphasize having students explore personal options in their lives, participate in visioning and goal-setting experiences, and practice reflective decision making. In many schools, both parents and students are encouraged to consider a variety of future pathways and are assisted in making specific plans for following their choice (LeBlanc-Esparza & Roulston, 2012). By asking students to assume positions of responsibility in the school and the community and engage in service learning (page 121), job shadowing (page 130), and career exploration (page 130), schools are helping students find their purpose and perhaps even their personal passion.

Schools with a Culture of Hope, especially at the middle and high school levels, also provide strong counseling and mentoring programs that support and guide students through school and graduation into positive postsecondary experiences. In rural schools, some middle and high school students work with adult mentors via the Internet in areas of career interest (Alliance for Excellent Education, 2011). This connection allows an ongoing dialogue between students and adults and provides a level of mentoring that may prove more effective than face-to-face mentoring.

Intrinsic motivation is closely related to autonomy. Students who have autonomy and make decisions about their learning are more likely to have intrinsic as well as extrinsic reasons for learning. Here are a few suggestions for increasing intrinsic motivation:

- Help students learn about their interests and talents through exposure to many activities. Career fairs, surveys, show and tell, community speakers, research projects, and service learning can provide this kind of exposure.

- Provide a wide variety of co- and extracurricular activities, offered at many different times of the day (before school, during lunch, after school, during an elective period, Saturday school, and so on).

- Create virtual or real scavenger hunts where students explore different careers, hobbies, sports, and arts and crafts.

- Allow students to "try out" activities before they commit. Some students will not try things because they want to be perfect, or think that if they try it they need to follow through.

- Teachers, administrators, and staff members should share their interests and talents. Consider having an adult talent show, where the adults perform for the students.

- Encourage students to participate in service learning, community volunteer projects, and school activities like cross-age tutoring.

- Talk with students and their families about the future and help students design life plans or personal plans. In chapter 10 (page 205), life pathways are provided to help in these conversations.

Engage Students in Reflective Inquiry

Ever since John Dewey (1916) talked about "learning by doing" and the importance of reflective inquiry, the field of social studies education has attempted to incorporate his ideas into the curriculum.

Dewey conceptualized that all learning occurred through a process that begins when a person feels uneasy or unsure about an issue or a personal belief or a decision that must be made. He called this *cognitive dissonance*. Out of this personal uneasiness, the individual begins to speculate on possible ways to resolve it, which is a process of reflective inquiry that leads to possible hypotheses and the search for factual information. The end of this process is the development of a growing number of tested personal conclusions or beliefs (Dewey, 1909).

Dewey and decades of social studies educators have argued that reflective inquiry is a skill that can and should be taught in schools and that the goal of instruction, at least for many social studies educators, is to "provoke" students to reflective thought and inquiry by confronting their unfounded beliefs. In a number of schools, reflective inquiry is being used to liberate students from passive, content-centered learning, freeing them to pursue important issues in their own lives, including one of the most important issues of all—what to do with their futures.

Journal

Noted psychologist William Glasser (1975, 1998) insists that the role of school is to confront students with questions, help them think about the implications of the choices they make for their lives, and assist them with making important decisions. In the late 1980s, I watched as Glasser demonstrated his theories with a number of high school students at Oregon State University. A typical discussion between Glasser and students would unfold like this.

Students: I hate school. School just sucks.

Glasser: Well, why don't you do something about it?

Student: I am. I'm going to drop out of school. Nothing you can say will change my mind!

Glasser (confronting the sullen and angry student with a number of questions): That's great, where are you going to live? Where do you plan to get a job? How much do you expect to earn at that job? Can you live on that salary? (No matter what the student replied, Glasser would say "Well that's fine . . ." and then ask him another question.)

In one encounter with a student, this discussion continued until the student grew more and more frustrated.

Student: Well, I can always join the army or maybe become a Marine!

Glasser (in a quiet voice): Did you know that no branch of the armed forces will take a high school dropout as a recruit?

Student (with tears in his eyes): Well what am I supposed to do?

Glasser then explained that only the student could answer that question, but that he would help him find some answers. Glasser slowly began to help the student think about options and talk about what he needed to investigate and how he could lay out some plans for himself and set some personal goals. He assured the student that he would find someone to continue to work with the student. It was absolutely captivating to watch a true master at work. —B.B.

There are a number of specific ways that teachers and counselors can use reflective inquiry to promote a sense of purpose. They can:

- Present ambiguous conflicts to students and encourage them to come to rational positions that resolve the conflict

- Hold debates in which students prepare to debate both sides of an issue and draw their "position" randomly right before the debate

- Present social dilemmas, such as what people do when someone drops an armful of books and papers, and how dependent their actions are on who is watching and how they feel about the person who dropped them

- Discuss human nature, and whether or how people can improve

- Use multiple pathways as encouraged by the Common Core State Standards to solve problems in mathematics. For students who are used to the "one right answer" emphasis of the NCLB years, this will create opportunities for cognitive dissonance that teachers can capitalize upon

- Confront students and lead them to think about personal decisions in their life and learning, using conversations like those described by William Glasser (page 118) using his famous "reality theory"

Provide Learning Options

Perhaps the best way to involve students and their families in important decision making is to provide educational options, including advanced placement and a challenging curriculum. Increasingly, school districts have stand-alone alternative schools, career-themed schools and programs, and even charter schools from which families can choose. The Vancouver, Washington, school district offers families options at the elementary, middle, and high school levels and has developed a sophisticated orientation program to ensure that all students and families have in-depth information about each program. The options available in Vancouver include:

- Challenge Program K–8
- Vancouver School of Arts and Academics Grades 6–12
- Lewis and Clark High School (an alternative/personalized learning program)
- International Baccalaureate
- Legal Studies Option
- Medical Arts Option
- Science, Math, and Technology Option
- Culinary Arts Option
- Portland VA Medical Center
- Clark County Skills Center

Over time, the high school program in Vancouver has looked more and more like a community college program than a traditional secondary school program. The district administrators believe that providing students and families with the opportunity to choose their educational programs enhances student motivation and commitment and helps the schools develop a sense of community and a sense of belonging among students and their families. It has also become an instrumental part of helping students find their personal purpose. The goals of the district, initiated first in the 1990s, are as follows (personal communication between Bob Barr and administrators in the Vancouver, Washington, school district, during the 2010 school year):

- To develop the individual interests, aptitudes, and talents of each student

- To link academic learning with career pathways relevant to higher education and the workplace

To develop relevant programs that accurately reflect the local work economy, the district set out to (Barr, 2010):

- Examine labor market statistics and community workforce needs
- Determine student needs and district and community assets
- Determine student interests
- Examine current programs
- Identify key personnel
- Conduct a symposium to answer essential questions:
  ▸ How can we maximize the schools' assets and best use our community resources?
  ▸ What are the critical content areas and applied learning opportunities?
  ▸ What marketing strategies can be used to promote the programs of choice?

The Vancouver district has also established *opportunity zones* serving fourteen schools in its most impoverished communities. These zones are an effort to address the needs of families and improve student achievement. Each provides parenting classes, coordination of social services, and connections with local food banks. Students in the zones receive additional tutoring, and the schools receive extra technology and teacher education (Von Lunen, 2012).

Some of the most powerful learning experiences for finding greater purpose and developing internal motivation and even passion for something students want to pursue in their lives relate to Dewey's (1916) concept of learning by doing. These learning experiences provide students with ways to question, explore, understand, and, ultimately, know. Learning by doing is a distinctly different approach to knowledge mastery, but it is loaded with intrinsic motivation. Since the 1970s, school approaches for learning by doing have been referred to as "experiential education," and a number of specific learning and teaching strategies have developed from this concept, including service, expeditionary, and legacy learning, which are discussed in the following sections. All of these programs are focused on getting students out of textbooks and classrooms and into their communities for real-world learning experiences. There is considerable research on each of these programs and the powerful impact they have on all students, but especially on students from low-income families. (Service learning was also discussed in chapter 6, page 93.)

A sense of purpose can be strengthened by making decisions about learning options. There are a number of ways that schools can support learning options. Teachers and staff can do the following:

- Provide options to choose from, such as electives, career pathways, small-school options, or after-school activities.

- Differentiate instruction so students are able to learn what they need to learn, and can choose how they might share it.

- Use the Workshop Model (minilesson, worktime, sharing) to provide choice, voice, and audience in writing, reading, science, art, and so on.

- Develop educational programs of choice (charter, magnet, or alternative schools; career clusters; mini-schools, and learning communities), being sure to plan for the enrollment of a diverse student population, so choices do not become elite islands of choice for students who have involved families.

- In the classroom, encourage students to personally select how to achieve a particular learning goal. This will encourage personal motivation and personal purpose in learning.

- Incorporate service learning, expeditionary learning, and legacy learning into classroom activities.

Service Learning

A service-learning project provides the same service as a volunteer project but with the added components of learning, reflection, and public sharing of findings. A defining characteristic of service learning is the transformative nature of the experience—students and community are changed by it (ETR Associates, 2012). Other examples of service-learning projects include the following (ETR Associates, 2012):

- Elementary school students in Florida studied the consequences of natural disasters. The class designed and distributed a kit for families in the community to use to collect their important papers in case of evacuation.

- Middle school students in Pennsylvania learned about the health consequences of poor nutrition and lack of exercise and then brought their learning to life by conducting health fairs, creating a healthy cookbook, and opening a fruit and vegetable stand for the school and community.

- Girl Scouts in West Virginia investigated the biological complexity and diversity of wetlands. Learning of the need to eliminate invasive species, the scouts decided to monitor streams and then present their findings to their town council.

Expeditionary Learning

An outgrowth of Harvard Graduate School of Education's Outward Bound project, expeditionary learning (EL) was conceptualized in 1991 in response to a call for school reforms to improve achievement for the lowest-performing students in the United States (Kearns, 1993; see also www.mcdonoughels.org). The EL model engages students with:

> in-depth learning through learning expeditions, which are interdisciplinary, project-based units of study that require students to engage in research, use the community in authentic ways, and communicate what they have learned through a culminating presentation of their final product to outside audiences. (Hartford Public Schools, 2010)

This model challenges students of all ability levels to accomplish high-level tasks and take active roles in their classroom and in their own learning. Forty-five thousand urban, rural, and suburban K–12 students were learning in 165 EL schools across the United States as of 2010 (Expeditionary Learning, 2011). When success is measured based on academic achievement, EL schools consistently outperform district averages on state and mandated tests in language arts and mathematics (Expeditionary Learning School, 2011).

Major characteristics of the expeditionary learning instructional model include the following (Hartford Public Schools, 2010):

- Student empowerment to pursue content knowledge on their own
- Student demonstration of knowledge through multiple presentation modes
- Student connections to community and field experts
- Integrated curriculum featuring Workshop Model instruction (incorporating minilessons, goal setting, student work time, and sharing, as described by Graves [1994] and Atwell [1998] among others)

As an example of expeditionary learning, students at Anser Charter School in Garden City, Idaho, conducted a two-year study of bald eagles along the Boise River that flows through the downtown area. The students conducted extensive research on eagle behavior pattern and mating patterns and diet. They conducted periodic counts along the river and compared them to earlier counts. They visited the Birds of Prey Center and interviewed a professional biologist and developed a set of recommendations for ensuring the survival and flourishing of bald eagles in their community. The students made a presentation of their findings to a variety of city councils and boards.

Legacy Learning

A special category of learning by doing, "legacy learning," makes a powerful difference by involving students in projects that focus on real problems or issues in the community. November (2011) uses the term *legacy learning* to describe learning experiences that result in a product other than a school assignment completed for a grade. Because these projects are deeply rooted in purpose and interest, they provide an incredible motivation for learning, and students of all ages connect with them. When this happens, students will work for hours, often on weekends and even in the summer, pursuing their projects. This purposeful work, which may cut across the entire curriculum, brings out the very best in students and seems to function with great power regardless of students' abilities going into them. The journal entry regarding students conducting a history investigation in Texas (page 91) is an example of legacy learning.

Expeditionary learning and legacy learning are two sides of the same coin. Legacy learning emphasizes work that continues to affect others long after the initial work is done, something that leaves a legacy, whereas expeditionary learning is a specific curricular and programmatic structure. Legacy learning has deep, personal meaning for each student and goes beyond any particular curriculum, pedagogy, or philosophy of learning.

Journal

When I picked up the February 2013 *Mendo Lake Family Life* magazine, I cheered when I saw the example of legacy learning on the cover. An eight-year-old girl named Vivienne decided to make a difference in ending child slavery by running a lemonade stand every day, rain or shine. Add some parental support, the *New York Times* breaking her story, and the help of Internet networking, and this child's dream ended up a fantastic reality. After 173 days, she had freed 550 people through the nonprofit organization, Not For Sale, and she has continued her crusade. The author of the story wrote, "We try to soften the blow of life's realities; we focus on the good things in life and try to help our children make sense of life's inequities. Few of us think our children can actually do something on a grand scale to change the world…[but] why can't a child change the world?" (Miller, 2013, p. 13). Vivienne said, "Gandhi was one person. Mother Teresa was

one person. Why can't you be one person?" (Miller, 2013, p. 13). That is the idea
behind legacy learning and service learning: students who act on their passions
to make the world a better place can truly make a difference. —E.G.

Often, legacy learning experiences are one of a kind and would be difficult to
repeat, but others seem to take on a life of their own and are passed on from one
classroom's generation of students to the next. In a video presentation, November
(2011) shared a number of student-inspired legacy learning projects, starting with a
description of his first project at an inner-city school in Boston.

In 1975, after purchasing an old storefront barbershop at a public auction for one
dollar, November challenged his biology and chemistry students at Roxbury High
School, a school serving a high-poverty community in Boston, to think about how
the building could be used to address a community problem or need. At the same
time, a local doctor friend expressed a concern that most community members were
not aware of the available free clinics and other health services for poverty-level
families.

After November shared this conversation with his high school students, the class
ultimately decided to gather as much information as possible and use the barbershop
as an information center for health services. The students became deeply invested in
the project. They contacted hospitals, health centers, and government health offices
and compiled a directory of all of the information that they had collected. Then,
after school, November and his students walked together to the storefront and spent
their evenings handing out the directory, answering questions, and encouraging
people to use the services that were available. They even got local bands to play at the
storefront and served donated refreshments to attract as much attention as possible to
the resources they had collected. The students worked night and day on this project,
which brought so many benefits to their community (November, 2011).

A few years later, in a more affluent Boston-area high school, one of November's
students created a database of resources for individuals with disabilities. When the
database impressed a university professor, the student agreed to his request to create
one that incorporated larger geographic areas, but refused to accept any payment.
When November asked why, the student explained, "This is my project. They are
helping me expand my work and help even more people. I should be paying *them* for
the help!" (November, 2011). As demonstrated repeatedly with stories of the power
of purpose and motivation, true ownership inspires greater effort and higher quality.
Students crave real work for real purposes.

Further examples of legacy learning include a math teacher in California whose
students created Internet-based tutorials on the entire sixth-grade math curriculum
and two history teachers in Ohio who created an online world history textbook that

is a living document, continually being revised and expanded by each year's classes. An outgrowth of legacy learning discussed by November (2011) is the opportunity for students to make real decisions about where and how they put their time and talents to use. The way students address this decision may take teachers by surprise: one student who published Harry Potter fan fiction on the Internet said she woke up each day and had to decide if she wanted to write for her teacher and grades or publish for the world (November, 2011). That students even need to wrestle with such questions is a testament to legacy learning.

Many existing schools and learning models, like the St. Paul Open School (page 92), and EdVisions (page 116), foster legacy learning as an outgrowth of their pedagogy and curriculum. Students are enthusiastically involved and learn more when their schools have projects like a school playground planned and built by elementary school students, school and community murals, or ecology studies. When students administer statistically correct opinion polls during election time, they are tapping into the value of legacy learning. And when teachers in Grand Rapids, Michigan, coach students in professional surveyor techniques in order to offer a zoning board alternative routing for a highway that threatened the environment, they are using the concept of legacy learning.

A specific and well-known example of legacy learning, Foxfire, began in 1966, when a Yale graduate took a teaching job in Georgia. After his frustration over not finding anything that would motivate his bored students, he began developing ways to bring relevance to writing for his poverty-level students at Rabun Gap–Nacoochee School District. When asked to design a purposeful task, the teacher and his students decided to collect the folklore of the region and publish a magazine. Still going strong, the folklore collected by students, year after year, is published in a national magazine and has been anthologized in a series of bestselling books. What started out as a first-year teacher's attempt to engage students at risk of dropping out became a multimillion-dollar business. Much of the profits have helped to support the school district as well as an outdoor Folklore Museum where the students have collected and displayed antiques and artifacts of their area. Other profits have been invested and managed by the students. The Foxfire program continues to motivate, inspire, and encourage students who go on to attend colleges and universities throughout the United States and has been replicated in schools across the United States (see www.foxfire.org).

Journal

While sharing information about the Foxfire program in a class I was teaching at Indiana University, one of my students raised his hand and confessed that he had gone to school in Rabun Gap, and had it not been for the Foxfire program, he was sure he would have dropped out of school, gone to work in the textile mills, and probably died of lung disease like his father. His job at Foxfire was to be part of the financial management team. This team was responsible not just for maintaining accurate records of the income and expenditures of the program; it was also responsible for investing the millions of dollars that the program earned from its various initiatives. While he was part of the financial management team, Foxfire actually bought out the local bank and assumed ownership of the institution.

He laughed and said, "Nobody could believe that a group of potential school dropouts owned and managed a bank. It was an incredible experience. For me, I learned that I could probably do anything that I decided to do. And, here I am, a college graduate and working on my master's degree." —B.B.

All of the provocative learning experiences described in this chapter represent specific school activities that have touched the lives of students, surely led to more internal motivation, and helped them find purpose and relevance in their learning—and their lives.

Develop Interests and Talents

Culture of Hope schools work hard to help each student identify areas of personal interest, often through clubs, activities, and school programs. Such activities include formal programs like 4-H, Junior Achievement, and student entrepreneur programs, as well as the more typical experiences of band, drama, dance, orchestra, and chorus. School newspapers, yearbook, and other student projects are always available at the high school level. The huge popularity of the movie *High School Musical* suggests the great power of students developing passionate interests and talents.

Journal

My wife and I were invited to attend the Indiana Science Teachers Association state conference in 2009, where our son was the keynote speaker. My son is known for his National Geographic TV show *Dangerous Encounters with Brady Barr* and his many appearances on the *Oprah Winfrey Show* and Jay Leno's *Tonight Show*. One of the joys of seeing our son speak is that he shows his school report cards (his mom had saved them over the years) and explains that he was a fairly average to below-average student throughout most of his childhood. He describes himself to teachers as the "kid at the back of the room"—that is, until he discovered biology and the wonders of nature. It was through going to zoos and national parks and through his school courses in biology that he became a teacher of biology for students from low-income families in North Central High

School in Indianapolis, Indiana. He explains that it was through experiences in nature and the world of science that he found not just his purpose in life but, more importantly, his passion.

He used this passion to earn his doctorate at the University of Miami and become a National Geographic resident herpetologist. That led him to become the only person to ever capture and study all twenty-three species of crocodiles—a study that took fifteen years and spanned thirty countries. He ends his presentation by speaking to the kids who always show up for his talks: "Let me share my secret with you. Don't start thinking about school coursework and college majors or what you are going to do with your life; it doesn't work that way. Find your own interest, find your personal passion; find what it is that you love. If you can find your passion, all of the rest will take care of itself." —B.B.

At the elementary level, teachers and other staff members can encourage students to identify their personal interests and talents and help them identify personal assets. All students, but especially students from low-income families, must be introduced to activities that may be far beyond their experiences, including music, theater, and other visual and performing arts, as well as the vast world of careers. During the middle school years, teachers often help students explore new learning experiences through survey courses that provide short samples of a variety of electives in art, computer technology, industrial arts, and so on. Such limited surveys can help students find an area of interest to focus on during their high school years.

Secondary schools open the world of possibilities to their students, especially through career-themed clusters, job shadowing, service learning, and career fairs with speakers from a variety of professions, careers, and vocations. With the development of alternative and charter schools, many students and their families can select from a variety of special schools. Specialized schools that emphasize the performing arts, for example, provide students with an opportunity to work with professional artists, dancers, actors, and performers. The film *Fame* depicts New York's famous High School of Performing Arts. Such schools transform the lives of students who may have never had an opportunity to identify and expand their personal talents.

Career exploration is an absolute must in helping students find purpose and meaning for their lives.

Journal

A teacher aide in Salem, Oregon, shared a learning experience she had that related to purpose: "On a day when the teacher was absent and I had no real plans for the class, I turned to the chalkboard and drew something that looked like the 'normal curve.' After dividing the curve into a number of seg-ments, I labeled each segment with sequential decades, starting with the decade when I had been born and ending with the decade when I would turn ninety. I placed an x to mark the date I was born, another x to mark my current age of forty-five, and a final x to indicate when I thought I might die. After explaining that my family tended to have long lives, I put the final x at ninety years of age. The kids all laughed and said, 'You'll never make it.'

"However, the students were surprisingly quiet and focused, something very rare for this class of unruly kids. I explained that the chart signified the curve of my life. I put x's on the curve at various places and described how I grew up, later went to school, got married and had a family, and finally became a teacher aide. I then talked about my life curve in the future beginning to narrow as my life slowed down and I aged.

"At that point, I erased my curve, and plotted a new one that would represent my students' lives, with dates that reflected their birth decade. I asked them to think about their own lives as I wrote in their decades. This class of tough city kids was totally engrossed as I shared the average life expectancy in the United States (around 80 years). I said, 'Now just look at your life! What do you plan to do with your life? What will you accomplish? Who will you become? Many of the students seemed to ignore the discussion, saying, 'We are going to live hard and die young.' But even as the class laughed, you could tell that so many of the students were thinking about their lives and futures.

"I tried to help the kids see that they needed to be careful with their decisions and actions, and try not to screw up their lives. I kept repeating, 'Just look at your life. Look at how much more living you have to do. Think about what you can do today that would make the rest of your life better.' I believe that it was one of the best discussions I ever had with my students." —B.B.

Counselors play an important role in helping students plan for the future, but many school counselors have typically worked with only the more affluent students who were expected by families and teachers to go on to college. Counselors must work with students from all backgrounds, introducing them to the vast array of postsecondary programs that are available, the requirements for those programs, and the complex world of financial aid.

Schools need to schedule trips to area community schools, technical schools, col-leges, and universities, so that students who have never set foot on a campus of higher education can experience this new and possibly foreign culture and talk to students from similar backgrounds who have successfully made the transition to higher edu-cation. Exposure to and discussions with students from diverse backgrounds who have been successful in college and career are absolutely essential as inspiration, mentoring, and modeling for high school students. In every way possible, schools must help students and their families open this remarkable door to opportunity and find a pathway out of poverty.

Journal

A student who was interested in becoming a veterinarian sat down with his tenth-grade biology teacher/advisory group leader to talk about his life plan. During that discussion, the student learned how much schooling it would take to become a vet. He wanted to give up the idea all together, saying, "Forget it, I can't do that. No way." His teacher asked him what he liked about the career of a veterinarian. The student indicated he enjoyed helping animals. They talked about other careers that could accomplish the same goal, including vet tech, animal hospital attendant, animal shelter worker, animal control officer, animal groomer, and animal trainer. After looking at the possibilities, the student selected vet tech. He then mapped out the science, mathematics, and technology courses he would need to take in high school, the co-enrollment courses he could take at the community college during his junior and senior years of high school to reduce the time and cost of his career training, and the community college that offered a vet tech certificate program, which happened to be near enough that he could live at home during the two-year program. While he could also do a four-year BS degree, part of this student's life plan included obtaining a good-paying job in as short a time frame as possible for financial reasons. The teacher also helped the student create a plan for community service hours at a local vet clinic to determine if being a vet tech was truly his passion and interest, since he was not aware of the negative aspects of the job, including the emotional toll it can take on workers. The teacher made a note to check in with the student in two months to discuss his volunteer experiences and revise or adjust his life plan as needed. —E.G.

Another absolutely essential activity that helps students find purpose and direction is creating a personal plan for life after high school. More and more schools consider these plans a prerequisite for graduation. Personal plans arise from careful work with faculty advisers and school counselors, with students selecting particular career areas, exploring possible job opportunities, and gradually honing in on career paths that are interesting and motivating. The use of advisory groups in middle and high school can facilitate the creation of personal plans (see chapter 9, page 182). The goal is for students to carefully narrow the range of options for their possible careers, learn as much as possible about requirements for accessing career interests, and finally make detailed plans that will help them reach their goals.

Journal

At a small alternative high school, staff structured the school week to allow students blocks of time on Fridays for career exploration and job shadowing. Near the end of a school year, I attended a session in which a young woman presented her "Plan Next" to a group of teachers and the school principal. She explained that she had completed an extensive career exploration and had chosen a career path of cosmetology school.

The student explained, "I visited a number of hair salons in the area and interviewed a large number of owners and workers in the salons. They convinced me to apply to the most expensive school in our area. It will cost $13,000 to complete the yearlong program, but everyone said that it is so much better than the other schools. If I go to this school, I will be practically guaranteed a job here." She continued, "A job in cosmetology will let me have a more flexible work schedule than in other careers, and I can get a job almost anywhere I might want to live. I might even want to have my own salon some day!"

I went away so impressed that this school not only offered students a solid academic program, but also graduated students with work-readiness skills. More importantly, the school had a program in place to help students think about the future and to make plans for their post–high school years. —B.B.

Developing interests and talents is the cornerstone of student purpose. When students have directions to go in, they will be more engaged in learning. There are many ways schools can promote the development of interests and talents. Teachers and staff can:

- Offer a variety of co-curricular activities as learning options during the school day, including lunchtime—electives, choice periods, and differentiating content

- Offer a variety of extracurricular activities outside of the school day, including sports, academics, arts, leadership, service learning, and focus groups. AmeriCorps workers, high school volunteers, college volunteers, seniors, and community and family members can help with offerings

- Use career fairs, research topics, student surveys, strengths assessments, and guest speakers to expose students to options

- Arrange for job shadowing, mentorships, and college and career field trips to help students visualize, as well as rule out, possibilities

- Create a life plan with a trusted counselor or advisory teacher

Master Strategies

After students focus on their goals and aspirations, schools must work hard to ensure they gain a realistic understanding of how to get from where they are as K–12 students to where they want to go. This type of detailed planning is absolutely essential if students are to make sound decisions about their future. Students need to be reminded, even confronted, with the realities of the work they face on the pathway ahead and even the sacrifices they may have to make. Students need to understand that hard work and perseverance will be needed to achieve their goals, especially if they hope to find a pathway out of poverty. In chapter 10 (pages 219–222), a detailed set of essential achievements is described for each student, from preschool through high school and beyond, so that each student and parent knows the learning requirements achieved and those that are yet to be mastered.

Finding a purpose for schooling, and for one's life, represents the highest step on Maslow's hierarchy of needs: self-actualization. This final point of Maslow's hierarchy is *not* a specific destination; it is, in fact, something attained throughout one's life. Self-actualization is a process of becoming. Few things help the process along more than gaining a personal purpose for school and life. Schools can play a powerful role in helping students get started on a path toward self-actualization and being lifelong learners who continue to grow and adapt to the changing world. When combined with the other three seeds of hope—a sense of optimism, a sense of belonging, and a sense of pride, self-esteem, and self-confidence—a sense of purpose provides a solid foundation for success in high school and beyond. When the seeds of hope are part of an entire school atmosphere focused on optimism, respect, safety, and success, a Culture of Hope exists, providing students with essential learning that enables them to progress on their personal pathways out of poverty, pathways to a better life.

Journal

While dean of the College of Education at Boise State University, I was asked to speak with a group of 250 high school students who were uninterested in and disconnected from learning at their large, comprehensive high school. These students seemed on a direct path to drop out of high school, and they continued to fail, despite a wide variety of intervention efforts.

When I walked into the school's auditorium, I saw what I expected: wild hair, lots of body piercings and tattoos, and the surly, sullen expression that so often typifies the teenage years. The talk and laughter were deafening. Acting on a hunch, I stood on top of a chair and yelled in my loudest voice, "HEY!" For just a moment, the kids stopped talking and turned their sullen stares at me. In an equally loud voice, I yelled, "How many of you would like to have a job making

$40,000 a year?" The reaction was as amazing as it was unexpected. You could have heard a pin drop.

In the moment of quiet, I began to talk to the students about the job opportunities in the area. I compared salaries for fast food restaurants, janitors, construction workers, and jobs at some of the local corporations. I talked about jobs at the post office, the fire department, and even the police department. I talked about careers in the military. The students were quiet and attentive.

We also talked about what sort of things they were planning to do after high school. We talked for over two hours until the principal, looking at his watch, said we had to end the discussion so the custodian could clean up. Because the session seemed to have been so successful, I told the students that I would come back the next week and we would continue our discussion.

I drove out to the community college campus that was near their school district to find someone who could help me with the next student session. On the college reader board was the message, "Now Taking Applications for Truck Driving School: Beginning Salary, $40,000."

"Oh boy," I thought, "this is perfect."

I met with the program director, explained what I was doing with the high school students, and invited him to join me for the next discussion.

The next week, the program director described the truck driver school's twenty-week program, which involved seven weeks of classroom work followed by thirteen weeks on a cross-country internship in a big rig truck with a master driver. He also showed PowerPoint slides of some of the 18-wheelers, with photos of the customized sleeping cabs, one with a built-in Jacuzzi.

The audience of high school students learned that if they passed the course work and the driving internship, they could move directly into a job with an average starting salary of $40,000 for both men and women. Experienced truck drivers earned up to $100,000 or $150,000 a year. According to the director, the United States had an extreme shortage of truck drivers, and this program had a 95 percent job placement record.

To say that the students were interested would have been an understatement; some of the boys were on the edge of their seats—they were mesmerized. One scruffy young man raised his hand and said, "Hey, dude, how do we get into the truck driving school?" The program director looked out over the auditorium at the students, and he slowly shook his head. "Are you kidding?" he asked. "Turn a huge piece of expensive equipment over to any of you to drive? I don't think so. I don't think any of you would qualify for our program."

In the midst of the silence that followed, another hand went up, and the student asked, "What would we have to do to get accepted into the program?" What followed was one of the best discussions I believe I have ever had with a group of high school students. Some were intent on finding out specifically what it would take for them to qualify. I had the feeling that lives were going to change as a result of this discussion, so the principal and I agreed to continue the weekly meetings.

Over the coming weeks, we had representatives from military recruitment offices, directors from community college degree and licensure programs, and technical training institutes. Students learned about a variety of job opportunities, including culinary arts, nursing, cosmetology, and computers. As the weeks went by, more and more students asked to join this impromptu career program, until the auditorium was packed. —B.B.

Next Steps

District and school leadership teams or learning community teams should complete the reproducible Staff and Team Questionnaire: A Sense of Purpose (page 135 and online at **go.solution-tree.com/schoolimprovement**) after reading this chapter. Following individual completion of the questionnaire, summarize the responses and compare them in small groups. Where there are significant differences, discuss why individuals perceive their school in such different ways. To gain maximum school effectiveness, there should be strong consensus on the basic beliefs of the school staff. Areas of disagreement should be the focus of extended discussions. The following chapter, "The Power of We," describes a process for overcoming disagreements and arriving at a consensus.

The reproducible Student Questionnaire: A Sense of Purpose (page 137 and online) can be used as the basis for a larger questionnaire by teachers and counselors for a specific school. Any survey of student perceptions should be anonymous and used only after careful orientation of the students and their families. If parents object to the survey, their children should not be asked to take it. A small group of teachers, administrators, and counselors could add questions that relate directly to their school and its programs. Obtaining student responses on their feeling about their sense of purpose provides a powerful "reality check" for school staff and, when administered again later in the school year, a way to monitor evolution of student attitudes.

If there is widespread agreement regarding needed improvements, those areas should become the focus of specific goals, discussions about interventions, and assessments of intervention effectiveness. Use the reproducible Discussion Topics: A Sense of Purpose (page 138 and online) to facilitate these collaborations.

Refer to the section in chapter 8 titled "Assessing the Institutional Culture" (page 154) for detailed information on conducting surveys and arriving at consensus.

Conclusion

In this chapter we discussed the fourth seed of hope, a sense of purpose. As with all the seeds of hope, purpose builds on and supports the others. Students who have a greater sense of purpose will have greater optimism, feel they belong, and have increased pride and self-esteem. Similarly, students will be able to engage more deeply with purpose and exhibit greater passion when they have pride, optimism, and a feeling of belonging.

The essential elements of purpose include focusing on intrinsic motivations, providing engaging learning options (service, expeditionary, and legacy learning), and helping students discover and develop their interests, talents, and passions. A fundamental task for schools is to bridge the gap between students' interests and talents and the prospective career fields that might provide stimulating and worthwhile employment. The use of mentors and advisory groups can facilitate this bridging.

Part Two has discussed all four of the seeds of hope, which correspond to stages of Abraham Maslow's hierarchy of needs—a sense of optimism; a sense of belonging; a sense of pride, self-esteem, and self-confidence; and a sense of purpose. Part Three, Implementing a Culture of Hope, details the nuts and bolts of creating cultures of hope in K–12 schools. In chapter 8, we look at the power of collaboration; chapter 9 discusses specific strategies for implementation at the high school level, and chapter 10 takes a final look at the faltering American dream and what we can do to restore it.

Staff and Team Questionnaire: A Sense of Purpose

Complete this survey, summarize responses, and then compare them in small groups. When there are significant differences, the groups should discuss why individuals perceive their school in such different ways and work toward consensus (see chapter 8, page 151).

Rank each statement using the following scale:

Needs Improvement   Effective Practices   Exemplary Practices

1   2   3   4   5   6

1. Our school helps students find a passion and purpose in their lives. _____

2. Our school helps students and their families consider a wide range of goals for their lives and make informed decisions about their future. _____

3. Our school helps students understand the knowledge, skills, and strategies necessary to achieve their personal goals for the future. _____

4. Our school helps students make specific plans designed to achieve their goals. _____

5. Our school is effective in developing internal motivation for learning. _____

6. Too many of our students seem bored and apathetic. _____

7. Our school counselors provide help with both college-prep and career education. _____

8. Most of our students seem to be "purposeful learners"—they see the relevance between what they are studying and what they would like to achieve in their lives. _____

9. Too many of our students seem more interested in their social network than their school network. _____

10. Our school has a counselor support program that helps all students and their families learn about alternative career opportunities and what is necessary to achieve the various opportunities. _____

11. Our school works hard to make sure students and their families understand the relevance of their schoolwork. _____

12. Our school helps students and their families learn about the variety of learning opportunities available after high school graduation. _____

Building a Culture of Hope © 2013 Solution Tree Press • solution-tree.com
Visit **go.solution-tree.com/schoolimprovement** to download this page.

13. Our school works hard to help families understand how important it is for their children to graduate from high school and go on for additional education or training. _____

14. Our school works hard to help students and their families explore a wide variety of career opportunities. _____

15. Our school provides ongoing student advisement and advisory groups. _____

16. Our school works hard to help each student make long-term plans about achieving his or her personal goals after high school and beyond. _____

17. Our school helps students make specific plans that will help them achieve their long-term goals. _____

18. Our high schools require each student to develop a detailed personal plan for his or her life after high school. _____

19. Our high schools require that all students complete advanced placement courses. _____

20. Our middle and high schools provide a wide variety of activities and learning experiences that help students explore a wide variety of career opportunities. _____

21. Our school involves students in personal responsibilities in the school and community. _____

22. Our high schools help students and their families learn about financial aid and college applications and help families complete all necessary paperwork prior to high school graduation. _____

23. Our school district monitors the progress of students after they graduate from high school. _____

24. Our school has a system in place that monitors each student's progress and immediately responds if a student begins to struggle. _____

25. Our school feels that career education is equally important as academic learning. _____

26. Our school ensures that each student is developing his or her talents and interests through participation in clubs, activities, or extracurricular activities. _____

Student Questionnaire: A Sense of Purpose

Respond with: 1 = do not agree; 2 = agree; 3 = strongly agree

1. I have a very strong understanding of what I want to do with my life. _____

2. I really have little or no idea what I plan to do after I graduate from high school. _____

3. My school has helped me to consider a wide range of possibilities for possible careers in my life. _____

4. My school has helped me understand what I would have to do in order to achieve my career goals. _____

5. Our school counselor has helped my family and me understand what I would need to do to go to college or community college. _____

6. My counselor believes that I can be successful in college or community college. _____

7. At my high school, career education is as important as academic learning. _____

8. My courses seem so irrelevant. _____

9. I am bored most of the time at school. _____

10. I am really encouraged by my teachers and counselors to go on to college or community college after I graduate from high school. _____

11. My school has helped my parents and me understand that the only way to really be ensured a good job with benefits is to continue with my education or training after high school. _____

12. As part of my graduation requirements, I must prepare a detailed plan for what I will do after high school. _____

13. I believe that I know what I want to do with my life and what I have to do in order to accomplish my goals. _____

14. I think I have a clear understanding of the various opportunities available to me, and my school has helped me make wise decisions about my future. _____

15. My school has helped me complete college-prep and advanced placement courses. _____

16. My school has an advising program through which I meet regularly with a staff member and peers. _____

Discussion Topics: A Sense of Purpose

After filling out individual questionnaires and examining the student questionnaires, staff members, teams, book groups, and other groups should come together to explore these topics of discussion.

1. How many students in our school have a personal purpose in their life?

2. How can our school help students find a personal passion or purpose in their life?

3. How can we help students have stronger internal motivation for learning?

4. Do too many students in our school seem bored and apathetic? If so, what can we do about that?

5. How can we help our students see the relevance of their studies?

6. How can we help students and their families set long-term goals and develop strategies to accomplish their goals?

7. Do student perceptions differ from those of the school staff? If so, why?

part three

IMPLEMENTING A CULTURE *of* HOPE

Chapter 8

The Power of We

Some changes are very hard to make alone. Developing and locally adapting a challenging new curriculum and mode of teaching, for example, is an extraordinarily difficult task that requires collaboration. It can energize participants, expose them to new ideas, and encourage them to take pedagogical risks in a supportive environment.

—David Tyack and Larry Cuban

A Culture of Hope is essential for teachers as well as students in high-poverty schools. For teachers, it offers professional rejuvenation, the opportunity to work together with other teachers, and the chance to become a team focused on improving the lives and learning of at-risk students. It brings optimism and energy to the work of educators, as well as strength through working together.

Visit a failing school, and defeatism, hopelessness, and blame seem to be everywhere. Teachers and administrators in ineffective or failing schools may also experience a learned helplessness. You may hear them say, "It is not we who are failing; it is the families. These families just don't care; these kids don't care." If a school is not being effective with poverty-level students, there is a tendency over time for teachers to "become resigned to their fate, nothing ever changes. . . . They drag others down with them, finding the worst in everything, or resisting other people's ideas but offering none of their own" (Kanter, 2010, p. 11). In any school, the interrelationships between students, parents, teachers, and administrators are so essential that they improve or deteriorate together. With blame comes loss of respect. Chenoweth (2009), after visiting both effective and ineffective schools across the United States, concluded, "One of the hallmarks of a dysfunctional school is the disrespectful attitude that pervades it" (p. 202). In such a school, everyone blames everyone. Chenoweth (2009) described visiting a large dysfunctional high school where uniformed guards and administrators roamed the halls telling students to find somewhere to be. The administrators spoke "harshly and condescendingly to students," and the students responded with sullen anger and resistance (Chenoweth, 2009, p. 202). A culture of failure and despair permeates an entire school, affecting everyone in a negative manner. Chenoweth concluded that the first step in transforming a failing or ineffective school is to improve the relationships, to replace the atmosphere of despair with one of respect.

We now know that confidence, persistence, and respect are essential for making and sustaining the changes needed to create a Culture of Hope, yet these are the very traits missing from schools where teachers work in isolation and feel the futility of their efforts (DuFour et al., 2010). As Snyder (1995) maintained:

> Hope is a *we* and not just a *me* concept. Hopeful people want to live and work in settings where shared goals can be met by the many and not just the few. As such, a hopeful work environment is one where common goals and willpower . . . to attain those goals occupy the minds of employer and employee alike. (p. 256)

Cooperation and collaboration are important ingredients in any organization, but they are essential in effective school reform. For a Culture of Hope, they are indispensable.

Snyder and colleagues (1991) defined the concept of workplace hope as "believing you have the will and the way to accomplish your goals, whatever they might be" (p. 579). While hope may not be a particularly effective organizational strategy, it does seem to carry along with it an organizational magic. Proponents of the learning community concept maintain that unusually talented teachers are not necessary to accomplish great things in schools. What is needed is a well-designed system in which even ordinary teachers and staff can achieve "stunning performance levels" (DuFour et al., 2010, p. 11). Successful systems identify and develop the capacity of those who know what to do and help them share it with those who don't (Elmore, 2008). They provide teachers with the support, encouragement, guidance, and time to work together.

Implementing and enriching a Culture of Hope requires profound changes in a school—changes that will challenge many to rethink how they view teaching and learning and how they view students. The Culture of Hope can of course be practiced in isolation in individual classrooms, but maximizing its impact on poverty-level students demands schoolwide collaboration and commitment. One teacher can have a powerful impact, but imagine the impact of surrounding students with a schoolwide environment that nourishes all the seeds of hope.

The Power of We can be characterized by the following set of beliefs:

- **We can build or transform school culture**—This culture supports strong interpersonal relationships and provides a caring and supportive atmosphere.

- **We can build a Culture of Hope for students as well as staff**—Such a shift provides an atmosphere of hope, optimism, and respect; a sense of belonging, pride, and self-esteem; and a strong sense of purpose in our work.

- **We believe in our students**—We believe that they can learn, succeed in school and graduate, and pursue a pathway out of poverty. We hold the highest expectations for their learning.

- **We believe that teachers can become stronger**—We can overcome the isolation of classroom teaching and come to trust and respect one another; we can ask for help; we can do great things together; working together, we are stronger and more effective than when we work alone.

- **We can improve instructional effectiveness together**—We improve by visiting and observing one another's classrooms, by planning together and developing curriculum and planning lessons, by each sharing our own unique strengths, by relying on the unique skills of each teacher, by relying on the most effective teachers on any particular topic, by bringing the power of the collaborative team to address difficult instructional challenges, and by sharing data and making decisions together.

- **We can create our own professional development**—With time to collaborate, access to an instructional coach, open acknowledgment of our problems, and careful monitoring of our progress in addressing those problems, the answer to any instructional issue can be found within our group.

Journal

Elementary school teachers at an Appalachian school district in western Kentucky reported on a meeting during which their principal drove them nuts talking about learning communities. He gave them books to read and tried to send some of them to a conference. When the principal started talking about collaboration, they tuned him out—what they did in their own classroom was nobody's business but their own, they felt, and certainly not the current principal's business! One of the teachers wrote:

"Then, at a Title I conference, we heard Dr. Barr speak about what he had been seeing all over the United States. He put up a slide that said 'The Power of We' and talked about what happened when teachers started meeting and sharing and working to improve. On our way home, I told my friend, 'You know, I think we could do something as easy as the Power of We.' At our next collaboration meeting, I wrote 'The Power of We' on the board, but then no one knew what to do. Finally, our most experienced teacher said, 'Let's stop here and agree to come back with something to share that we think we have done really well in

> our classroom, one of our success stories. Let's also be ready to share a problem we are having.'
>
> "Our next session was awesome! As each teacher shared, we all started taking notes and asking questions and really sharing, something we had really never done in our school. That was two years ago. Over time, we have come to trust one another, and we now talk a lot about specific kids and how we can help them. And oh, how we have helped each other! We now visit each other's classes and plan lessons together. In addition to our weekly school meetings, our 'We' team now meets once a month at one of our homes, and we just about work all night. Student achievement has just soared. We tell teachers at other schools: don't get too complicated, don't get too organized. Just get the 'me' out of the way and focus on the 'we' . . . and start sharing." —B.B.

The Collaborative School

The concept of teachers working in a consistent, schoolwide, unified effort flies in the face of the widely held traditional view of school as a collection of individual teachers working alone in their classrooms. Many still believe that teaching is practiced in "independent classrooms linked by a common parking lot, [which] leaves one with the impression that teaching is a relatively straightforward activity, bolstered as needed by outside course work and other occasional in-service activities" (Little, 1999, p. 256). But those who work effectively with low-income students know that teaching is anything but straightforward. According to Michael Fullan (2007), the more you develop a school into a learning community

> in which teachers observe one another's teaching, and work with school leadership to make ongoing improvements, the greater the consistency and quality of teaching across the whole school, at which point all students in the school benefit and keep on benefiting. And the more you do this, the more shared meanings and commitments, and related capacities, get generated. (p. 54)

There is, in fact, remarkable consistency among scholars regarding the essential conditions for implementing a collaborative school (DuFour et al., 2010; Elmore, 2008; Fullan, 2007). There must be:

- A consensus belief that all students can learn and achieve high levels of excellence
- Shared goals for the entire school
- Agreement that there should be a reliance on data
- Time for collaboration

- Time to monitor progress
- A plan for refining interventions

A schoolwide commitment to this simple process all but guarantees success, particularly if it focuses on only a few important goals at a time and progress is monitored carefully over time.

For example, after reviewing student data regarding behavioral referrals and bullying in the school, a group of teachers may brainstorm possible approaches to improve the school and classroom environments. They agree to talk with students about the concepts of respect and bullying and ask students for their own ideas about how to improve the school. Two teachers agree to attend a workshop on the peaceful settlement of conflict and share what they learn. Students who seem to be particularly prone to bullying behavior are scheduled extra time with a school counselor to try to determine the roots of the behavior.

Each week, the teachers review attendance data and behavioral referrals to determine if their efforts are proving effective and to continue their brainstorming. They discuss other measures they can take, such as contacting parents and asking for support and suggestions, visiting classrooms where there are almost no behavioral referrals for bullying, and finding curriculum materials that address this issue. The teachers meet regularly to compare how well particular students are learning with behavioral referral data, to see if their efforts are resulting in better student learning. This process continues throughout the year, until slowly the atmosphere of the school begins to change to a more positive environment; over time, behavior and student learning improve.

Another illustration of the Power of We in practice can be found in "Gaining Ground," a large study of middle schools in California, which involved 200,000 students in 303 middle schools during the 2008–2009 school year (Williams et al., 2010). The study found that teachers and principals in high-performing middle schools shared a personal and professional mission to get every student ready for high school and beyond. Teachers and principals met regularly to review student data. The high-performing schools also supported social and emotional growth, with an increased number of students involved in extracurricular activities and electives. They also reported high numbers of students enrolling in exploratory minicourses (Duncan, 2011).

In establishing a culture of collaboration, some ground rules are helpful to ensure that teachers' times together are not just gripe sessions. Chenoweth's (2009) Rules of Engagement offer some help:

If you don't say it in the meeting, don't say it in the parking lot.

Focus discussions on the things the school can control rather than what it can't.

Focus on specific objectives related to instruction.

Must have teachers willing to collaborate. (pp. 186–187)

Journal

For five years, I worked with small groups of teachers pursuing National Board Certification. Each year we would select about twelve teachers from among the large group who applied. They had to have letters of support from teachers in their school and their principal and were often former teachers of the year in their district. Occasionally, there were even a few state teachers of the year, as well. From this type of outstanding applicant, we then selected the very best. The expensive application fees were paid for by a local foundation and through private donation, and we hired teachers with national certification to serve as mentors. I had never been associated with such powerful, effective teachers. With our selection process and the group support that was provided, the pass rate was over 90 percent. Nationally, at the time, only about half the teachers who went through the process were successful.

Part of the National Board process was for teachers to describe their classroom demographics, plan and teach a lesson, collect student work samples as the lesson progressed, and then have someone videotape twenty unedited minutes of their teaching. During our first year, we quickly learned that sitting down and watching a videotape of themselves was the hardest thing any of the teachers had ever done. To have other teachers view their work in the classroom was simply excruciating. Few had ever had a colleague come into their classroom. Over the years, some teachers would actually have panic attacks: there were tears, upset stomachs, and even outbursts of anger. Remember, these were the best, most dynamic teachers in our area, and the lessons we watched were among the most powerful, often the most creative I had ever experienced.

Over the course of our weekly meetings, this all changed. Teachers began to relax and even look forward to the other teachers' reviews and comments. Our rule was that the teachers we were observing could not say anything until the group had completed its review and debriefing. During this time, the teacher being reviewed would take notes, often writing furiously so he or she did not miss anything, and would then be invited to react to what he or she had heard. Over the year, these discussions became more and more effective. Follow-up reviews almost universally reported that the most worthwhile parts of the National Board process were the classroom and video observations and discussions with other teachers. Long after our work was concluded, these outstanding National Board

Certified teachers were still visiting and observing one another and still spending time debriefing and brainstorming how to improve their instruction. —B.B.

Implementing a Culture of Hope requires teachers to perceive themselves as part of a web of professional relationships rather than solo practitioners (Elmore, 2008). Such a school climate is

characterized by an emphasis on collaboration and continuous improvement . . . where teacher effort is focused on skill acquisition to achieve specific goals. In such schools, experimentation and occasional failure are expected and acceptable in the process of teacher learning. Further, seeking or giving collegial advice is not a gauge of relative competence, but rather a professional action viewed as desirable, necessary, and legitimate in the acquisition of new skills. (Elmore, 2008, pp. 59–60)

According to DuFour (2005), Fullan (2007), and Schmoker (2005), purposeful teacher collaboration is a powerful way to shift a school's culture from one in which teaching occurs to one in which *learning* occurs (Barth, 2005; Darling-Hammond, 1997; DuFour, Eaker, & DuFour, 2005). The key to successful change is improving relationships, because teachers who work together and observe each other *will* improve (Fullan, 2007).

One of the most effective ways to promote teachers working together to develop a Culture of Hope is through the establishment of learning communities (DuFour et al., 2005). The path toward establishing learning communities begins with school leadership that creates a sharing culture. When the staff of a school shares and cooperates, students tend to do the same (Shannon & Bylsma, 2007). When leaders shift their focus from evaluating and supervising to developing grade-level and school teams' capacities for working collaboratively, the whole culture shifts from independent and competitive behaviors to interdependent and collaborative behaviors (DuFour et al., 2005).

As Schmoker (2005) wrote, "The right kind of continuous, structured teacher collaboration improves the quality of teaching and pays big, often immediate, dividends in student learning and professional morale in virtually any setting" (p. xii). In general, learning communities promote positive interdependence, support, relationship building, individual and group accountability, communication, trust, goal setting, and reflection (Marzano, Pickering, & Pollock, 2001).

Journal

Upon entering a high-poverty, high-performing, high English learner (EL) school in rural Idaho, I noticed the open, collegial environment everywhere— in classrooms between students, among grade-level teacher teams, and even in the office between staff and administration. The message I read on practically everyone's face was "We're in this together!" I asked the principal to tell me more about the school's culture.

She said, "In so many schools, when teachers see data, they get defensive and the walls go up, and it's like, 'That's not my fault! Do you know how many special ed kids I have? Do you know how many EL kids I have?'"

The principal explained that she feels very comfortable sharing grade-level reports, disaggregated by teacher, and helping teachers go over the data to analyze grade-level and individual strengths and weaknesses. She asks them to create a plan of action to bring up the weak areas and asks those strong in a particular area to share what they are doing.

"It is hard," she said. "You have to set up the trust first, or you aren't going to get anything from your teachers. The teachers I work with are wonderful to talk to, because the trust is there, and they know they can approach me. . . . The culture is the most important thing. The artifacts on the walls, the motivational posters—none of this matters until the teachers know they can trust each other and trust me, until they know that I am their biggest cheerleader and I will do everything I can to protect them. But I also have my requirements, so I ask them to please not fail me and to do the work that we outline to do. All agree to do it well." —E.G.

Principal Leadership

Transforming a school culture demands bold leadership with a vision for the future of the school. And while this leadership can come from teachers or instructional coaches, it represents a clear responsibility for the principal. The principal can quickly set the tone for the school and through his or her efforts and actions establish a clear, consistent vision. This vision must not just focus on the mantra "all students in our school can learn," it must demand that "all our students *will* learn!" This must be the mobilizing call for action; the rallying cry for everything that goes on in the school. It is the vision of "we can do it," but also a vision of "we must and we will do it."

The principal also demonstrates that the school will religiously focus on data to evaluate effectiveness and point the school toward issues that must be addressed. The principal demonstrates, for example, that disaggregated classroom data will be shared, discussed, and used to mobilize help, rather than being used to blame teachers. Along with a vision of greatness, effective principals nourish shared leadership with collaborative teams. In fact, collaboration is a catalyst for shared leadership (DuFour & Marzano, 2011, p. 56).

The principal also provides "celebration of staff effort and achievement," "challenges the status quo," establishes processes that "provide ongoing monitoring of the school's practices and their effects on student learning," develops trusting relations with each staff member in the school, and most importantly, helps shape the "beliefs, expectations, and habits that constitute the school's culture" (DuFour & Marzano, 2011, pp. 54–55).

Strategies to Build the Power of We

In the following section, we look at ways that staff and administration can work together to strengthen the Power of We. These include:

- Supporting the professional development of staff
- Building consensus
- Focusing on needs
- Assessing the institutional culture
- Gathering data for an early warning system
- Monitoring and maintaining the school's culture
- Engaging parents

Supporting the Professional Development of Staff

The concept of a Culture of Hope was first seen as bits and pieces of the cultures of both effective and ineffective schools. Over time, enough of the various components have been used to see an overall gestalt. And while there is certainly no blueprint to follow to get from a school's current reality to where the staff wants it to be, highly successful high-poverty schools and districts begin their efforts with an ongoing process of professional development. Everyone who comes in contact with students deserves and needs professional development, from the clerical and yard duty staff, to the paraprofessionals, teachers, and administrators. Teacher professional development is a key component of school improvement (Darling-Hammond & Sykes, 1999; Fullan, 2007; Shannon & Bylsma, 2007). This includes ongoing professional development for all staff, including paraeducators, as well as tailored ongoing support for new teachers with multiyear mentorship or training programs.

Journal

Working with teachers as the majority of states transition to the Common Core State Standards, I have seen two different reactions. Teachers who taught during the 1980s and 1990s remember project-based learning, workshop models, student-led conferences, hands-on math, student-generated content, and the first attempts at statewide writing, science, and math assessments that were hands-on and minds-on and scored by cadres of teachers who trained and calibrated during the summer. They remember developing units, planning curriculum, and designing learning activities that addressed the curriculum frameworks. The eyes of these teachers begin to sparkle, and they say, "Oh boy, I get to really teach again!" When they walk down the hall, there's a new spring in their step, even if they have no idea what exactly they'll be teaching. They have the tools and the know-how to dig in and get started. They have the self-efficacy.

However, teachers who have taught their whole careers under the guidance of NCLB are glad to see the hyper focus on discrete skills and high-stakes testing wane, but are uncertain of what their classrooms will look like. They have always been told what to teach, when, and how. They have been monitored by administration and curriculum coaches to make sure they were on the right page each day, teaching the curriculum with fidelity. They have been taught that doing a good job is determined by scores on a standardized summative test. When they look at the Common Core standards, these teachers often express anxiety: "What will I teach? Will we have curriculum? I don't know how to develop units. How will we know if students are learning?" Rather than seeing the era of the Common Core as a liberating opening to better teaching and learning, they see it more as a removal of structure, without knowing what will replace it. Many do not know how to start. Administrators, experienced teachers, and support personnel will need to provide scaffolding and many hours of professional development for many educators who joined the profession after 2001, until they get a taste of what teaching with the Common Core will be like. —E.G.

The following are research-based practices for nurturing successful professional development:

- Focus on concrete classroom applications
- Expose teachers to actual practice
- Offer opportunities for observation, critique, and reflection
- Provide opportunities for group support and collaboration
- Ensure evaluation and feedback by skilled practitioners (Elmore & Burney, 1999, p. 263)

The consensus on professional development is that it needs to be ongoing, embedded in the real work of students and teachers, and focused on improving student learning (Shannon & Bylsma, 2007). This means that a particular school district's professional development will be tailored to the specific needs of its student body, which will change over time. It should be kept in mind that in any given staff, the knowledge required to improve student learning (or the ability to access that knowledge) is almost always already present. What is needed is the willingness to roll up sleeves, collaborate, and get the work done (DuFour et al., 2005; Schmoker, 2005). In fact, schools that prematurely bring in outside experts and professional consultants or coaches miss the opportunity to reinforce confidence, build community, and empower staff by drawing on their expertise to improve student learning (Barth, 2005).

Thus, superior professional development is driven by a thorough assessment of the needs of the students and the knowledge and skills staff members must have to meet them, followed by a realistic inventory of the knowledge and skills they already possess.

Journal

A model for building teaching capacity can be found in the National Writing Project (NWP) and the associated state and regional writing projects scattered throughout the United States. In summer workshops on writing process instruction sponsored by the Redwood Writing Project (the regional writing project that services rural Northern California), for example, teachers are encouraged to write for themselves, for their own purposes, instead of for a course requirement or workshop assignment. This is a hallmark of the NWP: the best teachers of writing are, themselves, writers. It is also a hallmark of quality teaching in any subject area: teachers who are enthusiastic participants in the tasks of the subject area are more likely to inspire and engage their students.

Helping teachers get past negative emotional experiences with writing that they themselves had as children is part of the purpose of NWP professional development, as this reflection from one participant shows. "It was an amazing experience for me as an educator and as an individual. I was able to write the difficult piece about my daughter's birth that has taken me almost four years to write. I was able to face my own obstacles and insecurities as a writer, which will help me help my students. I am excited about creating a true writing community in my classroom."

When teachers have a powerful learning experience, when teachers experience real learning, they and their students benefit. What could be better than that? —E.G.

Building Consensus

Even with the professional development components in place, real change and improvement require the staff to come to consensus regarding foundational beliefs, policies, and goals. Although schoolwide consensus is difficult to achieve, maximum effectiveness demands consistency in practices and policies, which in turn requires consensus of beliefs on the following issues:

- All students can and will learn and achieve high levels of academic achievement.

- All students have talents and interests that will be developed.

- All students will achieve at the elementary, middle, and high school levels.

- All students will master basic skills and a rigorous core curriculum.

- All students will master a college-prep curriculum and succeed in advanced placement courses at the high school level.

- All students will graduate from high school and succeed in postsecondary training or educational programs.

- All students will have the chance to nourish their social and emotional growth.

If a school staff does not believe these statements of promise, there is little hope of students ever achieving them. The stronger the beliefs of teachers, the more positive the impact will be on students. Changing a school's culture is not a quick fix—it may take several months, it may take all year, and often it can be a two- to three-year process of consistent effort.

Journal

During observations at a high-performing, high-poverty, high–English learner school in rural Idaho, the principal spoke about the long road toward building a school culture that supported data analysis and learning communities that foster teachers as learners.

In reference to the Friday grade-level collaboration meetings, the principal explained, "Teachers are focusing on curriculum instruction and assessment during that time. . . . We encourage them to do lesson shares at that time, and we've trained our teachers in how to run a protocol—we call it the thirty-minute lesson-share protocol—where they bring a sample of student work and the lesson plan, tell the team about the lesson, and then evaluate the lesson. Each grade-level team gives me feedback on its collaboration and the lesson sharing."

Both principal and teachers indicated it took five years for them to feel like the Friday meetings were fulfilling the intended purposes of collaboration and sharing. While some staff may view examining data or having an instructional coach as a sign that they are ineffective and not doing their job, others embrace the idea wholeheartedly. It is the principal's job to set the tone for learning and relieve teachers' concerns about potential judgment and criticism.

Something that stood out about this school is the similarity between principal-teacher and teacher-student leadership roles. The principal differentiates instructional support for teachers by offering choices, providing support, encouraging, pushing to grow, honoring where they are, placing them into groups to develop relationships, and providing meaningful tasks for groups to work on. Similarly, the teacher differentiates learning support for students by offering choices, assessing students' needs, providing open ceilings so students can excel, placing students into groups, assigning meaningful tasks, monitoring progress, and adjusting instruction as needed. This theme of principals modeling for staff what staff need to model for students can be seen again and again in Culture of Hope schools. —E.G.

Focusing on Needs

Any school that seeks to develop or enrich a Culture of Hope must start with the recognition of needs. For example:

- Why does our school suffer from such high rates of absenteeism?
- Why are we being so unsuccessful in getting all of our students up to grade-level standards in reading and math?
- Why do we have so many students who are dropping out of school prior to graduation? Why do so many of our students seem to feel that they are not smart enough to do their schoolwork?
- Why do so few parents come to parent-teacher conferences?
- Why do so many of our students seem so unmotivated to learn?

Answering questions like these using school data can open the door to productive exchanges regarding the school culture and the students' social and emotional needs. Discussion may also be stimulated as a result of participation in professional conferences or workshops, when teachers return with ideas to share.

Consensus can also grow out of a reading and discussion program, a study group, or invited presentations to the staff. As teachers learn more about "locus of control," the conditions and needs of poverty, Maslow's hierarchy of needs, or dramatic changes in the economic world, they come to better understand the importance and relevance of their own work and the nature of the challenges they face. They may also begin considering ways to improve their school.

Journal

Though needs assessment is best done as a schoolwide process, individual teachers can improve the culture of their classrooms through student surveys as well. I conducted surveys of classroom climate several times a year, just to keep tabs on what was going on under the surface. With the first survey, students were concerned with hurting my feelings or being criticized for things they said, and were perhaps not totally honest. The surveys were always anonymous,

> but trusting in that anonymity was not universal. When I shared the data with the class, that's when the change and trust began to build. They saw how I handled criticisms: "Four students indicated they regularly can't see the board because I stand in the way. I am so grateful to get this information! Can you all help me come up with a solution for this?" I'd write down all their suggestions, and we'd make a plan for the best strategies.
>
> They also saw how I handled global comments like "I'm bored all the time," and requests like "Can we have water bottles at our desks?" with the same problem solving and genuine acceptance and grace. When the midyear survey came out, the comments and feedback were even more valuable for me as an educator, because students were even more honest and invested in making their learning environment better. They knew their feedback was valued and would be taken into consideration. —E.G.

Perhaps the most useful approach to improving a school culture is through collecting data that survey the attitudes and beliefs of teachers and students, as described in the next section.

Assessing the Institutional Culture

All of the personnel working in any school will have strong, concrete opinions regarding the institutional culture in which they work. And though people may use the same words and express similar feelings about their school environment, they often mean very different things. Research on high-poverty, high-performing schools has helped school leaders and educators understand the need to assess the beliefs, insights, and opinions of all of the school personnel regarding their school culture before beginning the work of consensus-building (Barr & Parrett, 2008; Barr & Yates, 2010; DuFour & Marzano, 2011; Lezotte & Snyder, 2011). When conducting school surveys, there are no right or wrong answers. The surveys are meant to uncover agreed-upon beliefs regarding students, learning, assessment, and instructional strategies. Schools creating or enriching a Culture of Hope must ensure there is a firm consensus agreement regarding these fundamental beliefs.

Additional resources for assessing a school's collective beliefs include the staff, student, and district surveys of the Idaho Building Capacity project. Links to these surveys are found in appendix B (page 235).

Regardless of which instruments are selected, all stakeholders, including teachers, administrators, school specialists, support staff, parents, students, and community leaders should complete surveys.

Following is a basic road map for assessing a school or district's culture:

1. Survey student attitudes.
2. Summarize responses.
3. Discuss diverse perceptions and beliefs.
4. Resolve differences.
5. Come to consensus.
6. Formulate school goals.
7. Collaborate and monitor.
8. Refine interventions and prepare for new surveys.

Survey Student Attitudes

Eric Jensen (2009) suggests that school staffs should start out by assessing the level of hope or hopelessness of students. He proposed a simple set of twenty-five or so questions in order to gain insight into how students view their life and their potential for the future. Examples of questions include:

- What is the likelihood of your succeeding in school and graduating?
- How much support do you feel you get from your teachers in your schoolwork and personal life?
- When you think about where you will be ten or twenty years from now, what comes to mind? (Jensen, 2009)

Other questions might include:

- How safe do you feel at school?
- When you arrive at school do you feel that you belong and are welcome?
- Do you often feel that no one at the school cares for you?
- Do you often feel alone and without friends?
- Do you feel that the coursework is too hard?
- Do you often feel that the coursework is simply beyond your abilities?
- Do your teachers ever praise you for your work?
- Would you rather stay home than go to school?
- Do you believe that your life in ten to twenty years will be better than your family's? About the same? Not as good?

(See student questionnaires at the ends of chapters 4–7, pages 61, 81, 103, and 135.)

Once a school staff has developed a student questionnaire, it should be used twice a year to monitor how student perceptions have changed during the school year.

The views of students often illuminate needed areas of improvement that adults are unaware of and can be a rich resource for the effects of school atmosphere and activities on students. As mentioned previously, students should be exempt from taking the surveys if they or their parents so choose, and the responses of those who do take it must be strictly anonymous. The responses should be routinely collected over time to determine the progress or lack of progress of the school.

Teacher and staff questionnaires must also be strictly anonymous, so that teachers feel that they can be totally honest. Any survey will help dramatize the degree to which a school staff has shared agreements as well as areas of disagreement. Identifying areas of disagreement is essential in helping a school staff establish specific goals, and regular use of surveys enables the school staff to assess whether or not they are achieving more or less shared agreement in the school. (See sample staff questionnaires at the ends of chapters 4–7).

For both student and teacher questionnaires, participants should be encouraged to be as honest as possible. Again, it is important to stress that there are no right and wrong answers.

Summarize Responses

Following the completion of the individual questionnaires, the responses should be tallied and summarized for the entire school. This will provide an overall snapshot of the perceptions of the entire school community. Next, the questionnaire responses should be summarized on the basis of "job-alike" groups, that is, teachers, administrators, specialists, parents and community leaders, paraeducators, and students; they could be summarized by teacher groups as well: all third-grade teachers, all high school English teachers, and so on, as long as groups are large enough that their size does not provide a clue to their identity.

Discuss Diverse Perceptions and Beliefs

The summarized responses can then be distributed for discussion to the school staff and school community. The large group of participants can again be organized into job-alike small groups for initial discussion and then into "jigsaw" mixed groups, each with representatives from all of the job-alike groups. The goal of these small groups is to compare the various responses and comments and work for understanding where there is disagreement about personal beliefs and perceptions of the school. It is especially helpful to compare responses among the various groups of people completing the questionnaire, such as among teachers, paraeducators, parents, students, and administrators. Disagreements can be identified and collected for further discussions.

Resolve Differences

The ultimate goal of any survey of staff attitudes and beliefs is to focus discussions on areas of disagreement. Discussions on areas of disagreement can serve as a catalyst for highlighting the need for and motivation for building group consensus on essential, research-based beliefs. As reported by some effective schools, this ultimately may require conflict resolution strategies, professional staff development, staffing changes, and careful recruitment and hiring to maintain or improve the school culture. For large schools, especially large comprehensive middle and high schools, consensus may be difficult, perhaps even impossible. To gain the consensus necessary for improvement, large schools may need to reorganize into smaller mini or optional schools (see chapter 10, pages 186–187, for a discussion of reorganization into mini schools).

Come to Consensus

In almost every school, there will be some opposition to the basic tenets of the Culture of Hope. Until a school staff has consciously worked to develop a unified school culture, there will be teachers, administrators, school specialists, and families who operate in fundamental disagreement with one another. Visit any low-performing or failing school, and it is quickly evident that the students are not failures; rather, the teachers and support staff do not believe the students can learn or, just as bad, have mixed beliefs about students. Often, negative attitudes about students reflect latent racism and class prejudice. And while the world, especially the world of education, has become more and more politically correct, racism and class prejudice are still huge negative forces in schools as well as society.

These negative attitudes often show up in classrooms as low expectations for learning. At their worst, schools can surround students with devastating social and cultural messages that either doom them to mediocre instruction or prompt them into reactions of anger and frustration. It is for this reason that teachers and administrators at effective schools will talk about the lengthy process—sometimes years long, in fact—it took to assemble a staff that shared a common set of beliefs about teaching, learning, and school culture, in particular the belief that all students can and will learn. As explained earlier in this chapter, this process requires careful observation and evaluation of classroom practices, a vigorous staff development plan, and an ambitious recruiting and hiring program. The end result can be awesome—a strong, unified, effective, and thriving staff.

The task of working toward school consensus is complex. It should start, as we have seen, with data about the school (attendance reports, student discipline referrals, student assessments in reading and math, records of parent conference participation, and so on) and the data from the Culture of Hope questionnaires. In the end, the goal is to move toward consensus on everything from foundational beliefs about teaching and learning (we believe that all our students can and must learn and achieve high levels of excellence) to group processes (we believe in a collaborative culture of professional sharing and decision making) and schoolwide goals (we expect our four-year cohort graduation rate to exceed 85 percent in three years).

Formulate School Goals

While most agreed-upon school goals focus on instruction, an understanding of the importance of students' social and emotional needs will help school staff consider goals that focus on school culture and the seeds of hope. Identifying a few targeted goals can lead to dramatic, often immediate school improvement, but the goals must grow out of documented concerns and provide some method of monitoring and evaluating the progress or improvements. The seeds of hope are so interrelated that addressing one area will lead to results in others. If a school staff can focus on even just one or two goals that relate to the school culture and the human needs of students, and can agree on a way of measuring and monitoring the impact of their efforts, students are likely to feel an immediate change in the school and classroom atmosphere. The school staff should agree on the goals and how to measure the impact of their work, and they should agree to meet regularly and monitor their work over time.

Simply coming to agreements like these heightens attention throughout the school and becomes a self-fulfilling process. Teachers, specialists, paraeducators, and administrators become conscious of their own actions and begin to address issues. Teachers are more alert to what is happening throughout the school. Multiply this by an entire school staff, and a sense that something important is occurring will grow. Imagine that the entire school sets out to ensure that each student believes he or she can learn and achieve high academic standards. Teachers surround their students with positive optimism and praise. They remind students day after day, "You can do this! You can learn this! You are doing such a good job! See, I told you that you could do it!" Teachers share their success stories. Older students are invited to return to their former classrooms and share their experiences. This does not just happen in one classroom, it happens throughout the school. Slowly, a Culture of Hope begins to emerge, and the students, in turn, respond with greater efforts.

Collaborate and Monitor

This process of school improvement demands that teachers have time each week to meet and discuss how well the school is doing. Wherever possible, data should be collected and reviewed. This might include data from student questionnaires or even from observations by teachers. Teachers talk about what they have done in their classrooms and what they have seen around the school. They tell success stories about specific students and how they may have responded to praise and high expectations. The following statements might be among those that teachers share in such a discussion (Jensen, 2009):

- "I use daily affirmations in my classroom, both verbally and on posters on the walls."
- "I have been asking students to share their hopes and dreams and offer positive reinforcement."
- "I tell my students each and every day why I know that they can succeed."
- "I help students set goals and develop goal-setting skills."
- "I tell my students true stories about students just like them who have succeeded, and I have been thinking about inviting some of the older students in the school to come in and offer encouragement ('Hey, if I could do it, I know that you can do it!')."
- "The best thing I have ever done is to begin to treat all of my students as talented and gifted."

Refine Interventions and Prepare for New Surveys

Out of discussions like these, teachers will learn new ideas from one another to try in their classrooms and will become better and better at positive reinforcement. Teachers might also look up books about "locus of control," building pride and self-esteem, or helping students find a sense of belonging in their classroom. They might set up a reading and discussion series. They could also visit one another's classrooms to see exactly what their colleagues are doing ("I loved watching you work with the students who are not up to grade level. I had never thought of doing that." "You are so successful; tell us how you do it."). The learning is occurring through teachers mutually trusting, sharing, and discussing. Behold the Power of We.

Journal

While having an expert come on site to do a one-time professional development training on the latest reform initiative can be beneficial, it is highly unlikely that a one-shot training will have a lasting impact on student learning without the ongoing support to implement and troubleshoot the new ideas. Ongoing support in the form of learning communities, book groups, monthly support meetings, and longitudinal training sessions is an example of how teachers and administrators lead themselves toward change.

For instance, in my capacity as a teacher-leader for the Redwood Writing Project, I've trained teachers through a five-day summer workshop on writing instruction, followed by an optional monthly support group throughout the school year. While the summer workshops are invigorating and inspiring, and teachers often tell me how their teaching practice has transformed, it is in the monthly support group that I see the true power of teachers teaching teachers. For the first two months of school, the group comes in bright eyed and bushy tailed, enthusiastic about the writing their students are doing and the way their students are crawling out of their seats to participate in minilessons and sharing. Then November rolls around, and the group comes in reluctantly, hesitantly. When we start the opening sharing of how things are going, the first teacher expresses how the luster has worn off, how he is worried, how he isn't able to schedule the kind of writing time he knows his students need. A collective sigh, accompanied with nods of agreement, goes around the group: "Phew. We are not alone, we are not failures."

We support each other through December and January, brainstorming solutions to concerns, and suggesting what has worked. Every teacher in the group sees that he or she has something to contribute to the others' growth. It isn't about my role as leader and expert, it is about my role as facilitator, connecting participants to each other as resources and colleagues. When we meet in February, their enthusiasm is back and they bring in student portfolios to show the progress students have made. Providing ongoing support over the course of a school year gives me a better chance of having a lasting, positive influence on student learning. Those teachers who might abandon a new idea when the going gets tough—as it almost assuredly will—have the encouragement to forge ahead with the reassurance that struggles are a normal part of everyone's process. —E.G.

Gathering Data for an Early Warning System

As a school year progresses, teachers may feel a need to gather different types of data to help them in their work. For example, effective schools have found that it is essential to be able to quickly identify students who begin to falter and fall behind in their learning. This has led many schools and districts to establish early warning systems. Too often, high schools wait until a student actually leaves school before stepping in to try to salvage the situation. By this time, it may be far too late. The high school dropout is typically significantly behind academically, with enough failed classes to make on-time graduation unrealistic. To truly reduce the dropout rate, schools must implement a K–12 system designed to effectively identify students in need or potential dropouts at the earliest possible time. Such a comprehensive system quickly responds to the needs of each of these identified students with an intensive intervention that does not let up until the student is successful.

These systems identify a number of significant indicators and follow data on each student. Some schools have extended the student questionnaires concept to carefully monitor social and emotional issues, such as students who may be isolated, bullied, or simply disconnected from school.

Journal

For a field-study class on school improvement while at Boise State University, I was able to intern for a year with Anser Charter School in Idaho. I showed up and was dispatched to the special education department ("the crow's nest"). At first, the director of the crow's nest, Lisa Cates, looked at me like a deer in the headlights. I could read her mind: "Oh no, another person I need to tell what to do. Yikes!" I smiled and asked her to tell me about what she wanted to get done, but couldn't do. I said, "I'm here to serve you, not the other way around. Put me to work!"

And that is how I got the job of redesigning the "pink sheets" that were used to collect behavior data across the school. When students had problems being learners and "crew" (an expeditionary learning term that refers to the role of learners as crew, not passengers), teachers and staff members filled out a pink sheet, which went to the crow's nest. Problem was, they stacked up, and there wasn't a way to collect the data for analysis. There was all this great data, just waiting to be used to improve the school. I created a database using Microsoft Access, with drop-down selections for each place on the pink sheet, trying to make it as streamlined and easy to use as possible for staff. Then the database was put onto the community drive so teachers could choose to enter information from their classroom computers and skip filling out the piece of paper.

The stack of pink sheets soon became a sortable, searchable database that was used to understand the challenges students experienced. We found out the days and times that students typically had the most behavior struggles, which led to modifications for individual students and whole classrooms, which resulted in decreased behavior struggles and more time spent learning and being crew. When students had to see the principal for discipline issues, she could pull up their pink sheet data to put their behavior in context. If a student had an individualized education plan (IEP) meeting, or a student study team meeting, again, the pink sheet data could be printed. What began as a task to deal with data grew to become an integral part of the behavior side of the school's response to intervention (RTI) protocols. —E.G.

Effective schools always monitor student achievement, but increasingly, research demonstrates the importance of collecting and monitoring data on social and emotional growth (DuFour et al., 2010). Some high-performing, high-poverty schools have discovered that focusing on academic strategies is not sufficient to keep low-income students learning effectively. For example, the Lincolnshire, Illinois, school district attributes much of its success in turning around a failing school to an emphasis on social and emotional growth:

> In the face of a growing research that (1) socially and emotionally competent students do better in school, engage in more pro-social behaviors, and are more likely to experience career success, and (2) social emotional competencies can be explicitly taught as an enhancement to rather than a detractor from the curriculum, the school district has taken steps to teach those competencies and monitor their presence in all of its students. (DuFour et al., 2010, p. 61)

The district developed a common vocabulary to describe the competencies, identified the most vital competencies—interpersonal, intrapersonal, stress management, and adaptability skills—ensured that all faculties understood how the competencies could be taught, and developed a survey to administer to all grades that identified and monitored the development of each student's growth. Student support teams implemented specific interventions to students identified with these needs (DuFour et al., 2010). In 2008, "almost 80 percent of the graduates had earned college credit" (p. 63). For reports on outcomes from Adlai E. Stevenson high school's 2008–2011 student surveys, see appendix B (page 235).

Identify and Use Predictive Factors

Research that was conducted by the Consortium on Chicago School Research, the Center for Social Organization of Schools at The Johns Hopkins University, and the Philadelphia Education Fund has identified three highly predictive factors that are associated with the phenomenon of dropping out (Bruce, et al., 2011). These initial findings were also validated in five-year longitudinal studies that were undertaken in a number of states and city school districts. In addition, some schools and districts have monitored two additional factors.

These five K–12 predictive dropout factors and the corresponding thresholds for intervention are as follows:

1. **Attendance**—Schools monitor attendance, including tardies and early pull-outs. Missing twenty days or having a 10 percent absence rate represents a significant setback in learning.

2. **Behavior**—Schools collect and monitor classroom and schoolwide behavior data. Students with two or more mild or more serious infractions are more likely to drop out.

3. **Course performance**—Schools monitor academic progress and communicate clearly across transitions to middle and high schools. Students who are unable to read at grade level by the end of third grade, who experience failure in English or mathematics in the sixth grade, or who fail to earn on-time promotion to the tenth grade are at serious risk of being dropouts.

4. **Social and emotional issues**—Using site-based instruments, schools monitor counselor referrals, course failures, family problems, and a large number of social and emotional issues. Without a foundation of strong social and emotional assets, even students who master the basics in the elementary years are at risk of dropping out in high school.

5. **Monitoring of students leaving school**—Effective high schools carefully monitor each student who leaves school in order to verify that he or she has actually enrolled in another educational option. Not all students who leave school are dropouts, but without follow-through from the school, some may slip through the cracks and fail to graduate.

To summarize, monitoring the social and emotional growth of students has great potential for stemming the tide of potential dropouts. In fact, according to Maslow's hierarchy, the first three predictive factors can be considered "symptoms" of problems that cannot be easily resolved until students' more basic human needs are met. For example, an attendance problem may actually reflect that a student and his or her family are homeless, that a student does not feel safe at school, or that a family is highly mobile and constantly moving. A reading problem may reflect that a student comes from a home with minimal oral communication and low vocabulary knowledge, that the student has not found a sense of belonging at the school, or that the student feels a cultural conflict with the middle-class values of the school and has chosen not to learn. If these social and emotional issues are addressed at a school's cultural level, these surface issues will likely be resolved.

Schools and districts interested in seriously addressing the achievement problems of low-income and minority students should use the factors of attendance, behavior, and academic success as warning signs, but they must understand that the problems that lead to these indicators are more personal and complex. The Hope Survey (www .hopesurvey.org) monitors social and emotional characteristics of hope, engagement, academic press, goal orientation, belongingness, and autonomy See also the information about student surveys in appendix B (page 235).

Regardless of the specific factors that are monitored, schools and districts must use the best available research as well as other agreed-upon indicators to proactively identify students who are likely to encounter school problems. All too often, schools are able to identify students in need but do not have a system in place that quickly and effectively addresses and remedies those needs.

Create a System for Addressing Students in Need

Such intervention cannot be a random, haphazard reaction to a student beginning to experience problems. An effective school knows immediately what to do and when to do it. The system's wheels begin to turn. Responses might include meetings with the school counselor, meetings between the counselor and the student's teachers, home visits, and in-depth discussions with parents. They may include immediate remediation, extended learning time before and after school, or summer intensive programs. Whatever strategies are used, a school must have a systemic response in place to surround, nurture, and support the student at the earliest possible moment, until he or she is re-engaged successfully in school.

It is essential that identification of students in need must also include full disclosure to and involvement of parents and families. Parents, especially poor and minority parents, want their children to succeed in school and may not understand that their child is struggling. The adults in a child's life can be highly supportive once they understand what they can do to help. And while effective elementary and middle schools tend to have a strong track record of partnerships with parents, this is an area in which high schools have less experience. As mentioned previously, Ricardo LeBlanc-Esparza, former principal in Washington State, believes that getting families involved in the education of their children was one of the primary factors behind the transformation of Granger High School. The school engineered this success in part by transforming parent-teacher conferences, resulting in 100 percent attendance of parents (LeBlanc-Esparza & Roulston, 2012), a rate that has persisted under new leadership (von Zastrow, 2009). (See the section on parent engagement, page 171, for more information about including parents as partners.) Parents represent strong effective partners in the education of their children and youth, but they must be involved; schools need to facilitate ways for them to learn how to help. Parents are powerful partners, but they must learn that the school is trustworthy and supportive and has their children's welfare clearly in mind.

Journal

Deep inside, every parent wants what is best for his or her child. No matter if a parent can act on it or not, he or she cares. If I can keep that in my mind when working with parents, especially parents who struggle to provide for their children, it helps me treat every parent with the respect and consideration necessary to establish communication and the beginnings of trust. It is not up to me to judge, it is up to me to help make a difference in each child's life. By working in partnership with parents, by asking parents about their children's strengths and problematic areas, and by keeping the focus on solutions rather than blame, I have a better chance of making that difference. —E.G.

Monitoring and Maintaining the School's Culture

An effective school, especially a Culture of Hope school, must also have a system of response in place for continual improvement. Without a clear and unified vision; without respect and trust among teachers, administrators, parents, and students; without an established process of meetings and collaboration; and without a way to work through difficult and divisive issues in a professional manner, teachers are likely to drift away on their own, close their classroom doors, and set out once again on the lonely path of teaching in isolation. If this happens, teachers may well begin to lose hope and sink into apathy and despair. All teachers will suffer if this begins to occur, but it is the students who suffer the most.

In addition to the task of establishing and utilizing a process of continuous professional development, there are a number of other ways an effective school will attempt to monitor and maintain the school culture: these include the use of instructional coaches and new-teacher induction programs.

Instructional Coaches

Every school needs support for teachers. This is often the principal or informal "buddy systems" with teachers across the hall. The most significant type of help, certainly the most powerful, is the use of instructional coaches or curriculum coaches for teachers. A teacher coach is needed in all schools, not just those that struggle or have challenging student populations. Similarly, coaches are not just for new teachers or teachers whose students have low test scores. Every teacher on staff deserves a coach. Professionals in any field who want to improve their effectiveness deserve a coach, and this is especially true for teachers. Continuous learning and growth are hallmarks of being a teacher; yet teaching can often be a lonely and isolated experience. Providing a coach can help signal that it is not only okay, but it is also assumed that teachers will share, collaborate, and talk about problems and successes. A coach is not there to bring everyone up to the status quo or to be the critical eyes and ears of the principal. Just like a teacher working with a classroom of diverse kids, the coach supports teachers as individuals and assists them all in reaching their greatest potentials. The child with learning difficulties, the child from poverty, the child who has a stable home life, and the child who qualifies for Gifted and Talented Education (GATE) services all deserve the teacher's time and attention. So too, all the teachers on a staff deserve the expertise and support of the coach, from the least experienced to the master, from the shyest to the knock-your-socks-off dynamo.

Journal

A district coordinator of curriculum coaches told me that her district had an instructional coach for every teacher. She said, "When you win the Super Bowl or the World Series, you still have a coach the following year. It isn't about how good a teacher you are, it isn't about the bells and whistles of your lessons. It's about being the best teacher you can be, every year. And that's measured by what your students do. Our coaches watch students more than they watch teachers." —E.G.

Instructional coaches represent a crucial ingredient in the implementation of a Culture of Hope. Just like kids, teachers can get so bogged down and stressed that they need a burst of professional optimism. Improvements in classroom instruction cannot occur in an atmosphere of intimidation and blame. Just like effective learning, improving classroom teaching needs a schoolwide, professional atmosphere of optimism; it needs teacher collaboration and supportive coaches. This is not the type of instructional coach who serves as "curricula police," making sure all fourth-grade classes are on the same page of the adopted text each week. These are coaches who serve as motivators, instigators, and invigorators. They help teachers collaborate with each other in grade-level teams and across grade-level teams. They identify areas for staff development and provide that staff development, or they identify another staff member who is capable. They free the principal to focus on other areas of leadership, and support the principal's efforts in establishing a learning community. They serve as a type of relationship glue that gets teachers positively connected with each other and connects teaching staff with administrative staff. Most importantly, by providing an instructional coach, the administration is sending the message that the school is a place where learning occurs, not a place where teaching occurs (Darling-Hammond, 1997). That may seem like a semantic splitting of hairs, but this idea carries weight when considered from a school culture perspective. It relates to creating a sense of optimism, safety, and belonging. When everyone within a school's walls sees him- or herself as a learner, when all adults and youth have their accomplishments celebrated, when mistakes are seen as signals of areas for growth rather than areas for sanctions and recriminations, teachers and students alike can invest more deeply in their work and their studies. When coaches are focused on growth, support, and encouragement, it helps teachers to engage more fully in improvement.

In order for a curriculum or instructional coach to be effective, the coach needs to develop clear communication and trust with the staff. There must be a firewall that allows information to come from administration to the coaches but filters information going from coaches to the administration to protect teacher confidentiality, at least until the atmosphere and school culture shift to one of trust. Teachers must be able to acknowledge their weaknesses without fear of reprisal, so they can focus on learning and truly grow. The coach helps teachers identify areas for improvement, both through observation and through facilitating self-evaluation. As professionals, teachers often know exactly what they need to work on, and just need the nudge to do so. Additionally, coaches help schools build their capacity to address learners' needs without bringing in a new curriculum or special speaker (for more on capacity building, see page 142).

A coach also facilitates the mapping of a staff's strengths, so when a grade-level team is examining mathematics data and discovers that three teachers have low student results in percentages and fractions, the coach can call in the fifth-grade teacher to demonstrate a sequence of lessons for teaching the concepts well. The coach focuses the team on solutions. No one is perfect, and we need to let go of the notion that teachers should already know it all. Even the winning NBA slam-dunk superstar needs a coach!

Journal

I was working with a second-grade teacher in Northern California, and one day I walked into her room for our coaching appointment to find her looking quite harried.

She was busily cleaning up her classroom after a long day and said, "I'm sorry, I'm not ready for you. I have no idea what I want to work on with you."

I sat down and said, "No need to apologize, you've been teaching all day!" And I invited her to tell me about her day.

She expressed frustration with the maturity level of her students at this point in the school year (March), compared to last year: "It's one of those groups where there must have been something in the water when they were born! The majority have the developmental maturity of kindergarteners. There is no way they can meet the standards for second grade."

She talked about how her students would rather crawl under the tables pretending to be dogs and cats than engage in more age-appropriate curricula. She knew they needed more hands-on and active learning, but she feared losing control, which with this group was tenuous at best. We brainstormed ways to incorporate more movement into the learning day.

I asked, "What are some areas of content knowledge that you feel they are weak in?"

She replied, "Parts of speech. They don't know verbs and nouns."

So we designed physical education (P.E.) activities around verbs and nouns, and I coached her in being explicit and using the terms she wanted students to know. When introducing the P.E. lesson, she would explain that they were going to practice recognizing verbs in a version of Simon Says. If she says a verb, they do what the verb says to do, and if she says a noun, they sit down. She left that meeting with a plan to make everything count for double duty. No activity was just P.E. or just math. *Integration* was the word of the day.

At our next coaching session, this teacher said, "I need to really thank you. You gave me permission to accept them just the way they were, and that alone has made all the difference. I'm not fighting them all the time. They haven't magically matured, but you really opened a door for me. It just perked me up and got me thinking and planning very different ways to get these energetic kids engaged and learning!"

Just like our students, teachers need encouragement and support to do the hard work of teaching. Creativity requires energy and motivation, both of which are hard to muster when you're facing the daily needs of a room full of energetic, very different kids under the stress of a constant push to be more effective. —E.G.

New-Teacher Induction Programs

Careful hiring and professional development for new staff members are integral to the process of creating and maintaining a school's Culture of Hope. So many poor rural school districts have difficulty recruiting and keeping well-trained and effective teachers. Their communities are often isolated, and salaries cannot compete with larger urban and suburban school districts. Recognizing this problem, some start recruiting teachers while they are still students in their schools. These students graduate from high school and go off to college, but they leave with a plan to return to their communities.

Journal

When I work in schools, especially when I speak to the entire school district staff in opening-day activities, I have come to ask, "How many of you went to school here when you were kids?" It seems that the poorer, more isolated a school district happens to be, the more hands that go up in the air. There seems to be a shared pride in not just being part of a school, but in being in the community where they grew up and in knowing that through their work, they are making a huge, positive impact. I have seen this in rural areas of Oregon, Kentucky, Virginia . . . just about everywhere I travel. There is a caveat, however: I see this pride only in communities where there are effective schools. It is the pride of being a part of a successful school, even as a student, that builds this connection and prompts people to want to return. —B.B.

Like high school dropout rates, the new-teacher dropout rate is shocking. Nearly 50 percent of new teachers leave the profession before the end of their fifth year—and urban and high-poverty schools lose upward of 70 percent of new hires (Muhammad, 2009). This tragic dropout rate disproportionately affects children coming from poverty, especially the urban poor. As Anthony Muhammad (2009) points out, "When the poorest and neediest students are consistently guided by novice professionals who never evolve into proficient instructors, they will constantly be behind" (p. 51). This loss greatly inhibits a school's ability to build institutional memory, which is the capacity to carry on from year to year with the goals and programs deemed worthy and important (Muhammad, 2009). A school's stability, which is so crucial to student learning, depends on its ability to retain administrative and teaching staff. Schools must be intentional about retaining new teachers.

The four seeds of hope are also necessary for new teachers. They need to feel a sense of optimism about their profession, their school, and their capabilities as professionals. They need to feel a sense of belonging within their school and district—that what they have to contribute is needed. They need a sense of pride, self-esteem, and self-confidence. They need to feel that they can handle the requirements of the job well and that students, colleagues, and need administrators see them as successful. And finally, they need to have a sense of purpose and feel that they are doing work that matters in the context of the community and the larger world.

Administrators and staff can ensure that new teachers are brought into the arms of the school in the following ways:

- Ask new teachers about their interests and hobbies, and find ways to utilize those interests and hobbies to connect teachers to the integral running of the school (Muhammad, 2009). Teachers who are interested in nature can be asked to supervise a Nature Explorers Club, and a teacher who enjoys needle arts like quilting and embroidery could be asked to create a display to ignite enthusiasm for an upcoming art elective.

- Provide safety and validation for teachers as learners by having staff share moments of learning at staff meetings. Have a "great idea" board in the staff room where individuals can post examples of lessons or strategies to share. Teachers need to view their classrooms as places where they learn as much as their students do. Teaching is learning.

- Help new teachers reflect on their practice and confront their apprenticeships of observation (Kennedy, 1999) by making thoughtful and particular pairings between new teachers and skilled educators who model appropriate teaching practice. Using PLCs (DuFour, Eaker, & DuFour, 2005) can provide new teachers with hope that they can live up to their ideals with the support of fellow teachers.

- Provide mentorship programs for new hires. In a high-performing, high-poverty school in rural Idaho, new teachers participate in a two-year mentorship program run by teachers with teacher leaders. During the first year, after-school classes focus on classroom management, Sheltered Instruction Observation Protocol (SIOP; Echevarria, Vogt, & Short, 2012), and Marzano's 9 Effective Teaching Strategies (Marzano, Pickering, & Pollock, 2001). During the second year, the emphasis is on assessment and curriculum alignment. Each new teacher works with a mentor, who receives a small stipend. Additionally, each new teacher gets five sessions with the instructional coach.

- Provide targeted professional development for new teachers. School leaders can do a lot to limit the normal struggles of new teachers by providing targeted professional development on classroom management, assessment, working with parents, lesson planning, and differentiation of instruction. In one school, the principal designed a new-teacher basic training program with an hour of professional development after school, every two weeks. True to the best of professional learning communities, staff members with capacity taught the sessions; the program began with three and expanded to twenty-one sessions within five years (Muhammad, 2009)!

Journal

Every new teacher faces his or her own feelings of inadequacy during the first few years on the job. In my first year of teaching, I remember stopping by a neighboring teacher's classroom after an especially trying day. She could see, by the look on my face and the droop of my shoulders, that I'd had a rough time with my fifth graders.

She said, "You know, some days you just have to pull the curtains, lock your door, and have a good cry at the end of the day. We all have bad days and lessons that flop. You just regroup, talk to a friend, and make a new plan!"

She patted my hand and helped me regroup. I no longer felt like a failure. Rather, I felt like I'd joined the team. —E.G.

The bottom line is that new teachers need to know that their struggles are a normal developmental milestone toward becoming expert teachers. They need ongoing mentorship from expert teachers who embody the Culture of Hope. And they need to be connected solidly to the school community with recognition and utilization of their personal strengths. Without support and ongoing professional development targeted to the needs of new teachers, schools set incoming teachers up for possible failure, manifested by dropping out of the profession or succumbing to the forces of mediocrity and jettisoning what is best for learners. As an elementary principal in Muhammad's (2009) study said, "When one student fails, that one student suffers, but when one teacher fails, 30 students fail" (p. 111).

Schools that expend the effort and resources to hire the best teacher candidates must plan to expend the effort and resources necessary to grow and retain their recruits. It is an investment that pays spectacular dividends.

Journal

The Kentucky superintendent laughed. "Well," he said, "we start recruiting teachers when they are in the second grade. We focus on each student, constantly telling them how important they are and how well they are doing in school, but we also remind them again and again that they have the good fortune of being a student in the 'best school district in Kentucky.' Our goal is to build community pride in each and every one of our students. As they grow older, we focus a lot of energy on exploring careers and selecting career areas. We make sure that a career in teaching is very prominent. For people living in our area of the state, a teaching job is a really good job and we want all of our students to consider that as a possible career area of interest. We work closely with Morehead State University, and we work to get as many top student teachers as possible working in our schools. When our former students graduate with their teaching degree, we want a job in our district to be their number-one choice. I believe that we have the strongest teaching staff in the state, and most of them, we raised ourselves." —B.B.

Engaging Parents

The final area for consideration by schools implementing a Culture of Hope is engaging parents. Lawrence Hardy (2007) writes:

For schools struggling to help at-risk children, it is essential to reach out to parents. But simply wanting "parent involvement" is not enough. Indeed, the families that stand to benefit the most from closer school ties—families living in poverty, English language learners, and others who find themselves marginalized by any number of misfortunes—are usually the hardest to attract. Districts, especially those serving low-income families, need comprehensive outreach plans to strengthen family ties and provide parents with the skills and information to help their children succeed. (p. 20)

The needs of families living in poverty are tremendous; schools must be mindful of the stress they are under and craft meaningful, purposeful ways for them to be involved and connected with their children's learning as early as possible and at every step.

Like their children, many of these parents feel sad, without hope, and helpless to turn their lives around. It is absolutely essential that schools work to build hope with parents as well as with children. Parents must come to see that their kids can achieve a far better economic life than they have and that the schools know how their children can do it. Schools must help parents understand an economic world that has baffled them. Parents need to understand that their kids can find a way out of poverty and achieve the American dream, though the path will not be easy or without sacrifice, and their children must have their help. Schools and families must work together to get the kids to school every day and help them every night with their studies. Just as the school must have a "college-going culture," families must have that same emphasis in the home and in discussions with their children. The belief expressed at home and at school must be, "You can go to college! You can excel! You can make it out of poverty."

Parents must understand that success starts at the preschool and elementary levels and progresses right through high school. There are essential benchmarks of success at every level along the way, and the continuum starts with their children learning to read and ends with advanced placement courses, high school graduation, and success in postsecondary training or education (see "A Modern-Day Rite of Passage," tables 10.1–10.5, pages 219–222 and online at **go.solution-tree.com/schoolimprovement**).

Impact of Stress on Parent Involvement

Stress affects families and kids. Children in families experiencing stress are more likely to exhibit low levels of engagement in their schoolwork. A family stress index compiled by Child Trends (Moore & Vandivere, 2000) listed six family stressors: (1) difficulty paying bills, (2) overcrowding in the house, (3) food insecurity, (4) lack of health care, (5) parent with poor mental or physical health, and (6) a child with a physical, learning, or mental health issue. Families with two or more of these factors are considered to be under stress (Moore & Vandivere, 2000). Schools serving high-poverty communities most likely have a majority of families under stress. Hardy (2007) writes:

> The findings appear to support the notion that improving the academic performance of at-risk children requires more than raising standards and monitoring test scores: It means reaching out to families and communities and engaging them in the difficult work of education. (p. 21)

Journal

The principal of a high-performing, high-poverty school in Boise, Idaho, told me, "We do whatever it takes to communicate with parents, because we know that every parent, deep down, wants what is best for his or her child. We connect with each parent, no matter what their job is, their educational level, or whether they take a bath every day. We want to conference with them about their children. If parents can't make it to school for a conference, we will go to parents' places of work, even if it is a bar downtown. We will go to jail or prison to meet with a parent. The message this sends children is that it doesn't matter who their parent is or what their parent has or hasn't done. Their parent is part of the learning team. We don't give up. We are persistent, and we don't take no for an answer." —E.G.

Meaningful Tasks for Parents

Parent involvement needs to be an integral part of building a Culture of Hope, not a secondary task. The consensus is that when it comes to parent involvement, highly effective schools in high-needs communities don't take no for an answer (Fullan, 2007). Bridging the gap between families and schools must start with the school. Fullan notes that "schools that have their act together have the confidence and competence to reach out to parents" (p. 194). But this reaching out must happen again and again, with persistence. When teachers and administrators give up after a few attempts, this reinforces for parents that they really aren't wanted or needed. The message must get through, loud and clear, that parents and community members are desperately needed as partners in the learning process.

The old model of parent involvement, having a few parents sit in on advisory committees or volunteer at the school, won't work for what is needed now. Instead, teams of school, family, and community members need to plan involvement activities throughout the year to connect the work of schools to the community and family. In high-needs communities, schools should provide a wide variety of pathways for involvement, including "options that accommodate family circumstances, provide choices, validate the family's culture and values, and explicitly emphasize the importance of family support of the students' learning" (Shannon & Bylsma, 2007, p. 120).

Although the traditional roles of helping at home and volunteering for field trips are important, family and community members should be invited (and expected) to participate in the school at all levels, including governance and planning, developing, and implementing new programs (Shannon & Bylsma, 2007). In-person contact and telephone calls are most effective. Home visits, parent-teacher conferences, and school community events like open houses or harvest festivals are excellent ways to open the conversation with families. Any textual information, such as newsletters, flyers, emails, websites, and classroom notes should be available in students' home languages if at all possible.

Part of the role of a Culture of Hope school is to support parents' needs for learning as well. Surveys of families can uncover potential themes for parent workshops (for example, English classes, résumé writing, or interviewing skills), family curriculum nights (for example, math game night or family literacy events), or first aid and CPR classes.

Journal

At Taft Elementary in Idaho, I heard many staff members voice variations of the same idea: "Families need to know they should be involved, they are capable of making a contribution, and they are invited in by the school and their children. There are many ways to invite families, but the critical factor seems to be consistent, repeated invitations. Once or twice or back-to-school night and a blurb in the newsletter are not enough. Seek out parental involvement." —E.G.

Conclusion

If the K–12 public school system in the United States has any hope of meeting the challenge of raising the country's graduation rate to 90 percent, teacher collaboration must be encouraged and schools, especially high schools, must be transformed into inclusive, personalized institutions fueled by the Power of We. Implementing a Culture of Hope takes focused leadership, with administrators who have building consensus and collaboration at the top of their agendas. Transforming relationships is the key to turning schools around (Chenoweth, 2009).

The path to a Culture of Hope requires an investment in professional development of staff and a systematic building of consensus on common beliefs. School leaders must focus staff attention on student needs through data collection and assessment of the institutional culture, which leads to implementing a systematic early warning system that identifies and provides support for students who are setting off the red flags of dropout indicators. Once a Culture of Hope is growing, efforts should include monitoring and maintaining the school's culture through purposeful hiring, induction, instructional coaching for staff, and thoughtful engagement of parents as partners in the learning process. Administrators with a vision for stability over time must plan to include targeted support for new teachers and parents in order to sustain the cultural shifts that take such effort to establish in the first place.

For teachers, the Culture of Hope promises the Power of We. It provides an approach to professional staff development that transforms schools and changes lonely, isolated teaching into a shared collaborative where teachers come to trust, share with, and support one another.

The next chapter will explore the implementation of the Culture of Hope at the high school level.

Chapter 9

A Culture of Hope at the High School Level

As an educator, I'm often haunted by one of my own students who went from failing every core high school class to making the honor roll in a year and a half. I worked in a high-expectations school where we all took pride in helping students reach their potential. But this student was dragging every risk factor in the book to school each day. In my deepest, darkest moments, I wasn't sure this student would graduate from high school. I finally concluded, in the absence of knowing any better, that we just have to treat each student like they are going to Harvard. If we are going to be wrong, let's at least do no harm.

—Alex Hernandez, 2012

It is not enough to be able to diagnose and document the destructive factors of high schools that continue to impact more than a million youth in the United States every year, or to track the disastrous impact of the failure of high schools on their communities. Nor is it enough to recognize how a 25 percent dropout rate relates to the U.S. national debt, unemployment, family violence, drug and alcohol problems, and even the explosion of the prison population. Understanding the scope and nature of the problem only brings us to the awareness level necessary for taking appropriate action. Before any true effort can be mobilized to help transform high schools, educators, policymakers, and community leaders must look to emerging research and best practices from effective schools to understand both what to do with our high schools as well as how to make it happen.

Previous chapters have presented numerous strategies and ideas; in this chapter, we outline a blueprint for high school reform built on the practices of high-poverty, high-performing schools with proven records of success (DuFour et al., 2010; Kennelly & Monrad, 2007; Parrett & Budge, 2012).

The *how to make it happen* question is more difficult to address. A marketplace of ideas surrounds the improvement of high schools—there is no shortage of proposals for turning around secondary institutions. The sad reality is that the high school, institutional icon of our society, is so steeped in tradition and constrained by the rules and regulations of teacher certification, binding contracts, state-mandated graduation requirements, textbook adoptions, departmental politics, and state legislature funding that it is not merely resistant to change, it has proven to be practically unchangeable (see chapter 3, pages 35–36, regarding institutional change and the characteristics of school culture).

On the other hand, more and more schools are breaking the grip of institutional memory and becoming places that work for all learners, but especially for poverty-level and minority students. This chapter describes in detail how these schools are making change happen, so that others can implement similar effective and necessary strategies.

The strategies and structures that follow draw upon the four components of a Culture of Hope, but also four specific approaches used by effective schools: (1) supporting students, (2) personalizing learning, (3) building academic rigor, and (4) laying the foundation for postsecondary success.

Supporting Students

Once students leave the support and small school size of elementary schools, it is essential that they encounter a sense of optimism, respect, safety, belonging, and success at the middle and high school levels. Without such an atmosphere, poverty-level students are likely to feel isolated and intimidated, leading to absenteeism and disengagement. Supporting students during high school actually begins during the middle school years, with a focus on the challenging transition ahead. Students continue to need targeted support during their first year of high school, a year that determines many students' high school successes or failures.

The transition between eighth and ninth grade is a critical period for the proactive prevention of potential dropouts. Many students who lack a sense of belonging or purpose begin to disconnect from school during the summer before ninth grade, or soon after they arrive on campus in the fall. Schools can provide a sense of optimism through orientation and counselor watch programs, summer and ninth-grade academies, and basic skills catch-up programs to provide an effective transition to high school.

Orientation and Counselor Watch Programs

In order to soften the shock of middle school students' first experiences in secondary school, a carefully planned orientation program—complete with guided visits or tours—is necessary for all eighth-grade students and their parents. The goal here is to help students experience the high school as a safe place where they belong. Every effort should be made to ensure that in this first contact with high school, every student is welcomed and feels safe, secure, and respected.

Successful high schools often have focused counselor or student "watch" programs that identify eighth- and ninth-grade students who are experiencing difficulties. At Adlai E. Stevenson High School in Illinois, the school counselors contact each of the principals of feeder middle schools and ask them to complete a counselor watch referral sheet for any students who meet criteria identifying them as needing special attention (DuFour et al., 2010). Identifying factors include poor academic progress, personal or family problems, poor attendance, peer relationship issues, and chronic underachievement.

After this initial identification, high school counselors follow up with a meeting at each middle school with teachers, counselors, social workers, and healthcare staff to clarify the needs of each identified student. On the basis of these discussions, well before students arrive on campus, the high school counselors have identified specific programs and services to address each student's potential needs (DuFour et al., 2010). A similar counselor watch program is used by California's Whittier City School District to identify and plan for the support of at-risk students (DuFour et al., 2010).

Whatever the name or overall district plan, some form of transition evaluation is essential to create a safety net for incoming freshmen. Components of that safety net may include an intense summer session, a ninth-grade basic skills remediation program, or a counseling program of support and referral. It is worth noting the importance of sharing information collected by transition programs with parents. High schools not used to working with incoming parents find that creating a partnership between the home and school to address students' problems has lasting benefits (LeBlanc-Esparza & Roulston, 2012).

Summer and Ninth-Grade Academies

The summer prior to ninth grade can be utilized positively by effective schools. For every eighth-grade student identified as being deficient in the basic skills, the summer must be used to provide intensive intervention. If a high school student is not up to grade level with basic skills, the intervention must be unrelenting until he or she has mastered the foundational basic skills.

Adlai E. Stevenson High School in Illinois provides arriving students with a high school survival course focused on high school expectations of ability with regard to note taking, annotating reading, organizing time, and other study skills (DuFour et al., 2010). At Cinco Ranch High School in Katy School District, Texas, a one-day summer "fish camp" is provided as an orientation and introduction for all students (DuFour et al., 2010).

Effective high schools provide a place within the larger school to protect, "incubate," and support freshman students, helping each find a personal sense of belonging. For many schools, this place has become the ninth-grade academy, where entering students attend classes in a restricted area, take a reduced instructional load, and participate in a required study hall or study skills support class (see Cinco Ranch High School in the Katy School District in Texas, DuFour et al., 2010).

An example is the Talent Development Program, developed by Johns Hopkins University's Center for Research on the Education of Students Placed At Risk (CRESPAR). This highly effective dropout prevention program was designed to transform urban schools with high dropout and low achievement rates by focusing on struggling ninth-grade students. The key to this program is its Ninth Grade Success Academy, which fosters belonging through reorganizing large comprehensive schools of more than 1,000 students into small groups of 150–350 who share common core classes with a small group of teachers who meet regularly to discuss each student's progress. The small group size helps students develop a sense of identity and special status. Students in the success academies report feeling close to their teachers and cohort of students (Quint, 2008).

Another effective high school model is First Things First, a program developed by the Institute for Research and Reform in Education and initially implemented in Kansas City, Kansas. This program uses small learning communities of two to three hundred students, much like the Talent Development Program, but groups of students are kept together throughout their four years of high school (Quint, 2008).

Key features of successful ninth-grade academies include basic skills catch-up programs, personalized support for struggling students, and co-curricular and extra-curricular activities.

Basic Skills Catch-Up Programs

Mastering the basic academic proficiencies is foundational to students' self-confidence and self-esteem. Thus, schools must identify, early on, all students who are struggling and then react quickly to address deficiencies. During the freshman year, any student who is not up to grade level in basic skills must have intensive intervention—though few things can be harder to accomplish than remediating basic skills with teenagers. And while most effective high schools use the ninth-grade academy, not all schools limit their support to the freshman year.

Some effective high schools have created a basic skills center with trained professionals who provide intensive assistance for all struggling students across the campus. If students are expected to complete a college-prep curriculum and advanced placement courses, they must master the basic skills before they leave the shelter of the ninth-grade academy. However, there are always students who continue to need support during their later high school years. According to one study (Bottoms & Anthony, 2005), many of these effective schools use a "double dose" of catch-up courses in language arts and English and mathematics during the fall semester of ninth grade to prepare students to enter English I and Algebra I during the spring semester.

Effective high schools do not simply retain low-performing students in the ninth grade until the students give up and drop out. Instead, these schools commit to using the entire ninth-grade year, including the summer prior to and the summer after, to help students catch up and become established on a path of success (Bottoms & Anthony, 2005).

Personalizing Learning

The research on effective high schools makes one thing very clear: helping low-income students succeed in secondary school takes far more than a strong basic skills program and rich academic curriculum. It also demands direct, personal support. This section looks at the eight ways learning can be personalized in high schools: (1) co- and extracurricular activities, (2) student advisory groups, (3) continuous progress monitoring, (4) a system of intervention, (5) counseling, (6) mentoring, (7) credit recovery, and (8) small school size.

Co- and Extracurricular Activities

Co- and extracurricular activities provide another venue for success, because they provide positive personal interactions with adults. The quantity and quality of interactions between students and staff improve when school personnel have time to know individuals and develop long-term relationships with them (RMC Research Corporation, 2008).

While working with schools in Kentucky and Texas, our review of high school data showed that over 90 percent of the schools' students participated in co-curricular activities. Some of these high schools had policies that no student should leave the ninth grade without finding a "home" in co- or extracurricular activities. If students can indeed find an activity home, almost everything regarding their performance improves: attendance, academics, even attitudes. And a student's activity home often leads directly to finding his or her passion and purpose in life.

The State of New York, in a study of benchmark high schools, concluded that participation in extracurricular activities has been associated with reduced rates of early dropout and criminal arrest among high-risk students (RMC Research Corporation, 2008).

At Cinco Ranch High School in Katy School District, Texas, part of the summer fish camp orientation prior to the start of the ninth grade is used to persuade entering freshmen to join co-curricular school programs. The high school offers more than sixty different clubs and activities: everything from fencing to guitar to ballroom dancing. Since it recognizes that students who are connected to an activity, club, or program are likely to feel more connected to the school and be more academically successful, every effort is made to help students find just the place their needs or interests connect with. Over 85 percent of the school's three thousand students participate in some type of co-curricular program (DuFour et al., 2010).

Student Advisory Groups

At the high school level, the cornerstone of a Culture of Hope is typically the student advisory group. Large high schools have come to use small student advisory groups as a primary way to provide personalized, continuous support during the high school years. These groups, typically composed of around twenty students and a faculty member, meet daily or weekly, and stay together for the duration of students' high school years. Schools use every full-time teacher as well as all school administrators and specialists as advisers. Adlai E. Stevenson High School in Illinois has a freshman advisory program, in which all freshmen meet four times each week with a faculty adviser for twenty-five minutes (DuFour et al., 2010).

Student advisory groups provide students with a safe place and an adult who knows their challenges and problems and offers ongoing information and support. The Center for Secondary School Redesign (2011) describes the importance of high school advisories in this way: "When done well, advisories build relationships between students and strengthen bonds with teachers, changing the way students feel about school and improving the educational experience for the entire school community" (p. 67).

Most student advisory groups in large comprehensive schools have the following responsibilities (LeBlanc-Esparza & Roulston, 2012):

- Monitor student attendance, family issues, and behavior problems.
- Monitor student grades, skills, and progress toward graduation.

- Assist students in exploring life/career choices and making decisions about their plans for the future.
- Provide advocacy for students in communicating with staff as well as families.
- Provide mentoring through sharing and personal encouragement, that is, faculty advisers do everything possible to help each student achieve his or her goals.

As participants in advisories, students will be well known personally and academically by at least one adult staff member, pushed to improve their basic skills, challenged to meet rigorous academic standards in appropriate educational programs, provided with opportunities to experience the benefits of community membership and to develop and practice leadership skills, and prepared for postsecondary success with a strong transcript, a career pathway, and a portfolio (LeBlanc-Esparza & Roulston, 2012).

Student advisory groups are a cornerstone of high school transformation. They provide the intimate, personal place of support that all students need, as well as a place of belonging. Most effective advisory groups refer to themselves as a surrogate family. At Granger High School in Washington State, Ricardo LeBlanc-Esparza worked to ensure that all of his faculty advisers treated their advisees "as they would their own kids, tracking their progress and coaching them to success" (LeBlanc-Esparza & Roulston, 2012, p. 82).

Journal

Ricardo LeBlanc-Esparza and I had worked together a few years earlier at the Institute for the Kids Left Behind, held in Tucson. I knew how committed he was to the use of student advisory groups during the high school years, but I wanted to hear him talk about the concept again. It doesn't take much to get this incredibly committed educator started. He was literally bouncing in his seat as he talked about his work at Granger High School: "We created little families throughout the school. We were so careful to select the students who were assigned to each group and then match them with a faculty adviser. We wanted our faculty adviser to really connect and to treat the students just like his or her own kids. We wanted the adviser to not only know the students better than anyone else in the school, but to know their teachers and family members as well. We wanted the advisers to advocate for the kids with their teachers and their families. We wanted the group to become a place of belonging, where students trusted and supported one another to be a part of a real family of caring and support. And we wanted this group to stay together throughout the high school years, something that only happens maybe in extracurricular activities. We also used the student advisory groups as a way to communicate with parents and to serve as the way of organizing our parent-teacher conferences. Doing this enabled us to achieve 100 percent family participation. The student advisory groups became the building blocks of our school and the single most effective strategy we found for caring for and supporting our students and ensuring that they succeeded in school and graduated." —B.B.

Continuous Progress Monitoring

Though ninth-grade academies are designed to ensure that all high school students have mastered the basic skills, found a place of belonging, participate fully in school, and are succeeding in their academic studies, some students will continue to struggle if their education is interrupted by personal and family problems. Every student must be carefully monitored throughout his or her high school years. In a case study of three high-poverty, high-performing high schools, the Education Trust (2005) concluded that without a clear, data-based system for identifying students who needed help and instruction, many high-risk students would fall through the cracks and ultimately drop out of school. As supported by the Building a Grad Nation reports (Balfanz, Bridgeland, Moore, & Fox, 2010; Balfanz et al., 2011; Balfanz et al., 2012), effective high schools carefully monitor attendance, grades, behavior problems, and involvement in co- and extracurricular activities. Most effective schools have installed sensitive data "trip wires" (see the discussion of early warning systems, page 160) that signal students who might need basic skills, before- or after-school programs, additional counselor sessions, home visits, consideration for a specialized program, and so on. Once problems are identified, schools must have a systematic approach for quick intervention.

A System of Intervention

As discussed in the previous chapter, effective high schools must have a straightforward early warning system in place that provides immediate, appropriate, individualized interventions in direct response to identified needs. There must be a system that enables everyone to know what happens next for a student with a specific issue.

Sanger Unified School District in Fresno County, California, established a districtwide response to address the needs of students who begin to falter academically or socially (DuFour et al., 2010). Rather than use a uniform plan, the district created a set of criteria to guide each school in developing its own individual plan to ensure that interventions are scheduled during the school day and that participation in additional instruction and support is a requirement, not an invitation. In addition to strategies focused on improving classroom instruction (developing objectives based on standards, monitoring student learning, and using curriculum to engage learners), Sanger High School provided specialized courses, including a corrective reading course in which students below grade level in reading are enrolled until they pass the California Standards Tests, and a variety of long-term and short-term English and mathematics intensive courses for tenth and eleventh graders. The high school's academic departments provide students with extra assistance when they need to retake an exam or make up late work, or need bilingual education support. Whenever a student shows signs of struggling, each school in the district responds immediately with a unique, established system.

Counseling

High school counselors, along with faculty advisers, are primarily responsible for working closely with each student throughout the high school years. Counselors and advisers must come to know each student's personal goals and plans, and help students stay on schedule to graduate and achieve their postsecondary goals. Successful schools "find ways to connect students to adults in the building" (Education Trust, 2005, p. 24). How each school goes about it may differ, but the end result is similar: "students are known by adults who care about them and their progress" (Education Trust, 2005, p. 24). In high-poverty, high-performing schools, students feel a connection with at least one adult on campus. The adult, whether an adviser, a counselor, a mentor, or a teacher of small learning groups, is responsible for connecting with students, showing genuine support and encouragement, and monitoring students' progress and problems (Education Trust, 2005).

Adlai E. Stevenson High School identifies struggling students for its counselor check-in program, which involves weekly meetings with a counselor for at least the first six weeks of ninth grade.

A look at follow-up evaluations of one hundred graduates of Adlai E. Stevenson High School revealed the importance of this ongoing connection with a counselor: 92 percent of those interviewed were attending a college or university full time, 3 percent were working, and 1 percent was in the military. Of those interviewed, 88 percent reported that the counseling department assisted them in their postsecondary plans (Martin & Perkins, 2011). High schools have always provided strong support services for college-bound students, but a concern is whether counselors can meet the increased student loads called for by high school reform efforts and whether they have the expertise to truly help the vocational or technical student make appropriate plans. As of this writing, most high school counselors carry an average load of 270 students, with some counselors serving as many as 500 (Symonds, Schwartz, & Ferguson, 2011). One of the authors visited a rural high school of 700 that had only one academic counselor!

Mentoring

Many effective high schools use adult and peer mentors to assist students as they move toward graduation. Some schools use "good friend" mentors, a system in which older, successful students work with those who are struggling; other schools invite college students and employed high school graduates to assist students who need support. At Sanger High School, sixty-five members of the school's staff volunteer as mentors. Adults in the Sanger community who work in occupations that overlap with students' career interests provide encouragement and support as students map out their futures. Increasingly, high schools are connecting students with online mentors, especially in rural areas where establishing in-person mentoring can be more challenging.

Credit Recovery

Every high school needs a number of ways to help students who are falling behind catch up on missed or failed credits. Credit recovery might include online courses or intense short courses in the summertime or even during Christmas break. Many effective high schools and most large school districts provide evening programs for credit recovery and working students (Barr & Parrett, 2001, 2008). Students who have fallen far behind or returned to high school after dropping out may best be served by moving directly into a community college program without earning a high school diploma. Some schools also remind students and their families that the goal is to graduate, not finish in exactly four years. Students and parents need to understand that some students will graduate in three, others in four, and some in five years. Graduation is not a race, it is a goal, and the goal is to gain the skills necessary to move forward.

In order to salvage the academic careers of some students, high schools must be very creative and flexible in helping those who fall behind and lack necessary skills. For students who have become bored or angry or who simply refuse to learn, dropping out or working for a while may motivate them to knuckle down and get to work. Often these students can return to become successful achievers (Allen, 2012).

Small School Size

Student motivation, student-teacher interaction, and close monitoring of students' academic progress are all easier to accomplish in the more personalized atmospheres of small learning communities. This concept of small learning communities is behind the small-school initiatives implemented in both New York and Chicago, funded in part by the Bill and Melinda Gates Foundation. In New York, where new minischools were designed from the ground up, a study found that students who attended the small schools were more likely to graduate from high school than teens in a large school (Hu, 2012).

One of the coauthors of the small schools study, Howard Bloom, reported that while school size was important, "it's certainly not just size. . . . It is how the size is used. These schools were organized from the ground up in ways that would be extraordinarily unusual" (Hu, 2012). These new small schools in New York were characterized by the common traits of rigorous curriculum; theme-based curriculum; personalized student-teacher relationships; and partnerships with community groups and businesses to offer hands-on learning experiences. While school size was not the single reason for their success, school size made it possible for these educational programs to be designed and implemented quickly and to provide an environment in which learning could be personalized.

There is little doubt regarding the effectiveness of small optional schools. They have been unusually successful at keeping struggling students in school, helping them gain basic skills, empowering them to master more challenging academic curricula, and perhaps best of all, helping them find a place of belonging (see Barr & Parrett, 2001). The vast majority of high schools recognized in *Newsweek* and *U.S. News*'s lists of the best high schools were small and specialized and were mostly magnet theme schools, charter schools, and college preparatory academies. Much of the media coverage on optional schools has focused on the size of these programs, but research has documented a number of effective approaches that can be transferred from small schools to large comprehensive high schools. These successful strategies include: volunteer participation, small school size (either small schools of choice or large schools reorganized into smaller learning teams), shared vision, caring and demanding teachers, a family-like atmosphere, customized curriculum, personalized learning based on the needs and interest of the students, and career themes (Barr & Parrett, 1997). As with many interventions and strategies, these schools support academic learning while addressing students' needs for place, pride, and the development of purpose.

One of the most powerful aspects of small optional schools is that they allow a redesign of the daily and weekly schedules. Such schools may teach academics for four days and use Friday for service learning, job shadowing, a career speaker series, and so on. Things that are all but impossible to do for an entire large high school can be done easily on a smaller scale. There may be very different organizations and schedules in various minischools, but in all of them, students' learning is assessed on the same basis as all other public school students. When developed carefully, small schools contribute to students' sense of belonging, are effective in keeping students in school, allow a focus on academic rigor, and lead to better jobs after graduation (Quint, 2008).

See the glossary (page 237) for an annotated list of the types of programs mentioned in this book that provide high school students with both academic rigor and personalized learning.

Building Academic Rigor

In the end, while all of the support programs are essential for keeping students in school and progressing, there is no substitute for a rigorous educational program. All of the support, monitoring, and remediation are focused on ensuring that each and every student is able to pursue a high school curriculum that prepares him or her for postsecondary education, training, and jobs. In the past, the college-prep program was reserved for the top 20–30 percent of the students, and those who were not excelling were placed in watered-down vocational education tracks with applied courses taking the place of rigorous academic study. That has finally begun to change. Not only have vocational/technical programs become more rigorous, but many schools now blend the college-prep and vocational/technical programs together and students are able to benefit from a more complete curriculum.

College Prep for All

Today, all students must have a college-prep curriculum in order to prepare them for the increasing demands of postsecondary education, training, and the workplace. A college-prep curriculum is no longer just for top students—it is for everyone. (It should be emphasized that "college prep" refers to the entire range of postsecondary learning options available to students, not just a four-year college program.) Today, all students must pass algebra. Many school districts have even moved algebra to the middle school level so that all students, whatever their ultimate goals, have time in high school to take geometry, calculus, and other advanced math. However, research in mathematics education, as evidenced in the Common Core standards for eighth grade, indicates that algebra should be an *option* in middle school, not a requirement (Liang, Heckman, & Abedi, 2012).

In New York, a study by Achieving Graduation (RMC Research Corporation, 2008) found that when high school/postsecondary "linkages are strengthened, and transitions eased for students," high school graduation rates increase significantly (p. 24). The study noted, that "students need current information about job markets to make informed post-graduation choices regarding education and training. High-impact high schools focus on preparing kids for life beyond school, not just graduation" (p. 24). To be effective, high school must "systematically cultivate aspirations and behaviors conducive to preparing for, applying to, and enrolling in college" (p. 24).

Concurrent Enrollment for All

In a similar vein, all high school students should participate in concurrent enrollment opportunities when available. Concurrent enrollment occurs when students enroll in college courses while still attending high school. This connects students to postsecondary education and training, as well as shortens the time between school and a job or career, since students are acquiring college credit at the same time as they are earning high school credits. Concurrent enrollment relates directly to helping students develop a sense of purpose for their education and their lives. Schools should encourage students to explore careers and focus their efforts on a particular interest. All students can benefit from concurrent enrollment: students interested in vocational/technical programs can get started in community colleges, and students interested in four-year colleges can help ease the academic load and expense of the required freshman-year courses. Few ideas are more rewarding and helpful than concurrent enrollment, which blends college with the pre-collegiate experience and provides credit for both, at a reduced cost.

Laying the Foundation for Postsecondary Success

Preparing for students to successfully enter college, postsecondary training, or a career directly after high school is receiving a great deal of media, political, and institutional attention. The work done during elementary and middle school to connect students with purpose and passions comes to fruition throughout the high school years, since students are now old enough and have the cognitive ability to think carefully about and plan for their futures and potential careers. For those students who know what they want to do after high school, some programs shorten the high school experience by using a 2-plus-2 program organization that enables students to complete two years of high school and two years of college (pages 190–191). Regardless of how the high school is structured, there are many strategies schools can employ to support students' transitions into young adulthood, including the following:

- Connecting purpose and passions to careers
- Organizing through career clusters
- Offering a fast track to college and careers

Connecting Purpose and Passions to Careers

Career education and experiences have become an essential part of any effective high school. Adding a career dimension to the high school curriculum adds relevance and student motivation for learning by connecting passions developed during the K–8 years to relevant career paths. Career planning is essential for helping students find purpose in their lives and connect what they are doing in high school with their plans for the future. Effective high schools and middle schools have developed curricula that integrate careers into the curriculum itself.

While often initiated in elementary schools and enhanced during middle school, the exploration of possible careers becomes more intense in the ninth grade. The goal is obviously not to make definite, specific decisions but to focus on and learn about particular areas. It is also fine for students to change their minds and explore various careers along the way. High school counselors will typically welcome students' decision changes, especially when they reflect serious and thoughtful investigation.

Organizing Through Career Clusters

By the end of the ninth grade, students and their families must begin to make preliminary plans regarding career areas and future postsecondary education or training. High schools using career clusters or a variety of optional career theme programs make this planning easier for students to follow (Quint, 2008). Career clusters provide a way to plan academic core courses that relate to the particular "career theme" that will be the focus of a student's high school studies. For example, students might choose to participate in a health professions career cluster if they are interested in everything from becoming a medical doctor, nurse, or nursing aide to becoming a medical librarian, paramedic, radiologist, anesthesiologist, or hospital administrator. Students would learn that a modern hospital is a small microcosm of society, with security guards, retail sales clerks, food and nutrition professionals, printing and design professionals, nonprofit development officers, volunteer coordinators, and even truck drivers and helicopter pilots.

The idea is for students to select large, general areas of careers; use the high school years to supplement their academic studies with career exploration, internships, volunteer opportunities, and job shadowing; and through these efforts help narrow specific job possibilities for the future. Other common career themes include law and legal professions, science and technology, education and childcare, and media and communications.

Offering a Fast Track to College and Careers

While the concept of a shortened high school experience was first used in vocational and technical programs, it is now being expanded and presented as an option for all students. Even some colleges are attempting to shorten their programs to three years for bachelor of science and bachelor of arts degrees. Such programs enable students to quickly move into good jobs or additional postsecondary training and education and are especially important for students from low-income families.

Like students bound for four-year college programs, students in 2-plus-2 programs also complete concurrent enrollment courses. In these programs, high school students often achieve certification or licensure while in high school or shortly after graduation. In the past, these fast-track options were limited to schools near community colleges or technical training centers, but this has changed with the advent of online courses and programs.

High schools are able to offer students opportunities to earn college credit through advanced placement and dual credit courses (courses that provide both high school and college credit). Many students are leaving high school with up to thirty credit hours of postsecondary education.

Some examples of fast-track programs include the following:

- In California, the Linked Learning network of high schools in nine districts is blending college preparatory studies with career and vocational education to create relevant and meaningful pathways to either a job or postsecondary education (Linked Learning Alliance, n.d.).

- In Dearborn, Michigan, an early college high school (which blended high school and college courses with some courses providing both high school and college credit) was created to respond to local labor shortages in the health professions. The program enables students to complete a high school diploma, an associate degree, and a certificate in a health-related occupation in five years (Swanson & Hightower, 2011).

- In Patton Springs, Texas, an isolated rural school seventy miles away from the nearest Wal-Mart and with over 80 percent of students from low-income families, provides students with thirty hours of college credit through dual enrollment (Courrege, 2011).

- In the Vancouver, Washington, School District, low-income and minority students are provided with specialized support in order to succeed in both traditional and online advanced placement courses (Webb, 2010).

Supporting the Transition to Postsecondary Education

In their final years of high school, learners should begin to conceptualize what their lives will be like outside the comforts of public schools. Turning the dream of college or technical training into the reality of enrollment and packing bags takes extensive support, especially for students from high-poverty backgrounds who may be the first generation to access postsecondary education. Preparation for the transition can come in the form of a speaker series, informative sessions with business leaders, and of course career and job fairs. High schools are also increasingly organizing peer counseling to connect older students, even college students and college graduates, with high school students. The type of one-on-one encouragement and advice they can give provides high school students with a reality check straight from someone they can trust and believe—a fellow student.

In addition to planned programs of information and orientation, many high schools provide their students with opportunities to visit postsecondary choices: community colleges, technical training institutes, colleges, and universities. These visits, coupled with conversations with college students, open the door to a world that poverty-level students may never have experienced. The leaders of the federal TRIO Programs believe that on-campus visitations and orientations, coupled with opportunities to meet and talk with poverty-level college students, provide an essential ingredient for first-generation college students' plans for the future (U.S. Department of Education, 2008). Other postsecondary topics that should be discussed with high school students include financial aid, the application and enrollment process, and the development of a personal plan.

Application and Enrollment Process

College, community college, and training programs often make the application and enrollment process a stormy sea of bureaucratic red tape. Affluent students and their families are often familiar with postsecondary educational enrollment procedures, since parents and often older brothers and sisters have gone through the process. For first-generation students, however, help is needed to navigate this bewildering, complex process. Effective high schools develop close ties with area colleges and training programs to develop approaches that simplify and streamline the process for families.

Financial Aid

In addition to registering for college, applying for financial aid can be a maze of bureaucratic requirements and complicated paperwork that defies understanding for traditional college students. For poverty-level students whose families have never considered or are not aware of the possibilities available to their children through higher education and training, it can be an insurmountable obstacle. High schools, community colleges, technical training centers, and universities must work hard to provide all high school students with a thorough understanding of the different ways students and families can finance higher education, including student work opportunities, federal grants or aid, student loans, and scholarships. A word of warning: the increasing school debt incurred by students in postsecondary education suggests that school officials must help students and their families make intelligent decisions regarding student loans and ultimately select institutions of higher education that they can afford.

Development of a Personal Plan

To foster students' personal responsibility for their postsecondary plans, a growing number of high schools now require students to create a personal graduation plan. Nothing is as powerful in helping students define their own specific "next steps," as in the development of a post–high school plan. In creating their plans, students develop detailed paths they can follow to reach their goals. They complete career explorations, on-site job shadowing, and internships; participate in counseling and advising sessions with counselors and group advisers; meet and discuss their futures with peer advisers and mentors; participate in career clusters or magnet schools; and slowly narrow their focus down to a particular career.

When personal plans are completed carefully, with ongoing advice and assistance from teachers, counselors, and parents, students know well in advance of graduation where they will go for postsecondary training or education. They will have completed admission forms and will know where and how to obtain financial aid. Often their plans are presented to a group of teachers, counselors, parents, mentors, and fellow students, just like a major senior project. Such a presentation provides a means of verification and reinforcement that helps the student make the difficult transition from dependent adolescent to an increasingly independent young adult. The creation of individual postsecondary plans that map a seamless transition to the world beyond high school should become as automatic as the transition from middle school to high school.

Succeeding at Mission Impossible

Given the dramatic magnitude of the school dropout problem, implementation of high school reforms demands the attention and urgent action of local, state, and national policymakers. While high schools have proven incredibly resistant to change, research on high-poverty, high-performing schools has provided more and more insights into effective institutional change processes (see DuFour et al., 2010; DuFour & Marzano, 2011; Lezotte & Snyder, 2011; Parrett & Budge, 2012). The following processes represent the best available insights into effectively changing U.S. high schools:

- Establish policy.
- Exert strong leadership.
- Implement strategies administratively.
- Become a professional learning community.
- Require professional development.

- Develop small learning communities within a high school.
- Blend academic and vocational education.

Establish Policy

The first order of business for high school reform is to ensure that policies are in place that cannot be ignored. The NCLB national policies, passed by the U.S. Congress with bipartisan support and signed into law by the president in 2001, had a dramatic impact on every school in the United States. For the first time, schools everywhere were required to focus on the learning of students from poor families. While some schools were more effective in addressing the instructional needs of these students, for the first time all schools had to focus their energies on all students, especially those living in poverty. There are few better examples of how policy can drive action than NCLB.

Unfortunately, the initial policy did little to document school dropout rates and may have even encouraged schools to ignore the dropout problem, because dropouts effectively remove lower scoring students from the testing population. Students who left school were not around to drag down the test scores of the school. Beginning in 2009, NCLB required schools and districts to monitor and report students who drop out and to use the four-year cohort model (the number of graduates in a given year divided by the number of freshmen four years earlier) to report graduation rates. More needs to be done, however. State legislatures, state departments of education, local school boards, and policymakers in Washington, DC must recognize the magnitude of the dropout problem and develop policies that require schools to track all students, by name, from the eighth grade through graduation. As an example of state policy, some states have raised the age for required school attendance to eighteen.

New policies should reflect the seriousness of the 25 percent dropout rate (Balfanz et al., 2012) by providing incentives for successfully increasing the graduation rate and adding sanctions for ineffectiveness. Bob Wise, the former governor of West Virginia, believes that all high schools should have a personalized learning environment, a rigorous curriculum, community collaboration, and effective leadership (Wise, 2012). He points out that since most U.S. federal funds go to elementary schools and higher education, with six million students in danger of dropping out in the United States, urgent funding must be made available at the high school level. While much can be done within existing budgets—such as establishing small learning teams by grouping teachers and students and freeing them to work together in new ways—true high school reform will surely be more expensive. Much of the development of minischools in New York and Chicago was funded by external grants. The new directions of career education and increasing counselors in high schools will demand extra funding at the federal, state, and local levels.

Regardless of funding issues, boards of education should have strong policies in place at the district level regarding school reform and monitoring of student progress. To achieve effective reform of high schools, there must be unified agreement among the school board, the superintendent's office, and high school leadership. Where appropriate, these policies should be integrated into teacher contracts or should be consistent with contracts. School boards should also have policies that require the monitoring and evaluation of the effectiveness of local high schools in implementing policies. Given the track record of high school reform, little change can be expected without strong local, state, and national policies.

Exert Strong Leadership

Almost every analysis of high-poverty, high-performing schools has identified strong leadership as a crucial factor in effective reform (Barr & Parrett, 2007; DuFour & Marzano, 2011; Parrett & Budge, 2012). To explain their success, effective schools almost always point to a leader with a clear vision for the future, one that helps mobilize the school and community around a set of school changes. In effective schools, leadership does not just mean the school principal and the administrative staff. Effective leaders involve leadership teams made up of teachers, counselors, specialists, administrators, parents, community leaders, and even representatives from the business community and higher education.

Before schoolwide consensus can be achieved, there must be consensus across the leadership team with a consistent, clear, uniform plan for school improvement. This school plan becomes the blueprint for effective change. The plan must include specific practices and strategies, professional development for the entire school community, small-group discussions, consensus-building sessions, and orientation and information sessions with parents and community members. Even a plan to encourage local media coverage is essential to help share future changes at the school with the entire community, many of whom will have graduated from the school and may have strong feelings about the direction of change. The goal is to have a plan for improvement developed by a well-supported schoolwide, communitywide team. Once a plan is developed, there should be scheduled opportunities for input and reaction and a way to revise the plan. Ultimately, the high school should have a well-reviewed and widely supported plan that represents a clear vision of the future that they can present to the local school board for approval and support.

Implement Strategies Administratively

Once a school reform plan is in place, many of the new practices and strategies can be implemented administratively—for example, having school counselors meet with their counterparts at the feeder middle schools to develop a "student watch" program (as described earlier in this chapter). The administration could also begin to systematically implement as much of the plan as possible—for example, by establishing programs to monitor and identify students who begin to struggle, establishing a schoolwide plan for quick intervention for students who falter, carefully monitoring students who leave school, and so on.

Become a Professional Learning Community

Effective schools are increasingly transforming themselves into professional learning communities (PLCs) (DuFour, Eaker, & DuFour, 2005). Because they involve the entire school, not just clusters of students and educators, PLCs represent an extremely demanding approach to school improvement. And for large high schools, developing schoolwide consensus, while not impossible, requires extensive work and institutional patience.

It is essential that the PLC begin with collaboration and the development of consensus, but because of the size and complexity of most high schools, this represents a significant challenge. Some high schools have invested as much as three years in planning to move to a block schedule for the academic programs, and even then, school leadership has found in some cases that as many as a third of the school faculty still opposes the move and resents the effort to move the school in a new instructional direction. Not only will some high school teachers object to changes designed to support low-income students, affluent parents may also object to this new emphasis, fearing that it threatens to water down and weaken instruction of the "more able" students.

In the absence of schoolwide consensus, high school leadership should move forward with those teachers who do support a new direction. Some of the most effective approaches to high school reform involve first creating small islands of change—minischools, career clusters, and alternative schools, or developing and adding one or two new instructional options if there are teachers interested in supporting this approach. The best place to start is the ninth grade, often staffed with those who are interested in working with the younger students. Developing a ninth-grade academy (see page 179) may prove less unsettling to core subject teachers than some other efforts to personalize instruction. The school principal and the school leadership team might also focus on developing consensus around a grades 10–12 student advisory structure.

High school leadership should work hard for consensus but not delay the implementation of the new direction of change. Some principals of effective schools have reported that it took as many as three years to begin to achieve a significant level of schoolwide support, and it was achieved only through the transfer of some teachers and the careful recruitment of new teachers.

Require Professional Development

A school- and communitywide plan for ongoing professional development is essential to help all stakeholders learn more about educational research regarding dropouts, learning communities, best practices, and the impact of the dropout problem on society. Superb consultants and a rich literature base are available as resources. Most informative and inspirational of all would be to have a team of stakeholders visit other high schools where some of the new practices have been implemented. Teams will come back talking about the problems and successes they observed and will have increased motivation for working on their own school program.

Develop Small Learning Communities Within a High School

Rather than trying to convince an entire school that it *must* change, a more successful approach may be to start with approximately 120 students (enough students for at least four teachers, at thirty students per teacher for the core subjects) and solicit teacher volunteers for each of the core areas (English, mathematics, science, and social studies).

The goal of this approach is for the team of teachers to cover all core subjects so the students will have the majority of their classes within the group. The goal is also to attract teachers who share a particular philosophy regarding teaching and learning or an interest in a particular career theme or pathway. The teachers would primarily teach students in the community but would also collaborate in creating the structure of the program, plan the implementation of their philosophy or career emphasis, and develop family, community, and higher education connections similar to what a group starting a charter school would do. What follows is the sequence of steps a school staff might follow to develop such an experimental program: (1) establish criteria, (2) recruit volunteers, (3) recruit and orient students and families, and (4) collaborate with the community.

Establish Criteria

The local school board must first sanction the development of a diversified high school through the formation of learning communities (that is, minischools, career clusters, and pathways). The school board or the school administration should also establish criteria: number of students and teachers, requirements concerning student demographics, the selection process, the use of state and local standards, and an evaluation plan to monitor the development of the new school. The board must require that the students in any new learning community reflect the diversity of the district or high school. Modest funding must be available to support professional development for the teachers starting any new learning community.

Recruit Volunteers

There is great power in asking for volunteers or inviting teachers to participate rather than assigning teachers to experimental programs. Teachers who choose to participate are typically highly motivated and throw themselves into the effort with great energy. They will often feel that they are creating the "dream school" they have always talked about and wanted to be a part of.

Schools might ask the group of volunteers to form a small team and develop a general plan for what they would do if given the chance. Administrators or a school improvement design team would then review the tentative plan and ultimately give a green light to the group of volunteers. Sometime in the fall semester, administration must provide these teachers with some relief from regular duties for the rest of the school year, either in the form of a release period or a number of professional development days where they can do intensive work together. The teacher volunteers must also be given compensated time over the summer to continue working together. As with other change processes, the team must be provided with professional development, essential readings, and opportunities to visit career clusters and alternative, charter, or minischools in other schools or school districts. The team should ultimately develop plans that are reviewed periodically, and by early spring a decision must be made to move forward toward implementation. A new school should not be overplanned, however; only so much can be done prior to starting a new school.

Recruit and Orient Students and Families

During the spring semester, orientations must be held to acquaint students and parents with the plan for the new school or minischool. There should be a clear idea of how many students will be chosen and what the process of selection will be. The most effective approach would be to both invite volunteers and use some type of lottery system. Some schools establish quotas to ensure that the demographics of the larger school community are represented.

Collaborate With the Community

Because the "new high school" must connect more carefully with the world outside the school, it is essential that any reform of the high school occur in close collaboration with business and industry representatives, community colleges, four-year colleges and universities, and even local business councils, business round tables, the Better Business Bureau, trade unions, and the Council for Economic Education. Such groups will bring to the table a host of ideas for cooperation and collaboration and perhaps even financial support. These groups are essential for support through the provision of mentors, service-learning opportunities, and adult models—all essential if low-income students are to be kept in school and motivated to develop plans for the future.

Some of the most exciting developments in high school education involve collaboration between high school staff and economic groups outside the school. For example, some high schools with career clusters have developed strong partnerships with specific business/professional groups. A health sciences career cluster might partner with a regional hospital and provide high school students as volunteers and service-learning participants, and in return, the hospital may provide mentors for students in the many health profession opportunities as well as speakers for classes and career fairs. Vocational/technical programs may have partnerships with trade unions and business groups who review curriculum to ensure that instruction reflects the most recent trends in the various trades and professions.

Blend Academic and Vocational Education

Perhaps the most encouraging development in high school education in the United States is the trend to merge the two distinct curricula of college-prep and vocational/technical education into a single, blended approach for all students, which has had impressive results. In California alone, there were more than 250 partnership academies, organized around the fifteen major business and industry sectors in the state, plus another 300 career academies. At least two school districts joined together to create regional centers to provide more advanced career and technical courses (Hoachlander, 2008).

In addition, there is a statewide effort underway in California to develop new blended curriculum and program specifications designed to help schools implement career clusters relating to sixteen major industries in the state. The hallmark of all of these efforts is to integrate real-world experiences into high school classrooms and to combine college-prep and vocational/technical programs into a single high school program. All of these efforts have come to be referred to as the Pathways Program.

The core components of the California Pathways Program are:

- **Academic**—Each student completes the required college-prep curriculum but integrates these subjects with real-world application in a particular career theme area.

- **Technical**—Each student studies concrete, industry-related knowledge and skills.

- **Work-Based**—Each student participates in intensive internships, virtual apprenticeships, and school-based enterprises.

- **Supplemental**—Each student receives intensive basic skills instruction as needed and a comprehensive counseling program designed to prepare students for college, postsecondary training, employment, or the military.

There is ample support for school districts interested in programs like the California Pathways Program. For technical assistance developing a pathways program or career clusters academy, see page 234.

A wide variety of research has shown that Pathways students excel academically, earn more after serving five years in the workplace, have lower dropout rates, and have higher success rates in postsecondary education than non-Pathways students (Hoachlander, 2008). This program offers a detailed look at the high school of tomorrow—and the progressive high school of today. It reflects the basic concepts of the Culture of Hope.

Other states are likewise moving in this direction. The state of Illinois is developing new instructional units that blend academic content and vocational/technical content into model online lessons. Illinois has developed over 1,300 lessons in four vocational/technical areas: family and consumer sciences; health occupations, business, marketing and computer education; and technology and engineering education (see www.ilcte.org). These new units are modeled after the 1,200 units in agriculture education that have been copied and used widely throughout the United States.

To help students find success in life, an increasing number of school systems are inviting them to begin thinking about jobs, professions, and careers no later than the middle school level, and are blending information, training, and experiences in these areas with rigorous academic content. Schools are helping students explore the widest possible set of life/education options and make specific decisions about their future. Leaders in the Pathways to Prosperity project at Harvard strongly support the concept of every student going to college, though not necessarily the typical four-year institution (Gewertz, 2011). Gewertz (2011) writes that every student must be able to "chart an informed course toward work, whether as an electrician or a college professor" (2011, p. 1). A growing number of school districts in the United States have found that combining college prep with vocational/technical training increases academic achievement, reduces dropouts, increases the number of advanced placement courses taken, and leads to good jobs with good salaries five years after high school graduation (Hoachlander, 2008). In blended programs, students are provided with hands-on connections to the world beyond the classroom walls, which increases students' perceptions of the relevance of learning tasks, potential applications of learning, and an understanding of the full range of career opportunities available to them (Hoachlander, 2008). The good news is that all of this effort seems to lead to increased student motivation and achievement.

Journal

While visiting a high-poverty, low-performing high school, I wandered into the auto shop class after sitting in on a core academic classroom in which many students seemed disengaged and unfocused. The bell had yet to ring, but the class was full of young men and women, some who I recognized from the previous disengaged class. All were seated, quiet, expectant. No one talked, everyone faced forward. The bell rang, the back door opened, and in walked the teacher. He gave the Auto Shop II students their assignments for the day: the cars they were working on and their goals.

To one student, he said, "John, when you find out what you need for the Chrysler, call and order the parts."

Respect permeated the room. The Auto Shop II students filed out the door to the shop while the teacher talked with the Auto Shop I students. Standing outside to observe the students working on the various cars, I was struck by their industrious, focused work, which was a far cry from what I had observed earlier in the core academic class. In a later visit to the woodshop, I found the same scene: groups of students intently focused on their meaningful work. —E.G.

To be effective, a blended program of college-prep and vocational/technical education should include the following organizing principles:

1. Prepare students for both postsecondary education and a career
2. Connect education programs to real-world applications
3. Lead to a full range of postsecondary opportunities (including two- and four-year education programs, formal employment, and the military)
4. Improve student achievement

The blending of college-prep and vocational/technical education into a single program for all students is a dramatic break with the traditional high school program. In the past, too many high schools operated under the idea that all students should not go to four-year colleges or universities (Symonds, Schwartz, & Ferguson, 2011). As a result, schools tended to operate a dual system of education that tracked all but the most academically talented students into a second-class curriculum. Many schools used this tracking system to separate college-prep students from "slow learners" and advanced placement students from the students found in "dumbed-down" hands-on vocational/technical programs. High schools have too often considered voc/tech as a "loser program"— a program for students who were "too dumb" to go to college. Such a belief could not be further from the truth (Symonds, Schwartz, & Ferguson, 2011).

Journal

The director of a heating and air conditioning program at a Delaware technical high school said, "My students and I quietly talk and even laugh about most people's perceptions of all of us that are here in this regional technical high school. I think high school teachers and counselors may be the worst. During my career, I have heard again and again: voc/tech is the 'dummy' program for students who have to work with their hands rather than their minds. We really have had a bad rap. But then my students start looking at the job opportunities that are available right now and the salaries they will make. Their salaries will be so much better than the salaries of the teachers. We just quietly smile when we are put down and think of the take-home pay we are going to earn." —B.B.

These types of separated programs are simply no longer viable today, if they ever were. For example, programs that train carpenters and sheet metal workers require trigonometry and calculus, and training programs in the various health professions demand advanced science studies. Still, transforming negative attitudes about vocational/technical programs remains a great challenge for high schools, and there is considerable reason for making the change.

At a time when many college graduates in traditional degree areas have difficulty finding good job opportunities (Klein, 2012), the opportunities in vocational/technical occupations are excellent. Table 9.1 shows a few examples of occupations and projected needs in selected vocational/technical areas. These are jobs that cannot be shipped overseas, and students who complete a one- or two-year training program in many vocational/technical fields are almost guaranteed job placements with good salaries. Today, all students need a blended program of college prep, advanced placement, career education, and vocational/technical experiences. This is the necessary curriculum of today.

Table 9.1: Examples of Vocational/Technical Occupations

Occupation	Projected Percent Increase, 2010–2020	Median Salary, 2011
Masonry Helpers	60 percent	$27,800
Vet Technicians	52 percent	$30,100
Iron/Rebar Workers	49 percent	$38,000
Physical Therapy Assistants	46 percent	$51,000
Medical Sonographers	44 percent	$65,200
Dental Hygienist	38 percent	$69,300
Radiology Technicians	28 percent	$55,100
Registered Nurses *	26 percent	$66,000
Automotive Technician	17 percent	$36,200

Source: Data collected from Occupation Profiles at CareerOneStop, 2012.

Note: A two- or four-year college degree, plus successful completion of the registered nurse exam, is required to become a nurse.

Journal

An English teacher in Texas said, "It took our high school about three years to finally get our career clusters up and running. But we used all of that time to begin working with local business and industry representatives, and they just completely altered my perceptions. These were some of the brightest, most interesting people, really committed to encouraging kids to learn about the world outside the schoolhouse.

"Over the summers, all of the teachers got to visit local businesses; we shadowed workers, worked with mentors, and were provided orientations to careers and professions. We went out in the community, but we really went 'back to school.' We suddenly began to see the relevance of what we were teaching. For the first time, a group of teachers began to meet together and discuss what we were learning. We were so energized, but not everyone agreed with the new direction of career education. Some of the teachers felt that it was simply destroying our academic integrity. But through continued meetings and discussions we at least came to respect one another's positions, and still work together. And we were finally able to talk about how to make our courses more meaningful and relevant. When we meet, there is much less 'I' talk and much, much more 'we' talk. We have come to realize that, together, we can get it done. We have also begun to see how excited our students are about learning in our classes and in the community. This is the new world of education. I am so glad that I am a part of it." —B.B.

Conclusion

In terms of promise and problems, the gateway for helping poverty-level students access pathways to future dreams is the high school. In so many ways, the high school, steeped in tradition and institutional culture, is almost totally irrelevant to contemporary students. The data on college freshmen remediation courses and the college dropout rate indicate our nation's high schools are not even serving our middle-class and affluent students well. Add to this the tragedy of the high school dropouts, and our secondary schools seem to serve primarily as a social milieu for adolescents and aspiring athletes. To be blunt, most high schools in poverty-level communities are total disasters. It is no wonder that so many high schools have been labeled as failure factories. If the poor are to have any chance at finding a pathway out of poverty, a way to somehow access the American dream, high schools must become the center of educational reform in the United States. They must become the focus for an improved future for American youth.

While there is an urgent need to address the problems of high schools, it is also essential that parents, students, teachers, administrators, and school policymakers understand that accessing the good life demands success at each step of the way, from preschool and kindergarten to elementary, middle, and high schools, on to college.

In the next chapter, we review the state of the American dream and what educators must do to ensure that it is passed on to future generations.

Chapter 10

Hope Fulfilled

Give us hope that the future will be better. We have tightened our belts every year so we could keep on going, thinking next year it would surely get better. Every day, we work with our students, providing the emotional, physical, and mental support they need to learn, often even the supplies that they need to learn. We work all day and often even into the evenings and weekends, giving all we have. We work hard, very hard, and we haven't stopped working hard. Give us some good news: please give us some modest ray of hope for adequate support. Fulfill our dream that we have something to work for next year other than our bedrock commitment that we will teach our students, no matter what.

—Teacher, speaking to a school board during contract negotiations

There is a deep and inseparable bond between public education in the United States and the American dream. Locally controlled public schools were started early on to provide a foundation for an informed citizenry. These schools taught the basics of reading, writing, mathematics, and what came to be called citizenship. These first schools began with the elementary grades, eventually extended into the middle and high school levels, and now include technical and vocational education as well as college preparation. At first, an elementary education sufficed to gain access to jobs and the American dream, but over the decades, an eighth-grade education, and then a high school diploma were necessary to secure careers with financial stability and security. Now that standard has changed yet again. Students need to obtain postsecondary training and education to access a solid economic future.

American public education has been the one unique institution that welcomed the families of the world, the poor and "huddled masses yearning to breathe free," and helped acculturate them into being "Americans." Public schools have often been described as the great American melting pot, a term too often tangled in confusion, controversy, and anger. As a result of this concept, many immigrants and Native Americans were stripped of their culture and language and punished when they resisted the U.S. government's institutional efforts to acculturate them. The negative impact of this acculturation on native populations and immigrants cannot be ignored, especially the impact of Bureau of Indian Affairs schools that removed indigenous children from their families and punished them for speaking any language other than English.

Journal

A doctoral student at Boise State writes, "Well, when we came up from Mexico I was twelve years old; my brother was eight. None of our family could speak English. It was a great struggle for each of us. For whatever reason, I learned English surprisingly quickly and did well in school. For years, I served as interpreter for my entire family. I remember going to social services offices and paying the rent and going to the utilities offices and doing the business of an adult for my family when I wasn't even a teenager. My brother really had difficulties in school. He just could not learn English. The school where he attended decided that he needed special education. I am convinced that he had no learning disability, just a problem like so many Spanish-speaking students of trying to learn a foreign language while trying to succeed in classrooms where he did not understand the teacher. My brother was so smart, and he had done so well in school in Mexico. I am sure that all he really needed was a strong bilingual program. The teachers and counselors did not see it that way. They assigned him to special education, and he never got out. He quickly grew so frustrated that he just gave up. He was not a special education student when they placed him there, but he was by the time he dropped out of school. The fact that this poor little kid had difficulties learning a new language led the school to make decisions about him that ruined his life. He never recovered from the stigmatism and discrimination he felt in school. He just never recovered. He never got even a basic education, and his life was ruined. He still to this day thinks of himself as a dummy. To think about what happened still breaks my heart." —B.B.

This clash of cultures continues, with the immigration of Spanish-speaking students from Mexico and South America. These students have been the focus of the "English only" movement that has worked to eliminate bilingual programs in public schools. However, schools have also served as an essential doorway of opportunity for students: teaching them a common language, giving them basic knowledge and a liberal arts education, and helping them learn and understand middle-class values. Perhaps most importantly, for those students who stayed in school and graduated, public schools have provided the necessary skills for living and working in the United States and pursuing their dreams.

Journal

In 2009, I was speaking to the teachers, administrators, and school board members of a large school district in Northern Texas. As part of my presentation, I described a story a Latino mother had shared at a community meeting the night before, about her bilingual daughter's experience transitioning to high school. Her daughter's middle school counselor had recommended the International Baccalaureate (IB) program for her daughter, based on her excellent performance in seventh and eighth grades. The counselor had been very careful to describe the incredibly demanding curriculum of the IB, which included learning French, while also insisting the daughter was a superb student and would excel in the demanding program. Both mother and daughter understood that the IB program would open many doors of opportunity. But when the family attended the end of summer registration session, the daughter was denied admission to the IB program and ended up in a vocational track, taking Spanish as a foreign language, even though she already spoke the language fluently. The mother said, "It was only after I reported this to the middle school counselor, and after she got involved as an advocate for my daughter that the school granted her admission to the IB program."

While telling this moving story, I was interrupted by a district school board member who was attending my session: "That story is simply not true. That would never, ever happen in one of our high schools." The board member then pulled out her cell phone and walked out of the room, slamming the door. I apologized to the group for sharing a story that I had not verified, but as I resumed talking the door burst open again and the board member returned. In a very soft voice she said, "I am so sorry to interrupt again, but I am just thoroughly humiliated. I have made a few calls and learned that the story that you just shared with this group was absolutely true. So I apologize to you from the bottom of my heart. I also want you to know, that if I have anything to do with it, no Latino student will ever be denied access to one of our programs due to their race or ethnicity or native language. For goodness sake, this is America." —B.B.

The American Dream

The American dream has always been a significant and unique strand in the fabric of our culture, woven into the country's foundational documents by Thomas Jefferson in 1776, when he wrote about a person's natural rights including life, liberty, and the pursuit of happiness. The pursuit of happiness was a unique concept at that time, but one that came to characterize U.S. culture. Much later it became known as the American dream (Adams, 1931). From the very beginning, citizens and immigrants dreamed of a better, richer, happier life. Adams (1931) says this uniquely American "dream of hope" had been there from the start with the original colonists and may well have bestowed the United States with its most defining characteristic, optimism. The American dream provided the United States with a built-in motivation to aim high and shoot for the stars, or as it turned out, to shoot for the moon. What could be a more appropriate expression of this characteristic than public schools consciously striving to enrich their learning environments with optimism, to surround students with a Culture of Hope?

In the past, there were two things that seemed to be inextricably related to the American dream. First, there was the belief that all that was needed to achieve a better life was hard work and determination. Second, given the country's vast areas of land and natural resources, there was the consistent promise of a new beginning, another chance to start all over again. These ideas were what so captured the attention of Alexis de Tocqueville, a nineteenth-century French aristocrat who traveled and wrote about the Americans he encountered. It was not where individual citizens found themselves on the socioeconomic ladder, but their absolute belief that their life could be better, that they had a chance to move up that ladder. Such optimism, de Tocqueville concluded, was a defining characteristic of the United States. It was not so important that people were poor, as long as there was a chance that they could significantly better their situations. The phrases "go west, young man" and "rags to riches" encapsulate this idea; it was what the Oregon Trail, the California Gold Rush, oil-seeking "wildcatters," and homestead laws were about. There were always bold new opportunities just beyond the western horizon. That hope is upward mobility—the unique key to American culture. Today, this hope is no longer just beyond the western horizon; today the horizon of hope is education.

There was never any promise that the "pursuit of happiness" would be easy. The good life seemed to demand sacrifice and hard work. The dream has survived in our country during particularly difficult times, even the Civil War. The optimism has survived bad weather and bad crops; it has survived falling prices for crops and livestock. It has survived plant closings and layoffs as well as union busting and outsourcing. Somehow the dream of a better life has even survived the Great Depression, when so many Americans, broke and unemployed, traveled from town to town and state to state searching for opportunities, seeking only a chance to work. Yet even in the depths of the Depression, people continued to believe that life would get better if they could work hard when they got the chance. That was what the fictional Joad family did during the Oklahoma dustbowl years; they packed up and moved to California looking for jobs, pursuing their special form of hope and happiness down a very difficult road (Steinbeck, 1939). America has always been the land of opportunity, but it has also been the land of hope and optimism.

With hope, optimism, and the freedom to pursue happiness came the ability, perhaps the responsibility, to acknowledge and address disparities in access to the American dream. Thus, out of the American dream came the various civil rights movements, including rights for women, different racial and ethnic minorities, disabled individuals, and individuals who speak languages other than English. President Johnson's "War on Poverty" also attempted to address socioeconomic disparities during the 1960s (Siegel, 2004). Many education programs started at that time have continued today, including Head Start, the Federal TRIO programs, and domestic job corps, but most school desegregation programs were discontinued during the 1980s.

Death of the Dream?

Everything is changing. As we write, millions are receiving unemployment benefits and food stamps, and millions more have defaulted on their mortgages and lost their homes to foreclosure. What is left of the American dream is beat up and battered; in the increasingly sad news coming not just out of Wall Street but throughout the world, it seems that hope and optimism may be disappearing. It seems this difference is more than just a market correction or an economic adjustment; something fundamental seems to have changed. Cities have gone bankrupt. Some states, drowning in debt, have invalidated the contracts of public service employees and teachers and suspended collective bargaining rights to unions. Jobs in every sector of the economy have been eliminated. For minorities, the challenges during this recession have been even greater. Rather than upward mobility, more and more Americans are experiencing a slide into a declining economic status.

There is also a growing divide between the haves and the have-nots in the United States, even between the most affluent and the middle class. Poverty and homelessness have grown to unprecedented levels. The economic inequalities, coupled with a growing new conviction that there is a diminishing hope of upward mobility, have transformed our perceptions of the good life. The optimism of the United States has begun to wither and wilt; pessimism seems to be flourishing.

Talk to anyone over sixty years of age, or maybe even fifty, and you'll hear unprecedented anxiety about the future: "Our kids and grandkids are not likely to have nearly as good a life as our generation." When in our long history have you ever heard that? If Americans ever agreed on a single thing, it was that although their life was hard, the lives of their kids and grandkids would be better.

Despite all that the American dream has survived, there are forces at work that could well do it in. In 2011–2012, *Time* magazine published a series of articles titled "Keeping the Dream Alive" (Meacham, 2012), "What Ever Happened to Upward Mobility?" (Foroohar, 2011), and "Middle of the Road" in the special issue "The

Return of the Silent Majority" (Klein, 2011). All of these articles focus on the question of whether or not the dream is dead. Their conclusions are sobering.

In terms of upward economic mobility, it is estimated that the United States has fallen behind other industrialized nations: the United States is now ranked behind Denmark, Norway, Finland, Canada, Sweden, Germany, and France (Foroohar, 2011). Researchers have become much better at analyzing the American dream and upward mobility. It is now understood that economic mobility is not just dependent on hard work and sacrifice—it seems to be tied up in a "complex mix of geography, race, health and education" (Foroohar, 2011, p. 30). It is now estimated that a person from a lower-income family has only a 52 percent chance of achieving middle-class status during his or her lifetime. It is also difficult for particular racial groups to move up to middle-class status; Hispanics have a 59 percent chance and African Americans have only a 50 percent chance (Foroohar, 2011). In a 2011 report, "Whither Opportunity?," compiled by the Russell Sage and Spencer Foundations (Duncan & Murnane, 2011), a number of sobering research conclusions were revealed: in one study, comparing standardized test scores of students from families in the 90th percentile of income with students from families in the 10th percentile of income, the achievement gap between these two groups grew by 40 percent between 1960 and 2007, while the gap between white and black students regardless of income had shrunk substantially. Sadly, the upper socioeconomic scores remained rather stable while achievement for students in the 90th percentile of income declined. In another study, researchers at the University of Michigan found that "one of the important predictors of success in the workforce"—the imbalance between rich and poor students in college completion—"increased by 50 percent since the mid-80s" (Tavernise, 2012, p. A7).

If not dead, upward mobility—expressed by the collective dream of life, liberty, and the pursuit of happiness—has certainly been tarnished, or perhaps transformed. In today's economic recession, everything seems to have changed: laid-off workers have found that as the economy has improved, their previous jobs have been outsourced or filled with temporary workers. Workers everywhere have experienced declining investment accounts that have led them to postpone their retirement plans; the values of homes not lost to foreclosure have declined. There is now talk of "being upside down" on a mortgage and selling homes "under water," or below their mortgaged value. The rock-solid expectation of home ownership is slipping away, becoming increasingly elusive in America.

The reasons for these changes in the economic realities of American families are fairly evident. The main factors (reviewed in chapter 1) include the rapid development of technology and the resulting displacement of human workers, the international workforce of cheap labor and the resulting outsourcing of manufacturing and other jobs to developing nations, the failure of financial institutions, the collapse of the mortgage industry, and the momentous level of debt in most of the industrialized nations. The result is that the twin pillars of the American dream—being willing to work hard and perceiving an opportunity to move on and start anew—have all but disappeared from the American marketplace.

One result is that education has emerged as the new horizon of opportunity in the United States. A high-quality education must now be considered an inalienable birthright of every American. It is no longer moral or ethical to merely provide "equal opportunity" to education. It must be a guaranteed civil right.

Education and the American Dream

Education is now considered to be the single factor that "is more closely correlated with upward mobility than any other" (Foroohar, 2011, p. 34). As long as educational achievement keeps up with the technological changes in the marketplace, job opportunities are created; similarly, job opportunities are available to individuals who keep up with technological changes in their fields (Foroohar, 2011).

There also is a growing understanding that education has a developmental aspect—that it provides the foundation for further learning. In this way, achievement in high school and beyond can be jeopardized or supported by the experiences of earlier years of schooling. Researchers at the Pew Charitable Trusts have been examining this concept as it relates to upward social mobility; they have even run the odds on this provocative concept. For example, if individuals can achieve essential educational standards at each level of human development, from early childhood through young adulthood, it is estimated that their chance of achieving middle-class economic status increases to 85 percent for all socioeconomic, gender, and ethnic/racial groups, which is even higher than the probability of achieving a middle-class standard of living when born to an upper-income family (Brookings Institution, 2011).

This does not mean that a young adult can be ensured the good life if he or she graduates from high school lacking other essential knowledge, skills, social and emotional development, or is semiliterate or lacking social integration. To have a solid chance of achieving middle-class status during one's lifetime, researchers now believe that individuals must achieve essential education standards at *each* of the developmental levels of life: at the family and preschool level, elementary level, middle childhood years, adolescence, and young adult years. And it is important to understand that success seems to be cumulative—it builds on each preceding level. This of course was what Abraham Maslow maintained about human needs, and it is what the Culture of Hope is all about. It is building educational successes in ascending layers of knowledge, skills, and social and emotional learning. For children of poverty, this is a concept of significant, long-lasting consequence, for it is this continuously ascending movement that best represents a potential pathway out of poverty.

If the researchers cited in this chapter are correct in their assessment that economic mobility is dependent on a series of sequential developmental achievements, then they have provided educators with an incredibly useful road map. This sequence of developmental achievements could serve as a modern-day rite of passage for school students as they make the long, complex transformation from childhood to adulthood.

We know that schools can teach all types of students effectively, so no school can shirk responsibility by saying, "We gave all of our students every opportunity to learn; some just did not take advantage of that opportunity. They didn't care; they weren't motivated." The data on high-poverty, high-performing schools dictate that it can be done; scholars in the field now maintain that it must be done. To actualize the inherent potential of every person, each must be provided a high-quality, world-class education. Each child and adult must successfully complete a set of essential learnings at each level of development. In effect, they must complete a modern day "rite of passage." It will take the entire community of schools, parents, and leaders from all career areas and all sectors of society to accomplish this task, but research now provides the insights that make it a realistic possibility. It can be done. And, to ensure that every student achieves the opportunity of accessing the good life, it must be done.

A Modern-Day Rite of Passage

Societies throughout history have had cultural processes that were designed to help youth bridge the transition from the dependence of childhood to the independence of adulthood. This process has often been referred to as a "rite of passage" (Campbell & Moyer, 1988). And while these rites can be traced back to antiquity, they have been all but lost in the increasing complexity of modern Western civilization. Yet, developments in a variety of related fields have begun to identify just such a set of cultural learnings that could be regarded as a modern-day rite of passage for American youth.

In the 1970s, a haunting movie produced in Australia, titled *Walkabout*, became popular in the United States. It told the story of an aboriginal boy who struggled through a long walkabout in the Outback, and through surviving, learned skills that were necessary for the survival of his tribe. The movie prompted a Canadian educator, Maurice Gibbons, to write an article for *Kappan* titled "Walkabout: Searching for the Right Passage From Childhood and School" (Gibbons, 1974). The article prompted considerable interest among educators in North America and led to discussions about what a modern-day rite of passage might look like. And with support from Phi Delta Kappan and private foundations, discussions and symposiums were held throughout the United States and ultimately led to a number of high schools being reformed around this. The most prominent of them was a small alternative school, Learning Unlimited, in Washington Township, Indiana. This school envisioned a walkabout as being structured around consumer skills, citizenship skills, and career skills.

While the walkabout concept attracted considerable interest for a while, few of the efforts at developing a modern-day rite of passage survived over time. What is so interesting today is that research from a number of sources has begun to identify specific components that seem to be absolutely essential for youth moving toward an independent and successful adulthood. At last, a modern-day rite of passage is emerging from educational research.

Quite remarkably, the identification of these essential components has begun appearing from a number of independent sources in the form of reports, initiatives, and research, as well as effective practices in effective schools. These efforts bring together some of the best minds in a variety of different fields and provide helpful guidelines that lay out what schools need to do and what students must accomplish at each level in order to achieve the best chance of economic success and independent adulthood.

At least four major sets of recommendations hold great promise for helping families, especially families living in poverty, to understand what is necessary for their children to accomplish at each developmental level in order to gain economic independence. The recommendations and conclusions of these four developments are remarkably consistent. They were first presented in three major reports and a summary of research— *Building a Grad Nation* (Balfanz et al., 2010; Balfanz et al., 2011; Balfanz et al., 2012), prepared by the America's Promise Alliance; *Opportunity Nation*, a report of the Pew Economic Mobility Project (Brookings Institution, 2011; Pew Center on the States, 2011); the report from the Commission on the Whole Child (2007); and last of all, research on poverty, learning, and the Culture of Hope.

Building a Grad Nation

Recognizing the enormous social and economic problems associated with the failure of students to achieve high school graduation, the America's Promise Alliance (Balfanz et al., 2010) recommended a major national initiative that focuses attention on both academic learning and social and emotional issues. The very first step in trying to transform schools and help students find a better economic life is to reduce the huge number of students who drop out of school each year. Everything begins with that goal in mind. Referred to as a national "Marshall Plan" for high schools (named after the U.S. program that helped rebuild Europe after World War II), America's Promise sets two goals: first to achieve a 90 percent graduation rate nationally by the class of 2020 and, second, to achieve the highest college-attainment rates in the world. America's Promise recommends a number of specific goals for meeting these two benchmarks, goals that cut across K–12 education and blend academic issues with social and emotional concerns. The goals align perfectly with and support the use of the predictive factors identified by the Pew Charitable Trusts in their Pathways to the Dream, described later in this chapter. The 2012 America's Promise report recommends the following benchmarks toward ending the dropout crisis:

Elementary and middle school goals:

- Substantially increase the number of students reading with proficiency by fourth grade. . . .

- Reduce chronic absenteeism. . . .

- Establish early warning indicator and intervention systems that use the Early Predictors of Potential Dropout (attendance, behavior, and course performance in reading and math). . . .

- Redesign the middle grades to foster high student engagement and preparation for rigorous high school courses. . . .

- Provide *sustained* and *quality* adult and peer support to all students who want and need these supports, continual supports from adults serving in school as "success coaches" for all off-track students, and intensive wrap-around supports for the highest-need students. . . .

High school goals:

- Provide transition support for struggling students in grades 8–10 in all schools with graduation rates below 75%, as well as their feeder middle and elementary schools. . . .

- Transform or replace the nation's dropout factories with effective schools. . . .

- Raise the compulsory school attendance age to when students graduate or age 18 in all states, coupled with support for struggling students. . . .

- Provide all students (including those who have dropped out) clear pathways from high school to college and career training. . . .

- Support comprehensive dropout recovery programs for disconnected youth. (Balfanz et al., 2012, pp. 7–10)

Opportunity Nation

The Pew Economic Mobility Project (Brookings Institution, 2011; Pew Center on the States, 2011) has identified a process of educational development that depends on a sequential set of learning achievements that must occur at each of four age levels. Achieving the various knowledge and skills at each level could not only lead a student out of poverty, but would increase the likelihood of upward mobility into the middle class—a pathway to the American dream. The following represents the accomplishments that Pew Charitable Trusts scholars concluded are fundamental to such a pathway:

Pathways to the Dream:

- Early Childhood: 0–5 Years
  - ▸ Pre-reading and math skills; school appropriate behavior; no major health problems

- Middle Childhood: 5–12 Years
  - ▸ Basic reading and math skills; self-regulated behavior

- Adolescence: 12–19 Years
  - ▸ High School diploma with GPA greater than 2.5; not convicted of a crime; if female, has not given birth

- Transition to Adulthood: 19–29 Years
  - ▸ Post-secondary degree or equivalent; family income greater than 250 percent of poverty level (Foroohar, 2011, p. 31)

These recommendations represent a bold new vision designed to address the magnitude of the problems facing not just high schools in the United States, but the social and economic future of our country. They also focus attention squarely on the needs of poor and minority students. The report emphasizes how essential it is for students to achieve certain academic goals at each developmental level, such as the ability to read effectively by the start of fourth grade, which has a direct and powerful relationship to high school graduation.

The Pew Project concludes that if students meet all of the necessary requirements for each age level, they have an 85 percent chance of reaching the middle class in the United States. If they fail to make the requisite achievement at any or all of the various age levels, the probability of achieving economic stability falls off dramatically (Foroohar, 2011). If a student meets the educational accomplishments of the first two levels, that is, the early and middle childhood levels, but then drops out of school (as 25 percent of all students did in 2011), the chance he or she will achieve middle-class status drops to only 44 percent.

Reviewing conclusions from other, more targeted educational research provides a way to enrich, expand, and refine the Pew's Pathways to the Dream and perhaps make the construct even more useful.

Commission on the Whole Child

In 2006, the Association for Supervision and Curriculum Development sponsored a national commission that focused on the social and emotional needs of children and youth. During a time when most of the educational establishment was focusing on the new policies of the NCLB federal legislation and the instructional requirements to teach all students to read at grade level, as well as on age-appropriate knowledge and skills in mathematics, ASCD was reminding parents, policymakers, and educators of the importance of social and emotional growth in public school students. As we have reported, when the basic needs of children and youth were satisfied, academic achievement was likely to increase (Commission on the Whole Child, 2007). The Commission on the Whole Child (2007) also warns of the opposite: if basic human needs are not satisfied, students are "more likely to become less motivated, more alienated, and [perform] poorer academically" (p. 12).

Just as the two preceding reports recognize how essential it is for learning to occur at each stage of development, the scholars and public school educators on the commission explain that failure to address the basic needs of children at an early age could lead to unfortunate circumstances later. If the basic physiological and safety needs of children are not satisfied, they are not only likely to do poorly in academic affairs but also in their contributions to the school and community and the development of personal social skills and understandings (Commission on the Whole Child, 2007). The Commission on the Whole Child (2007) also describes Maslow's hierarchy of needs and explains how important it is for schools to develop the social and emotional growth of all students, particularly children of poverty, at each level of human development. Once again, a major report emphasizes the importance of schools helping ensure that all students achieve established goals at each level of their development.

The Culture of Hope

The final set of research and recommendations that offers help in designing an effective rite of passage for today's youth and in guiding poverty-level students toward a better life is the collected research base on poverty and learning and on the Culture of Hope. This research, described in chapters 3–7 (see, for example, Jensen, 2009; Maslow & Lowry, 1973; Newell & Van Ryzin, 2007; Tileston & Darling, 2008; Lezotte & Snyder, 2011; and Damon, 2008), provides yet another set of age-based developments that contribute to the effective learning of students at all ages and to providing a foundation of self-confidence necessary to find and pursue personal purpose. The first step in opening up the door to middle-class opportunity for poor youth is to keep them in school, help them succeed academically, and push them to graduate from high school. To accomplish these demands, schools must make sure that students feel a sense of belonging in school, have the self-confidence to do the work, and find relevance in their work through a personal sense of purpose. The secret of success for poverty-level students in school is to have the personal internal strength to do what needs to be done. It is not just effective schooling. It is building a foundation of personal strength through social and emotional learning.

Taken together, these four sets of research and recommendations provide a consistent plan for improving public education and providing a new and powerful atmosphere of optimism for all students, especially those living in poverty. Taken together, this research offers a profound new view of public school. It transcends the traditional grade- and school-level organization that has always characterized public education. For example, it is now evident that organizing the years of schooling into elementary (typically grades K–5 or K–6), middle (grades 6–8 or 7–9), and high school (grades 9–12 or 10–12) may be an antiquated and dysfunctional approach. It is now evident that the early grades must focus an intense effort on ensuring that each and every student learns to read well and as quickly as possible and begins to develop a strong social and emotional foundation. So many effective schools are reorganizing these early years into nongraded classrooms, looping experiences in which students stay with the same teacher and cycle through two or more grades with the same peer group, and multi-age classrooms in which students from multiple grade levels are working and learning together in the same classroom. All of these creative efforts are designed to make sure that each student achieves grade-level standards in reading by the end of the third or fourth grade and finds a secure sense of belonging during the early elementary years. The research is powerful: if a student is not reading up to grade level by the end of the third grade, that student's chance of graduating from high school is all but nonexistent without intense intervention (McPartland & Slavin, 1990).

In much the same way, American middle and high schools must be transformed from large, comprehensive institutions into small, personalized learning communities and the traditional academic content transformed and blended with new career education standards like those that have occurred in International Baccalaureate programs. A new organizational emphasis must be designed for public schools that is built around the specific achievement standards—standards that reflect the best that we know about human growth and development, the social and emotional needs of children and youth, and the demands of the current world of economics and technology. This new design could become a powerful set of pathways out of poverty.

Using the Pew's Pathways to the Dream construct as a model, and supplementing it with educational research on poverty, learning, and students' social and emotional needs, we've devised a detailed series of sequential benchmarks of learning and development that are a prerequisite to upward mobility—essentially, a modern-day rite of passage (tables 10.1–10.5, pages 219–222 and online at **go.solution-tree.com /schoolimprovement**).

Pathway Models

Today, with a strong and growing research foundation, it is finally possible to help students and their families explore a variety of "pathways to the future" and for students to consider what type of life they would like to live as an adult, how hard they are willing to work to achieve that life, and what they need to know about salaries and lifestyles to help them make informed decisions. These various pathways are surprisingly simple—and consist of just the kind of clear, focused information that families, even poverty-level families, can understand with help of school personnel. The following pathways use the Pew model, enriched with other research.

- **Pathway #1—Without High School Graduation** (approximately 25 percent of all high school students in 2011 [Balfanz et al., 2012]):

  ▸ Profile—Students may arrive at school academically behind with a limited vocabulary and do not catch up, fail to learn to read quickly and well during the first three years of school, begin to miss school and fail courses, and become increasingly difficult behavior problems. They may be involved in risky behavior, and when arriving at the ninth grade, feel lost and isolated and ultimately drop out of school. Some students fall victim to drugs and alcohol. Other students, while being academically capable, may simply become detached, apathetic, and lack any clear purpose for their life.

  ▸ Economic forecast—The economic possibilities for the "good life" are dramatically diminished for the dropout. The probability of the dropout living out his or her life unemployed, underemployed, or unemployable are greatly increased, as is the likelihood of a variety of risky behaviors: drugs, alcohol, gangs, unsafe sex, and even crime. Large numbers of dropouts end up in prison (see chapter 2 on the "pipeline to prison," page 20). The youth who drops out of school will not qualify for the military service, and most of the jobs available—such as a retail sales clerk—are at the minimum pay level, earning a median salary of $21,000 in 2011. Jobs might include day laborer, construction helper, service worker at franchise fast-food restaurants, and a variety of sales clerk jobs. Some of these students, realizing the futility of their life, return to school for adult education courses and GED programs that might open up new avenues for employment. Others may go

Table 10.1: A Modern-Day Rite of Passage for Children of Poverty—Birth to Preschool

	Essential Learning	Essential Conditions for Learning
Cognitive	Children gain pre-reading and math skills. Children are exposed to rich and varied vocabulary. Parents engage children in conversation and ask questions requiring in-depth response (more than yes/no answers).	Extensive parent/mother education and support by school, hospitals, and other agencies Birth-to-three program: education and support groups for young mothers Good nutrition
Social and Emotional	Children engage in respectful and playful learning with other children. Children develop positive self-esteem and self-worth. Children learn to self-regulate in social situations and in the family.	Healthcare checkups and vaccinations Safe and caring family atmosphere Early school intervention program for young children (e.g., Healthy Start)

Table 10.2: A Modern-Day Rite of Passage for Children of Poverty—Preschool to Grade 5

	Essential Learning	Essential Conditions for Learning
Cognitive	Students learn to read and read up to grade level no later than the fourth grade. Students achieve grade level in mathematics, writing skills, and basic technology.	Attendance at same school for at least three years Attendance at Head Start, preschool, and all-day kindergartens A welcoming atmosphere of optimism, respect, and safety
Social and Emotional	Students learn an internal locus of control and come to believe that they can learn effectively. Students find a sense of belonging in the school and classroom. Students learn self-regulating behavior and develop effective relationships with other students and adults in the school. Students learn or enrich a sense of self-esteem and self-worth.	Effective instruction, caring, supportive teachers with high expectations, and careful monitoring of students' progress A variety of activities and experiences to ease the transition from home to first school experiences, including orientations, periodic sessions with families and preschoolers, home visits by teacher prior to school, and a welcoming atmosphere Regular teacher collaboration regarding student progress Partnership between schools and parents regarding mobility, attendance, health and nutrition, and reading Regular attendance

Table 10.3: A Modern-Day Rite of Passage for Children of Poverty—
Grades 6–8

	Essential Learning	Essential Conditions for Learning
Cognitive	Students enrich their basic skills, achieving grade-level standards as they grow and develop. They learn appropriate knowledge and skills in required content areas: math, English, social studies, and science and technology so they are prepared for high-school-level studies and advanced placement courses. Students complete algebra no later than the eighth grade so that they can complete advanced math at the high school level. They complete their exploration of careers involving knowledge and experiences.	Effective transition programs for all new middle school students and their parents A welcoming atmosphere of optimism, respect, and safety Partnerships with parents Parent education regarding pathways available for their children Student watch program to identify and address students who experience academic or social problems Basic skills catchup Career education and exploration blended into the academic curriculum College-going culture
Social and Emotional	There is a welcoming atmosphere of optimism, respect, and safety. Through clubs and extracurricular activities, students begin to explore talents and interests and find a sense of belonging. Students develop positive, respectful relationships with other students and school adults. They continue to develop self-regulating behavior. Students continue to develop a positive sense of self-esteem and self-worth. Through the exploration of talents, interests, and careers, students begin to consider a purpose in learning and life.	Personalized and engaging learning Positive experiences in the community A wide range of clubs, activities, and extra-curricular experience Teachers regularly collaborating regarding student progress

Table 10.4: A Modern-Day Rite of Passage for Children of Poverty—
Adolescence

Essential Learning		Essential Conditions for Learning
Cognitive	Students master and enrich basic skills and grade-level standards.	Effective transition to the high school
	Students participate successfully in a college-prep curriculum including advanced placement courses.	Welcoming atmosphere of optimism, respect, and safety
		Ninth-grade academies
		Small learning communities where teachers meet regularly and collaborate
		Learning options and career clusters
	Students experience a career education curriculum that includes knowledge and experiential activities.	Student watch program identifies students with academic or social problems
		Basic skills catch-up and summer skills programs
	Students begin to implement postsecondary plans.	Student advisory program: grades 9 through 12
		Recovery and reentry program for dropouts
	Students graduate high school with a 2.50 minimum GPA.	College-going culture
Social and Emotional	Students learn about careers and select a career area for further study.	Extensive counseling for careers and college
		Career and academic program blended into a single set of standards
	Students find a sense of belonging in the school.	College-prep curriculum for all students
	Schools continue to enrich students' self-esteem.	Advanced placement courses for all students
		Career exploration program
	Schools focus on personal purpose in school and life.	Blended classroom and community experiences
	Schools enhance students' self-esteem and strengthen their internal locus of control.	Opportunities for volunteer and service-learning activities
		Program to help students and families arrive at long-range decisions for students' lives and find purpose in their future
	Students prepare detailed plans for life after high school.	Program for students to make detailed plans after high school
	Students avoid risky behavior of drugs, alcohol, and unsafe sex.	Transition program for leaving high school
		Orientation to and planning for training programs, associate degree programs, college programs, military, or work
	Students celebrate graduation with network of family and friends.	2-plus-2 programs with area community colleges
		Successfully complete program, college application, and financial aid plans

Table 10.5: A Modern-Day Rite of Passage for Children of Poverty—Transition to Adulthood

	Essential Learning	Essential Conditions for Learning
Cognitive	Each graduate must complete one or more of the following postsecondary options: • Obtain employment after graduation with an appropriate salary, benefits, and opportunities for advancement, such as retail sales or food service. • Complete active military service or military training: college ROTC, service with Coast Guard, Army, Navy, Marine, Air Force, or military contractors. • Complete a job training certificate or licensure program: for example, hair stylist, truck driver, local/state government jobs. • Complete a one-year associate degree. • Complete a two-year associate degree. • Complete a BS/BA degree. • Complete an additional professional degree (for example, law, medicine, or graduate degree). Regardless of pathway, graduates find a stimulating and motivating job in a chosen career or area of interest.	Extensive counseling program at high school and college level Transition programs: high school, college, and careers Extensive partnerships with job training and community and four-year colleges Remediation courses and programs for postsecondary students Successful high school graduation with a minimum 2.50 GPA Successful completion of advanced placement courses and college-prep curriculum Successful exploration of careers and personal decision-making for future Successful completion of personal plan for post–high school
Social and Emotional	Graduates avoid risky behavior: for example, no juvenile crime, no teenage pregnancy, no addictions. Graduates find sense of belonging in postsecondary path. Graduates develop strong network of friends. Graduates continue to benefit from support of family.	

to work with their parents in their family business (farming, fishing, construction, and so on) and enjoy a decent financial life.

▸ Median starting salary—$21,000

- **Pathway #2—High School Graduation** (no additional education or training; currently, approximately 32 percent of high school graduates, according to the Bureau of Labor Statistics [2012]):

    ▸ Profile—Students learn to read adequately by the end of third grade, have reasonable attendance and behavior, and pass their courses as they progress up through the grades; some, even with marginal grades, may not be particularly motivated to do well in school but stay in school and graduate. This person can expect a better set of opportunities than the dropout, but not by much. Many who graduate lack adequate literacy skills.

    ▸ Economic forecast—There are few opportunities for a student with only a high school diploma. Some branches of the service will accept recruits with only a high school education, and there are a large number of retail sales jobs, cashier jobs, and jobs as servers and hosts in restaurants. Jobs might be available in construction. There are also many local and state government jobs available to the high school graduate. Salaries for the high school graduate are somewhat better than the dropout, and the jobs usually provide better benefits.

    ▸ Median starting salary—$29,900

- **Pathway #3—Completion of Job Training, One- or Two-Year Associate Degree** (Editorial Projects in Education Research Center [2011], estimates one-third of the working-age population has some form of sub-baccalaureate postsecondary training):

    ▸ Profile—Students have satisfactorily completed a high school diploma with good grades but are uninterested in or cannot afford a college degree. Many lack the academic confidence to pursue college. They have a record of good attendance and have focused on a particular job or a general career field.

    ▸ Economic forecast—Job training and associate degree programs lead directly to a large number of excellent jobs, most with good benefits. Job placement for many of these jobs, especially in the health field, is unusually high. Each of these programs is specifically designed to prepare a person for a specific job, unlike college, which often provides a degree in a particular field, like psychology, liberal arts, history, sociology, and so on, that might not necessarily prepare a person for a specific job. And there is the added benefit that this pathway has a relatively short preparation time. For example, truck-driving school, leading directly to high-paying jobs, is only twenty weeks long. Some of these jobs have high salaries. Licensed heating and air conditioning workers, electricians, plumbers, auto mechanics, and a wide variety of computer workers can earn in the $30,000 to $150,000 range, often far better than many college graduates. There are also dozens of jobs in the health and law enforcement fields that lead to immediate employment with excellent salaries and benefits. Other jobs like beautician, bartender, and work in the culinary arts promise early employment and good salaries and benefits. This pathway includes firefighters, police, postal workers, utility workers, guards, private security workers, airport security workers, all sorts of health-related occupations, and so on.

  ▸ Median starting salary—$37,000

- **Pathway #4—College Graduation** (approximately 68 percent of high school graduates go on to college, of those only 30 percent graduate [Bureau of Labor Statistics, 2012]):

  ▸ Profile—Students have completed high school graduation. During high school they have completed a college prep and a career curriculum and taken the ACT and/or the SAT. Many college students arrive at college unprepared and must take remedial classes. Many students lack a personal purpose for their studies and have difficulty selecting an academic major that truly excites and motivates them. Some will major in areas that lead directly into careers and jobs as teachers, nurses and other health professionals, and so on. Some will major in areas that do not lead directly to a job—for example, philosophy, liberal arts, and communications. A number of majors will typically require additional graduate work to enter the job market, for example psychology; and some degrees may require additional professional work—for example, pre-law, pre-medicine, and business.

  ▸ Economic forecast—In the years since the 2007–2008 U.S. economic recession, new college graduates have not been ensured of gainful employment in their areas of study. Jobs in business have been dramatically cut back, and with state budget shortfalls, jobs in teaching have been reduced. In some cases, new college graduates may be more employable than experienced workers. They are more mobile and usually cost far less. Some college graduates unable to find employment may return to pursue focused associate degrees that lead directly to a particular job opportunity.

  ▸ Median starting salary—$45,000 but with long-range opportunities for advanced study and extremely high salaries—$50,000 to $300,000 in selected fields (law, business, and medicine)

If there is any hope of helping students find a way out of poverty, information about these various pathways to the future must become an integral part of the K–12 curriculum. School staff should conduct conversations with parents about the various pathways at the earliest possible level, because all of the paths except the first one demand academic success beginning at the preschool and early elementary levels. These conversations must continue throughout the school years. As students grow and develop, conversations must include each of these options, for it is essential that students and their families have a clear awareness of the forecasts for high school dropouts, as well as high school graduates and the other pathways.

Journal

The former principal of Granger High School in Washington State, Ricardo LeBlanc-Esparza, told me how he would explain to students the salary levels that go with three different groups. The first group earns $15,000 or less, the middle group $20,000–$40,000, and the top group $40,000 and above. He used a poster in his office to help explain the various opportunities. The poster had three arrows, one labeled "low income," one "average income," and the other "good to great income." He also added to his poster information about health benefits, retirement, sick leave, and paid vacations and illustrated each of the three levels with photos of people taken from *Parade* magazine.

The photos, some of average people and others of famous actors and athletes, included the job of the person along with his or her salary. Ricardo's job, he explained, was to confront the students with their possible futures, to push them to think about their lives. He pushed them to make conscious decisions about what kind of life they wanted for themselves and helped them understand that they could fulfill their dreams. He felt that these discussions led to personal decisions by the students that helped transform their lives and had a greater impact than any of the instructional programs his staff used to help students succeed. Once a student really begins to think about a particular way of life and a particular job and asks, "What would I have to do to get that job?" educators know they have opened a door to the future for that student. —B.B.

How do we get it all done? All teachers and school administrators have full-time jobs apart from the added responsibilities that a kindergarten through college and career program demands. And while these expanded responsibilities may be easier to assume in small optional and charter schools, regular public schools offer greater challenges. Responsibilities must be part of job descriptions and be approved in teacher contracts. To be of maximum benefit, state and national policy makers must support this expanded responsibility—even in a time of budget cuts at the national, state, and local levels and reduced funding for public education across the board. The recognition that many local jobs go unfilled or are filled with temporary workers from abroad may evoke support for education from business organizations and lobbying groups like the Better Business Bureau.

A growing number of organizations are already working to help schools and families focus on kindergarten through college and career. The Albertson Foundation in Boise, Idaho, has launched a campaign urging students to graduate from high school and go on to postsecondary training or education. The "go on" information is found in newspaper ads, highway billboards, and animated TV commercials. These materials emphasize that Idaho is forty-eighth among all states in terms of the high school graduation rate and that large numbers of jobs in the state remain empty, because there are no applicants with the necessary training.

The Urban League likewise has a national campaign called Pathways to Prosperity that encourages students, especially minority students, to stay in school and pursue postsecondary education.

A number of states have made the kindergarten-through-college-and-careers concept a major goal. Reading national and regional education media, such as ASCD SmartBrief and Ed Now, articles highlighting schools' and districts' efforts to promote college-career readiness are evident.

For example, the state of Delaware has funded college tuition for all residents who graduate from high school in the state (Woodruff, n.d.). These Delaware scholarships provide support for a two-year technical degree at the Delaware Technical Community College or the University of Delaware Associate Arts degrees. In Oregon, the legislature has reorganized education funding at all levels, combining the functions of the state superintendent of public instruction as well as the chancellor of higher education. That state is now moving toward one system for funding K–12 public education, community college, and higher education, and using an "outcome" funding model to encourage cooperation and coordination across all levels of education, from kindergarten through graduate school (Melton, 2011). The new goal in Oregon is for 100 percent of all students to graduate from high school, 40 percent to earn a community college degree, and 40 percent to earn a college degree.

Another interesting proposal, the DREAM Act, would allow illegal immigrants to gain citizenship after a six-year conditional path that includes either military service or completion of at least a two-year college degree (Abbadon, 2010). Introduced to the U.S. Senate in 2001, and then reintroduced in 2009, the Dream Act is a dramatic new concept for addressing the issue of illegal aliens. Though as of this writing it has yet to earn legislative approval, the proposal highlights the needs of low-income undocumented youth. Different states have added state-level legislation that offers similar benefits and protections to the children of illegal immigrants, such as California's Dream Act, which was approved in 2011 and went into effect in January 2013 (Castro, 2013). In 2012, President Barack Obama used an executive order to allow illegal aliens who have been in the U.S. since childhood to remain in the country for two years and apply for work permits as long as they meet certain criteria, including being in school, having graduated high school, having served in the military, and having no criminal record (Mason & Cowan, 2012). This act will relieve an estimated 800,000 individuals from deportation. Again, as of this writing, there appears to be growing bipartisan agreement on a number of new immigration initiatives that could well tie education and service to citizenship.

The federal government is supporting the kindergarten-through-college-and-careers concept in a number of ways. The Common Core State Standards in English Language Arts and Mathematics emphasize college-career readiness across K–12. There are, of course, the Pell Grants for student financial aid for low-income college students, without which most poverty-level students could not attend college. Information about preparing for college as well as information about financial aid are increasingly available to students, families, and school districts. The U.S. Department of Education provides a brochure about college preparation that includes detailed checklists of information relevant to different stages of high school education, as well as essential steps for students to take along the way (see the Checklists for Academic and Financial Preparation at https://studentaid.ed.gov/students/publications/checklist /sitemap.html).

There are also a number of federally funded programs with a long record of helping low-income and minority students stay in school and attend college. The TRIO programs begin supporting low-income students with academic potential at the middle school levels, continuing through high school and college. Additional federal programs help migrant workers and their offspring earn high school diplomas (HEP: High School Equivalency Program) and enter college (CAMP: College Assistance Migrant Program). Where available, these programs provide a range of supports and have proven to be especially effective in helping poverty-level students stay in school, graduate, and later succeed in college.

Conclusion

Given the social and economic changes occurring in the United States and throughout the world, the only hope for poverty-level students is to help them open the door of opportunity and pursue the American dream of optimism and prosperity with education. Education is the new horizon of hope for low-income Americans; it has emerged as more than just a door of opportunity—for most students it is the only hope for a better life. And based on research and observation, no approach seems as powerful or to have as much potential to help the children of poverty remain and thrive in school as developing and enriching a Culture of Hope in every district, school, and classroom.

Enriching all who inhabit schools with optimism and opportunity through the four seeds of hope, the Power of We, and the redesigning of the high school has the potential to dramatically change the dropout crisis in our nation. Utilizing the modern-day rite of passage and providing students and families with clear information about the four basic pathways into adulthood have the potential to transform the relevance and importance of K–12 public schooling. Academic rigor and relevance are at the heart of education, but it is the social and emotional learning celebrated in a Culture of Hope that provide the foundation of personal strength that is so necessary to keep youth traveling a pathway toward a better life, a pathway out of poverty.

Appendix A

Methodologies of the *Newsweek* and *U.S. News & World Report* Studies

To make it onto *Newsweek*'s list, America's Best High Schools 2012, schools needed to complete a detailed survey based on 2011 data (Daily Beast, 2012). Over 10,000 schools received the survey, with 2,300 completing it. No details were given about how schools were selected; nor were there statistics about responders versus nonresponders, so the quality of the data is in question. With over 24,000 public high schools across the United States, and only one in ten completing the survey, this list is not comprehensive. However, it does include a measure of income (subsidized lunches), which allows for sorting of the data along this criteria as well as type of school, resulting in our ability to identify schools that met our search parameters.

Criteria for data collected by *Newsweek*:

- On-time graduation rate for 2011
- Percent of 2011 graduates accepted to college
- Advanced Placement/IB/Advance International Certificate of Education tests per student, 2011
- Average AP/IB/AICE score
- Average ACT/SAT score
- AP/IB/AICE courses offered per student
- Type of school (open enrollment, magnet, charter, selective enrollment, or lottery admission)
- Subsidized lunches as a measure of socioeconomic status

Newsweek ranked all schools that submitted complete data, with the final 1,000 schools ranked based on their level of success.

Our criteria for selection of high-poverty, high-performing high schools were: current data from 2010-2011 school year; enrollment of over 800 students; open

Table A.1: Database of the Thirteen Schools

Note: All are open enrollment except for Medgar Evers, which had a small percentage of selective enrollment for one specialized program within the larger school.

U.S. News & World Report Rank	Newsweek Rank	Enrollment	School	City	State	Grad rate	AP/IB tests	College bound	Avg SAT	Avg ACT	Subsidized lunch	Avg AP
Not Ranked	259	1,500	Eastside	Gainesville	FL	85	2	67	1500	24	60	2.7
Not Ranked	298	557	Penn-Griffin School for the Arts	High Point	NC	95	0.7	100	1626		55	2.5
24	409	1,024	Yonkers	Yonkers	NY	94	0.8	99	1456		68	3.2
156	447	2,500	Valencia	Placentia	CA	93	0.5	98	1675	26.6	57	3.8
Not Ranked	491	802	Medgar Evers College Prep	Brooklyn	NY	98	0.8	99	1345		88	2.5
795	592	2,408	Mark Keppel	Alhambra	CA	98	0.4	93	1617	24.7	59	3.7
566	690	1,690	Glen A. Wilson	Hacienda Heights	CA	95	0.5	91	1701	23.9	52	3.2
371	783	1,800	University City	San Diego	CA	95	0.5	94	1683	23.2	56	2.9
844	785	230	Coast Union	Cambria	CA	99	0.2	98	1513		57	3.0
Not Ranked	833	979	Hidalgo Early College	Hidalgo	TX	99	1	87	1257	17.1	100	1.4
196	866	2,038	La Quinta	Westminster	CA	90	0.5	97	1573	23	68	3.4
Not Ranked	983	1,835	Woodside	Woodside	CA	94	0.3	96	1532		53	2.9
1,842	989	721	Carpinteria	Carpinteria	CA	95	0.3	95	1516	23.9	56	2.8

enrollment; a diverse student body with over 50 percent subsidized lunches; on-time graduation of over 85 percent; and documented success of low-income students. Because *Newsweek*'s list incorporated all of the data we required, we mined its list for potential exemplary Culture of Hope schools. Due to design flaws (discussed in the next section), our list is in no way exhaustive or comprehensive. However, the resulting thirteen schools had graduation rates above 85 percent, and college acceptance rates above 85 percent, with the exception of Eastside's 67 percent. Average AP test scores ranged from 2.8 to 3.9 (except Hidalgo with 1.8). Subsidized lunch ranged from 52 percent (Glen A. Wilson) to 100 percent (Hidalgo). Student enrollments on our list ranged from 230 (Coast Union) to 2,408 (Mark Keppel). The two schools in our list of thirteen that had enrollment well under 800 (Coast Union and Penn-Griffin School for the Arts) remained on our list for comparison with the other schools because they were exemplary high schools with unique programs, serving diverse neighborhood populations, and they represent how truly short the list of *larger*, successful high schools is!

Another large ranking of high schools, produced by *U.S. News & World Report* (*U.S. News*, 2012), Best High Schools Ranking 2012, examined data for every high school that had twelfth-grade enrollment and sufficient data for analysis (resulting in over 21,000 schools). (The entire state of Nebraska was excluded from the study due to insufficient data.) *U.S. News* used three steps to identify top schools:

1. Academic proficiency was measured by high school achievement tests and then filtered by schools' percentage of disadvantaged students (black, Hispanic, and low income).

2. Schools' scores for disadvantaged students were compared to those of similar students across the state, and schools with achievement scores at or above the state's average for disadvantaged populations moved on to step 3 of the ranking process. Schools that passed step 1 and did not have populations of disadvantaged students automatically passed to the third step.

3. The resulting schools were judged on college readiness based on AP/IB test data, with 75 percent of a school's ranking comprised of twelfth graders who *passed* an AP/IB exam with a score of 3 or higher at some point during high school, and 25 percent of a school's ranking comprising the percentage of seniors who *took* an AP/IB exam at some point during high school. Then, an average was calculated for all high schools in the study, and those schools that had scores above the average were included in the final ranking and given a number and a medal. Schools that fell below the average and schools that did not offer AP/IB exams or courses were not eligible for final ranking and medals.

Thus, for the final ranking on *U.S. News*'s list, high schools that received ranking and medals passed all three steps and had a college readiness score above the average. Those high schools that are not ranked either did not pass the first two steps or did not have a high enough college readiness score. There are high schools that may do very well for disadvantaged students in respect to test scores and have a high graduation rate, but do not offer college prep courses.

The main flaw in *U.S. News*'s ranking, as we see it, is the lack of using graduation rates and college acceptance rates as part of the criteria. Thus, we used *Newsweek*'s list to locate schools that met our criteria and then looked for the same schools on the *U.S. News* list to see how they ranked on that list. For this reason, for the thirteen schools that met our criteria on the *Newsweek* ranking, we have also given *U.S. News*'s ranking (table A.1, page 232). Of the thirteen schools identified as high-poverty, high-performing, open-enrollment neighborhood schools in *Newsweek*'s list, eight are ranked on *U.S. News*'s list, meaning eight passed all three steps. For those that did not receive a ranking on *U.S. News*:

- Penn-Griffin had a 100 percent college readiness score, but did not report scores for math and science, and thus was eliminated at the first step.

- Medgar had a college readiness score of 29.9 (above the average) and academic measures above New York's average. It is not clear why it did not receive a ranking.

- Hidalgo had test scores far below the Texas average and did not have a college readiness score.

- Eastside had test scores and college readiness scores far above the Florida average. It is not clear why it did not receive a ranking.

- Woodside had test scores below California's average and was excluded at the first step.

Other Culture of Hope High Schools

In addition to the schools identified in the *Newsweek* and *U.S. News* rankings, there are a few other large comprehensive high schools that the education literature has identified as examples of excellence. And while the literature discusses aspects of the Culture of Hope, each of these schools likewise suffers from problems regarding data—for example, too few low-income students, lack of enrollment data, or lack of current comprehensive data. Because these schools have appeared prominently in education literature, we list them here with the data that are available and with their ranking in the *Newsweek* and *U.S. News* lists. But because these schools did not meet all our criteria for outstanding, large, open-enrollment high schools serving high-poverty, high-minority populations, they have not been included on the list of thirteen schools.

Schools Highlighted in Education Literature

- Elmont Memorial Junior-Senior High School, Elmont, New York, serves nearly 2,000 students. Elmont did not participate in *Newsweek's* list, and did not rank on *U.S. News's* list. It serves a 99 percent minority, 24 percent subsidized lunch population, and 43 percent of its students take AP tests. Although its graduation data are out of date, the school demonstrated a significant improvement in students passing the state Regents exams, with 69 percent of all students earning a Regents diploma, which requires scores of 65 percent or better on five or more Regents exams (Chenoweth, 2007). The New York Benchmark Schools study (RMC Research, 2008) profiled Elmont High School, noting it for the following Culture of Hope components: comprehensive guidance and advisory support, extracurricular connections, new teacher induction, and collaborative learning opportunities for staff.

- Adlai E. Stevenson High School in Illinois (see DuFour et al., 2010) serves over 4,000 students and has a solid record of academic success, high graduation rates, and high postsecondary success. It ranked 153 on *Newsweek's* list and 162 on *U.S. News's* list, but was eliminated during our search due to its modest minority population (23 percent) and relatively low percentage of subsidized lunches (4 percent). This school has well documented use of Culture of Hope components.

- Cinco Ranch High School in Texas (see DuFour et al., 2010) serves nearly 3,000 students, with 35 percent minority and 7 percent subsidized lunches. It ranked 354 on *Newsweek's* list and 580 on *U.S. News's* list. Again, it has a documented track record of success and use of Culture of Hope components, though they did not meet the criteria for our search because it does not serve a high-poverty population.

- Whittier Union High School District in Los Angeles County has five comprehensive high schools, with a total district enrollment of 14,000 students. The district has reduced the dropout rate to 9 percent, and between 2005 and 2008 over 99 percent of the students in the district passed the state exit exam for high school graduation (see DuFour et al., 2010, p. 149). One of the district's schools, Whittier High School, ranked 1,336 on the *U.S. News* list, with 92 percent minority and 65 percent subsidized lunches. It did not participate in the *Newsweek* list.

Schools Highlighted in the New York Benchmark Study

- Information about the New York Benchmark Schools (RMC Research, 2008): Data provided in this report are pre-2008, and two of the schools are too small to be included in the authors' list. However, the information in the report is quite extensive and could be very helpful for high schools seeking pathways toward improvement.

- Brentwood High School, Brentwood, New York, did not participate in *Newsweek*'s list, and did not rank on *U.S. News*'s list. It serves nearly 4,000 students, with 89 percent minority and 42 percent subsidized lunches. Twenty-one percent of its students take AP tests. Brentwood has the following Culture of Hope components in place: personalization and student support, with progress monitoring, interventions for at-risk students, monitoring of transition to high school with a "small learning communities" program, postsecondary exploration, and new teacher induction and support.

- Sleepy Hollow High School, Sleepy Hollow, New York, ranked 986 on *Newsweek*'s list, and did not rank on *U.S. News*'s list. It serves 828 students, with 67 percent minority and 35 percent subsidized lunches. Forty-two percent of students take AP tests. Culture of Hope components used by Sleepy Hollow are: personal plans for progress for all students, progress monitoring for at-risk students, guidance and advisory support, and parent, family, and community involvement.

School District Visited by Authors

- An exemplary district that provides extensive options is the Vancouver, Washington Public Schools, which has developed a comprehensive program of school choice at all levels. At the high school level, these learning options include legal studies; medical arts; culinary arts programs; Vancouver School of Arts and Academics; careers in education; habitat planning and civil engineering; welding and machine technology programs; science, mathematics, and technology magnet; International Baccalaureate diploma program; college in the high school; and the Internet learning academy. For an overview of the depth and breadth of programs and pathways offered by Vancouver (Washington) Public Schools, see the Magnet and CTE Opportunities chart at www.vansd.org and the Career Clusters, Pathways and Programs of Study at http://portalsso.vansd.org, which has links to PDFs of each program of study students take (Vancouver Public Schools, n.d.a; Vancouver Public Schools, n.d.b). Students and their parents at the middle school level are involved in a thorough program of information, experiences, and guidance to help ensure that high school learning choices are carefully considered.

Surveys of Students and Staff

Adlai E. Stevenson High School

Following are links to reports summarizing the results of Adlai E. Stevenson High School's student surveys for the years 2008–2011. Results are for each survey question given to all students at the school, graduates from the year before, and graduates from five years before to see how they are doing in the larger world. We provide these links to share the types of questions to ask to monitor school/staff effectiveness in preparing students for postsecondary success. Visit **go.solution-tree.com /schoolimprovement** to access these resources.

- www.d125.org/assets/1/Documents/student_survey_2011.pdf
- www.d125.org/assets/1/Documents/student_survey_2010.pdf
- www.d125.org/assets/1/Documents/student_survey_2009.pdf
- www.d125.org/assets/1/Documents/student_survey_2008.pdf

Idaho Building Capacity

The following URL offers links to staff, parent, and student surveys on school climate, culture, and academics: www.uidaho.edu/cda/ibc/resources

Center for Educational Effectiveness

This organization offers scoring and data analysis services for the surveys used by Idaho Building Capacity: www.effectiveness.org/default.aspx

Pathway Programs: Technical Assistance

- **ConnectEd, The California Center for College and Career** (www .connectEdCalifornia.org)—Resource base for California's Linked

Learning pathways, including videos, blogs, curriculum, lists of schools, and so on. Click on "Online Toolkit" for help.

- **College and Career Academy Support Network, University of California, Berkeley** (http://casn.berkeley.edu)—The College and Career Academy Support Network provides a Planning Guide for Career Academies.

- **National Academy Foundation, New York City** (www.naf.org)—This organization provides the academy development model.

- **Ford Partnership for Advanced Studies, Ford Motor Company** (www. fordpas.org)—This partnership provides technical assistance to help schools build programs to assist students interested in careers in business, engineering, and technology.

- **Career Clusters, CTE Works for America** (www.careertech.org /resources/workforce-education.html)—Developed by the National Association of State Directors of Career Technical Education Consortium, CTE works with schools and businesses to develop curriculum and program specifications designed to help high schools implement career clusters relating to sixteen major industries (Hoachlander, 2008).

Glossary

alternative schools. Large numbers of school districts still offer small off-site alternatives for struggling students.

career clusters. These schools might include academic programs that emphasize the health professions, science and technology, the legal professions, business, and so on. Students take courses within a cluster based on their interests.

charter schools. A growing number of communities now have opportunities to participate in these semiprivate, public schools. Often they reflect distinctive learning philosophies or approaches not available in traditional public schools. These include Montessori schools, continuous progress schools, Paideia schools, Waldorf schools, multiple intelligences schools, and so on (see Barr & Parrett, 1997, for established models for alternative, magnet, and charter schools).

early college academies. These options enable students to complete college courses during senior year and provide a chance to finish college in three years.

early college high schools. Usually located on college campuses and offering students an opportunity to leave the traditional high school campus and attend school in a new, demanding setting, these programs provide opportunities to take dual-credit courses so that as students complete required classes for high school graduation, they are building their vita of college courses as well. College professors usually teach these courses.

International Baccalaureate program. These programs require a rigorous high school curriculum leading to the widely recognized IB examination.

magnet schools. These schools are designed to attract a diverse population of students to a school that would have a high-minority, high-poverty student population if it only took students from the surrounding neighborhood. Programs of study are thematic, such as visual and performing arts, technology, science, or college preparatory.

performing arts schools. These schools serve students who possess special talents with opportunities to work with professional artists in the community.

virtual schools. Every state now has high school options for virtual classes or virtual diplomas. Some states are now requiring all students to complete a number of courses online via virtual academies. Enrollment in virtual programs often makes them the largest high school in a state.

vocational and technical schools. Schools often provide these programs, which may lead to certification or licensure programs, in conjunction with business, industry, unions, and community colleges. These programs can lead quickly to high-quality jobs with high salaries and fringe benefits.

References and Resources

Abbadon. (2010, July 16). *Basic information about the DREAM Act legislation.* Accessed at http://dreamact.info/students on February 20, 2013.

Adams, J. T. (1931). *The epic of America.* Boston: Little, Brown.

Allen, L. (2012). *Back on track through college in the Rio Grande Valley: From dropout recovery to postsecondary success.* Washington, DC: First Focus. Accessed at www .firstfocus.net/sites/default/files/BI2012%20-%20DropoutRecovery_0.pdf on April 23, 2013.

Alliance for Excellent Education. (2011, November). *The high cost of high school dropouts: What the nation pays for inadequate high schools* (Issue Brief). Washington, DC: Author. Accessed at www.all4ed.org/files/HighCost.pdf on November 28, 2012.

Apple, M. W. (1971). The hidden curriculum and the nature of conflict. *Interchange, 2*(4), 27–40.

Atwell, N. (1998). *In the middle: New understandings about writing, reading, and learning* (2nd ed.). Portsmouth, NH: Heinemann.

Aud, S., Hussar, W., Planty, M., Snyder, T., Bianco, K., Fox, M., et al. (2010). *The condition of education 2010* (NCES 2010-028). Washington, DC: U.S. Department of Education, Institute of Education Sciences, National Center for Education Statistics. Accessed at http://nces.ed.gov/pubs2010/2010028.pdf on December 19, 2012.

Balfanz, R. (2009). *Putting middle grades students on the graduation path: A policy brief.* Westerville, OH: National Middle School Association. Accessed at www.amle.org /portals/0/pdf/research/research_from_the_field/policy_brief_balfanz.pdf on February 9, 2012.

Balfanz, R., Bridgeland, J., Bruce, M., & Fox, J. (2012). *Building a grad nation: Progress and challenge in ending the high school dropout epidemic—Annual update, 2012.* Washington, DC: Civic Enterprises. Accessed at www.americaspromise .org/our-work/grad-nation/~/media/Files/Our%20Work/Grad%20Nation /Building%20a%20Grad%20Nation/BuildingAGradNation2012.ashx on December 19, 2012.

Balfanz, R., Bridgeland, J., Fox, J., & Moore, L. (2011). *Building a grad nation: Progress and challenge in ending the high school dropout epidemic—2010–2011 annual update.* Washington, DC: Civic Enterprises. Accessed at www .americaspromise.org/our-work/grad-nation/~/media/Files/Our%20Work /Grad%20Nation/2011%20Summit/Reports/GradNation_Update_March2011 .ashx on December 19, 2012.

Balfanz, R., Bridgeland, J., Moore, L., & Fox, J. (2010). *Building a grad nation: Progress and challenge in ending the high school dropout epidemic.* Washington, DC: Civic Enterprises. Accessed at http://pearsonfoundation.org/downloads /BuildingAGradNation_FullReport.pdf on December 19, 2012.

Barr, R. D., & Parrett, W. H. (1995). *Hope at last for at-risk youth.* Boston: Allyn & Bacon.

Barr, R. D., & Parrett, W. H. (1997). *How to create alternative, magnet, and charter schools that work.* Bloomington, IN: Solution Tree Press.

Barr, R. D., & Parrett, W. H. (2001). *Hope fulfilled for at-risk and violent youth: K–12 programs that work* (2nd ed.). Boston: Allyn & Bacon.

Barr, R. D., & Parrett, W. H. (2007). *The kids left behind: Catching up the underachieving children of poverty.* Bloomington, IN: Solution Tree Press.

Barr, R. D., & Parrett, W. H. (2008). *Saving our students, saving our schools: 50 proven strategies for helping underachieving students and improving schools* (2nd ed.). Thousand Oaks, CA: Corwin Press.

Barr, R. D., & Yates, D. L. (2010). *Turning your school around: A self-guided audit for school improvement.* Bloomington, IN: Solution Tree Press.

Barth, R. S. (2005). Turning book burners into lifelong learners. In R. DuFour, R. Eaker, & R. DuFour (Eds.), *On common ground: The power of professional learning communities* (pp. 115–134). Bloomington, IN: Solution Tree Press.

Bassuk, E. L., Murphy, C., Coupe, N. T., Kenney, R. R., & Beach, C. A. (2010). *America's youngest outcasts: 2010.* Needham, MA: National Center on Family Homelessness. Accessed at www.homelesschildrenamerica.org/media/NCFH _AmericaOutcast2010_web.pdf on December 19, 2012.

Beaumont, L. R. (2009). *Learned helplessness: Why bother?* Accessed at www .emotionalcompetency.com/helpless.htm on September 28, 2012.

Benard, B. (1996). Fostering resiliency in urban schools. In B. Williams (Ed.), *Closing the achievement gap: A vision for changing beliefs and practices* (pp. 96–119). Alexandria, VA: Association for Supervision and Curriculum Development.

Benard, B. (1997). *Turning it around for all youth: From risk to resilience.* New York: ERIC Clearinghouse on Urban Education.

Benard, B. (2003). Turnaround teachers and schools. In B. Williams (Ed.), *Closing the achievement gap: A vision for changing beliefs and practices* (2nd ed., pp. 115–137). Alexandria, VA: Association for Supervision and Curriculum Development.

Benson, P., Galbraith, J., & Espeland, P. (1998). *What kids need to succeed: Proven, practical ways to raise good kids* (Rev. ed.) . Minneapolis, MN: Free Spirit.

Billig, S. (2000). Research on K–12 school-based service learning: The evidence builds. *Phi Delta Kappan, 81*(9), 658–663.

Bloomberg, M. (2011, June 14). *NYC high school graduation rate hits all-time high* [Web log post]. Accessed at www.mikebloomberg.com/index.cfm?objectid =8F537A57-C29C-7CA2-F9960B491507142E on December 21, 2012.

Bottoms, G., & Anthony, K. (2005). *Raising achievement and improving graduation rates: How nine High Schools That Work sites are doing it.* Atlanta, GA: Southern Regional Education Board.

Brookings Institution. (2011, November 14). Opportunity nation: Pew's economic mobility project. *Time, 1/8*(19), 30–31.

Brown, J. H., D'Emidio-Caston, M., & Benard, B. (2001). *Resilience education.* Thousand Oaks, CA: Corwin Press.

Bruce, M., Bridgeland, J., Fox, J., & Balfanz, R. (2011). *On track for success: The use of early warning indicator and intervention systems to build a grad nation.* Washington, DC: Civic Enterprise and the Everyone Graduates Center at Johns Hopkins University. Accessed at http://new.every1graduates.org/wp-content /uploads/2012/03/on_track_for_success.pdf on December 21, 2012.

Brudevold-Newman, B. (2006). *The cost of dropping out.* Accessed at www.npr.org /templates/story/story.php?storyId=5300726 on September 28, 2012.

California Department of Education. (2005). *Getting results: Update 5, student health, supportive schools, and academic success.* Sacramento, CA: CDE Press.

CareerOneStop. (2012). *Occupation information: Occupation profile.* Accessed at www.careerinfonet.org/Occ_Intro.asp?id=1,&nodeid=1 on September 28, 2012.

Carroll, J. A., & Kirkpatrick, R. L. (2011). *Impact of social media on adolescent behavioral health in California.* Oakland, CA: California Adolescent Health Collaborative. Accessed at www.californiateenhealth.org/wp-content /uploads/2011/09/SocialMediaAug2011.pdf on February 10, 2013.

Castro, T. (2013). *California DREAM Act now law*. Accessed at www.voxxi.com /california-dream-act-now-law on February 20, 2013.

Center for Secondary School Redesign. (2011). *Advisory*. Accessed at www.cssr.us /advisoryN.htm on December 21, 2012.

Chenoweth, K. (2007). *"It's being done": Academic success in unexpected schools.* Cambridge, MA: Harvard Education Press.

Chenoweth, K. (2009). *How it's being done: Urgent lessons from unexpected schools.* Cambridge, MA: Harvard Education Press.

Child Trends. (2012). *Home computer access and internet use.* Accessed at www .childtrendsdatabank.org/?q=node/298 on February 22, 2013.

Coalition of Essential Schools. (2006). *Measuring up: Demonstrating the effectiveness of the Coalition of Essential Schools.* Oakland, CA: Author. Accessed at www .essentialschools.org/d/3/Measuring_Up_Report.pdf on September 28, 2012.

Coley, R. J., Cradler, J., & Engel, P. K. (1997). *Computers and classrooms: The status of technology in U.S. schools.* Princeton, NJ: Policy Information Center. Accessed at www.ets.org/research/policy_research_reports/pic-compciss on February 20, 2013.

Comer, J., Joyner, E., & Ben-Avie, M. (2004). *Six pathways to healthy child development and academic success: The field guide to Comer schools in action.* Thousand Oaks, CA: Corwin Press.

Commission on the Whole Child. (2007). *The learning compact redefined: A call to action.* Alexandria, VA: Association for Supervision and Curriculum Development.

Conrath, J. (2001). Changing the odds for young people: Next steps for alternative education. *Phi Delta Kappan, 82*(8), 585–587.

Courrege, D. (2011, July 29). How two rural schools prepare kids for college, part 1 [Web log post]. *Education Week.* Accessed at http://blogs.edweek.org/edweek /rural_education/2011/07/two_rural_schools_prepare_kids_for_college_part_1 .html on September 28, 2012.

Crawford, D., & Bodine, R. (1996). *Conflict resolution education: A guide to implementing programs in schools, youth-serving organizations, and community and juvenile justice settings.* Washington, DC: U.S. Department of Education, U.S. Department of Justice. Accessed at www.ncjrs.gov/pdffiles/conflic.pdf on February 22, 2013.

Crawford, D., & Bodine, R. (2001). Conflict resolution education: Preparing youth for the future. *Juvenile Justice: School Violence, 8*(1). Accessed at www.ncjrs.gov /html/ojjdp/jjjournal_2001_6/jj3.html on February 22, 2013

Cromwell, S. (2002). Is your school's culture toxic or positive? *Education World, 6*(2). Accessed at www.educationworld.com/a_admin/admin/admin275.shtml on September 28, 2012.

Cromwell, S. (2010). *Student-led conferences: A growing trend.* Accessed at www .educationworld.com/a_admin/admin/admin112.shtml on September 28, 2012.

Daily Beast. (2012). *America's best high schools 2012.* Accessed at www.thedailybeast .com/newsweek/2012/05/20/america-s-best-high-schools.html on December 19, 2012.

Damon, W. (2008). *The path to purpose: How young people find their calling in life.* New York: The Free Press.

Darling-Hammond, L. (1997). *The right to learn: A blueprint for creating schools that work.* San Francisco: Jossey-Bass.

Darling-Hammond, L., & Sykes, G. (Eds.). (1999). *Teaching as the learning profession: Handbook of policy and practice.* San Francisco: Jossey-Bass.

Davis, T., Fuller, M., Jackson, S., Pittman, J., & Sweet, J. (2007). *A national consideration of digital equity.* Washington, DC: International Society for Technology in Education. Accessed at www.k12hsn.org/files/research /Technology/national-consideration-DE.pdf on September 28, 2012.

Deal, T., & Peterson, K. (1999). *Shaping school culture: The heart of leadership.* San Francisco: Jossey-Bass.

Delpit, L. (1995). *Other people's children: Cultural conflict in the classroom.* New York: The New Press.

Dewey, J. (1909). *How we think.* Boston: Heath.

Dewey, J. (1916). *Democracy and education.* New York: Macmillan.

Dillon, S. (2009, October 8). Study finds high rate of imprisonment among dropouts. *The New York Times*, p. A12. Accessed at www.nytimes.com/2009/10/09 /education/09dropout.html on September 28, 2012.

Domhoff, G. W. (2011). *Power in America: Wealth, income, and power.* Accessed at http://sociology.ucsc.edu/whorulesamerica/power/wealth.html on September 28, 2012.

Dryfoos, J. (2010). Centers of hope. In M. Scherer (Ed.), *Keeping the whole child healthy and safe: Reflections on best practices in learning, teaching, and leadership* (pp. 213–221). Alexandria, VA: Association for Supervision and Curriculum Development.

DuFour, R. (2005). What is a professional learning community? In R. DuFour, R. Eaker, & R. DuFour (Eds.), *On common ground: The power of professional learning communities* (pp. 31–44). Bloomington, IN: Solution Tree Press.

DuFour, R., DuFour, R., Eaker, R., & Karhanek, G. (2010). *Raising the bar and closing the gap: Whatever it takes.* Bloomington, IN: Solution Tree Press.

DuFour, R., Eaker, R., & DuFour, R. (Eds.). (2005). *On common ground: The power of professional learning communities.* Bloomington, IN: Solution Tree Press.

DuFour, R., & Marzano, R. (2011). *Leaders of learning: How district, school, and classroom leaders improve student achievement.* Bloomington, IN: Solution Tree Press.

Duncan, A. (2011). *Making the middle grades matter: Secretary Arne Duncan's remarks at the National Forum's Annual Schools to Watch Conference.* Accessed at www .ed.gov/news/speeches/making-middle-grades-matter on September 28, 2012.

Duncan, G. J., & Murnane, R. J. (Eds.). (2011). *Whither opportunity? Rising inequality, schools, and children's life chances.* New York: Sage.

Echevarria, J. J., Vogt, M., & Short, D. J. (2012). *Making content comprehensible for English learners: The SIOP model* (4th ed.). Columbus, OH: Pearson.

Editorial Projects in Education Research Center. (2011). Diplomas count 2011: Beyond high school, before baccalaureate—Meaningful alternatives to a four year degree. *Education Week, 30*(34). Accessed at www.edweek.org/ew/toc/2011/06/09 /index.html on September 28, 2012.

Editors of Rethinking Schools. (2012). Stop the school-to-prison pipeline. *Rethinking Schools, 26*(2).

Education Trust. (2005). *The power to change: High schools that help all students achieve.* Washington, DC: Author. Accessed at www.edtrust.org/sites/edtrust.org/files /publications/files/ThePowerToChange.pdf on December 21, 2012.

Education Trust. (2009). *Closing the gaps.* Washington, DC: Education Trust. Assessed at www.edtrust.org/issues/pre-k-12/closing-the-gaps on April 16, 2013.

EdVisions. (2010). *What is the hope survey?* Accessed at www.hopesurvey.org/about -the-hope-survey on September 28, 2012.

Elmore, R. F. (2008). *School reform from the inside out: Policy, practice, and performance.* Cambridge, MA: Harvard Education Press.

Elmore, R. F., & Burney, D. (1999). Investing in teacher learning: Staff development and instructional improvement. In L. Darling-Hammond & G. Sykes (Eds.), *Teaching as the learning profession: Handbook of policy and practice* (pp. 263–291). San Francisco: Jossey-Bass.

ETR Associates. (2012). *What is service-learning?* Accessed at www.servicelearning.org /what-service-learning on September 28, 2012.

Expeditionary Learning. (n.d.). *Academic achievement.* Accessed at http://elschools .org/our-results/academic-achievement on March 6, 2013.

Fletcher, M. A. (2011, September 13). Nearly one in six in poverty in the U.S.; children hit hard, census says. *The Washington Post.* Accessed at www.washington post.com/business/economy/us-poverty-rate-hits-52-year-high-at-151-percent/2011 /09/13/gIQApnMePK_story.html on September 28, 2012.

Foroohar, R. (2011, November 14). What ever happened to upward mobility? *Time*, *178*(19). Accessed at www.time.com/time/magazine/article/0,9171,2098584,00 .html on September 28, 2012.

Friedman, T. (2012, January 24). Average is over. *The New York Times*, p. A29. Accessed at www.nytimes.com/2012/01/25/opinion/friedman-average-is-over .html?_r=0 on February 22, 2013.

Fullan, M. (2007). *The new meaning of educational change* (4th ed.). New York: Teachers College Press.

Gathercoal, P. (2006, April). *Judicious discipline: Preparing students for living and learning in a free, democratic society.* Paper presented at the American Educational Research Association (AERA) Annual Convention, San Francisco, CA.

Gewertz, C. (2011, March). *Harvard report questions value of "college for all."* Accessed at www.lcti.org/cms/lib02/PA03000052/Centricity/Domain/159/March_2011 _DR.pdf on February 22, 2013.

Gibbons, M. (1974). Walkabout: Searching for the right passage from childhood and school. *Phi Delta Kappan, 55*(9), 596–602.

Glasser, W. (1975). *Reality therapy: A new approach to psychiatry.* New York: Harper & Row.

Glasser, W. (1998). *Choice theory: A new psychology of personal freedom.* New York: HarperCollins.

Gonzales, P., Williams, T., Jocelyn, L., Roey, S., Kastberg, D., & Brenwald, S. (2009). *Highlights from TIMSS 2007: Mathematics and science achievement of U.S. fourth- and eighth-grade students in an international context.* Washington, DC: U.S. Department of Education, Institute of Education Sciences, National Center for Education Statistics. Accessed at http://nces.ed.gov/pubs2009/2009001.pdf on January 3, 2013.

Goodall, T. (2012, March 21). Student focus, better data create fewer Portland high school dropouts. *The Oregonian*, p. C7. Accessed at www.oregonlive.com/opinion /index.ssf/2012/03/graduation_rates.html on January 3, 2013.

Graves, D. H. (1994). *A fresh look at writing.* Portsmouth, NH: Heinemann.

Hardy, L. (2007). Children at risk: The family. *American School Board Journal, 194*(6), 19–23.

Hartford Public Schools. (2010). *McDonough Expeditionary Learning School.* Accessed at www.hartfordschools.org/files/McDonoughDesignSpecs.pdf on April 16, 2013.

Hecker, D. (2005). Employment outlook: 2004–14. *Monthly Labor Review, 128*(11), 70–101.

Heller, K. M. (n.d.). *Isolation at core of adolescent woes.* Accessed at www.drheller.com /isolashn.html on September 28, 2012.

Henderson, N., & Milstein, M. (1996). *Resiliency in schools: Making it happen for students and educators.* Thousand Oaks, CA: Corwin Press.

Hinduja, S., & Patchin, J. W. (2012). *School climate 2.0: Preventing cyberbullying and sexting one classroom at a time.* Thousand Oaks, CA: Corwin Press.

Hoachlander, G. (2008). Bringing industry to the classroom. *Educational Leadership, 65*(8), 22–27.

Hollis, J. (2005). *Finding meaning in the second half of life, how to finally really grow up.* New York: Gotham Books.

Hu, W. (2012, January 25). City students at small public high schools are more likely to graduate, study says. *The New York Times*, p. A26. Accessed at www.nytimes .com/2012/01/26/education/new-york-city-students-at-small-public-high schools -are-more-likely-to-graduate-study-finds.html on January 3, 2012.

Huitt, W. (2007). Maslow's hierarchy of needs. *Educational Psychology Interactive.* Valdosta, GA: Valdosta State University. Accessed at www.edpsycinteractive.org /topics/conation/maslow.html on January 3, 2013.

Illinois State Board of Education. (2001). *High poverty-high performance (hp-hp) schools.* Chicago: Author. Accessed at www.isbe.state.il.us/nclb/csa/appendices /appendixM.pdf on January 3, 2013.

Ingrum, A. (2006). *High school dropout determinants: The effect of poverty and learning disabilities.* Accessed at www.iwu.edu/economics/PPE14/Ingrum.pdf on September 28, 2012.

Jackson, A. W., & Davis, G. A. (2000). *Turning points 2000: Educating adolescents in the 21st century.* New York: Teachers College Press.

Jackson, J. (2011). *Education redlining in New York City: Preface.* Accessed at http ://schottfoundation.org/publications-reports/education-redlining/preface on March 6, 2012.

Jensen, E. (2009). *Teaching with poverty in mind: What being poor does to kids' brains and what schools can do about it.* Alexandria, VA: Association for Supervision and Curriculum Development.

Jensen, E. (2011). *Teaching with poverty in mind: 5 secrets to high-performing schools.* Accessed at www.jensenlearning.com/workshop-teaching-with-poverty-in-mind .php# on September 28, 2012.

Junger, S. (2010). *War.* New York: Twelve.

Kanter, R. M. (2010). *Confidence: How winning streaks and losing streaks begin and end.* New York: Three Rivers Press.

Kantrowitz, B., & Wingert, P. (1999, October 18). The truth about tweens. *Newsweek, 134*(16), 62–79.

Kazdin, A. E. (1993). Adolescent mental health: Prevention and treatment programs. *American Psychology, 48*(2), 127–141.

Kearns, D. T. (1993). Toward a new generation of American schools. *Phi Delta Kappan, 74*(10), 773–776.

Kennedy, M. M. (1999). The role of preservice teacher education. In L. Darling-Hammond & G. Sykes (Eds.), *Teaching as the learning profession: Handbook of policy and practice* (pp. 54–85). San Francisco: Jossey-Bass.

Kennelly, L., & Monrad, M. (Eds.). (2007). *Easing the transition to high school: Research and best practices designed to support high school learning.* Washington, DC: National High School Center at the American Institutes for Research.

Klein, J. (2011, October 24). Middle of the road. *Time, 178*(16). Accessed at www.time.com/time/magazine/article/0,9171,2096838,00.html on September 28, 2012.

Klein, J. (2012, May 14). Learning that works. *Time, 179*(19). Accessed at www.time.com/time/magazine/article/0,9171,2113794,00.html on September 28, 2012.

Kliff, S. (2008). The popularity gap. *Newsweek.* Accessed at www.thedailybeast.com/newsweek/2008/05/14/the-popularity-gap.html on February 9, 2013.

Kohl, H. (1994). *"I won't learn from you." And other thoughts on creative maladjustment.* New York: The New Press.

Korman, A. K., Greenhaus, J. H., & Badin, I. J. (1977). Personnel attitudes and motivation. *Annual Review of Psychology, 28,* 175–196. Palo Alto, CA: Annual Reviews.

Kozol, J. (2005a). Apartheid education. *The Nation.* Accessed at www.alternet.org/print/story/29174/apartheid_education on February 18, 2013.

Kozol, J. (2005b). *The shame of the nation: The restoration of apartheid schooling in America.* New York: Crown.

Kreite, R. (2002). *Morning meeting book* (Rev. ed.). Turner Falls, MA: Northeast Foundation for Children.

Krovetz, M. L. (1999). *Fostering resiliency: Expecting all students to use their minds and hearts well.* Thousand Oaks, CA: Corwin Press.

Lawler, E. E., III., & Suttle, J. L. (1972). A causal correlational test of the need hierarchy concept. *Organizational Behavior and Human Performance, 7,* 265–287.

Layton, L. (2012, March 19). High school graduation rate rises in U.S. *The Washington Post.* Accessed at www.washingtonpost.com/local/education/high-school-graduation-rate-rises-in-us/2012/03/16/gIQAxZ9rLS_story.html on January 3, 2013.

LeBlanc-Esparza, R., & Roulston, W. S. (2012). *Breaking the poverty barrier: Changing student lives with passion, perseverance, and performance.* Bloomington, IN: Solution Tree Press.

Leithwood, K., & Jantzi, D. (2009). A review of empirical evidence about school size effects: A policy perspective. *Review of Educational Research, 79*(1), 464–490.

Lenhart, A., Madden, M., Smith, A., Purcell, K., Zickuhr, K., & Rainie, L. (2011). *Teens, kindness and cruelty on social network sites: How American teens navigate the new world of "digital citizenship."* Washington, DC: Pew Research Center's Internet & American Life Project. Accessed at http://pewinternet.org /Reports/2011/Teens-and-social-media.aspx on January 3, 2013.

Lezotte, L. W., & Snyder, K. M. (2011). *What effective schools do: Re-envisioning the correlates.* Bloomington, IN: Solution Tree Press.

Liang, J.-H., Heckman, P. E., & Abedi, J. (2012). What do the California standards test results reveal about the movement toward eighth-grade algebra for all? *Educational Evaluation and Policy Analysis, 34*(3), 328–343.

Little, J. W. (1999). Organizing schools for teacher learning. In L. Darling-Hammond & G. Sykes (Eds.), *Teaching as the learning profession: Handbook of policy and practice* (pp. 233–262). San Francisco: Jossey-Bass.

Marshall, S. (2012). The educational effects of social interaction. *The Thunder Project: Taking education by storm.* Accessed at www.thethunderproject.org /the-educational-effects-of-social-interaction on February 10, 2013.

Martin, P., & Perkins, L. (2011). *Adlai E. Stevenson High School student surveys, 2010– 2011.* Accessed at www.d125.org/assets/1/Documents/student_survey_2011 .pdf on January 3, 2013.

Marzano, R. J. (2003). *What works in schools: Translating research into action.* Alexandria, VA: Association for Supervision and Curriculum Development.

Marzano, R. J. (2007). *The art and science of teaching: A comprehensive framework for effective instruction.* Alexandria, VA: Association for Supervision and Curriculum Development.

Maslow, A. (1943). A theory of human motivation. *Psychological Review, 50,* 370–396.

Maslow, A. (1970). *Motivation and personality* (2nd ed.). New York: Harper & Row.

Maslow, A. (Author), & Lowry, R. (Ed.). (1998). *Toward a psychology of being* (3rd ed.). New York: Wiley.

Mason, J., & Cowan, R. (2012, June 16). Obama spares many illegal immigrants deportation. *Reuters.* Accessed at www.reuters.com/article/2012/06/16/us -usa-immigration-idUSBRE85E0VA20120616 on September 28, 2012.

McDonough, P. (2009, October 26). *TV viewing among kids at an eight-year high* [Web log post]. Accessed at http://blog.nielsen.com/nielsenwire/media _entertainment/tv-viewing-among-kids-at-an-eight-year-high on September 28, 2012.

McPartland, J. M., & Slavin, R. E. (1990). *Increasing achievement of at-risk students at each grade level.* Washington, DC: U.S. Department of Education, Information Services, Office of Educational Research and Improvement.

Meacham, J. (2012, June 21). Keeping the dream alive. *Time, 180*(1). Accessed at www.time.com/time/specials/packages/article/0,28804,2117662_2117682_2117680,00.html on September 28, 2012.

Melton, K. (2011, February 11). Gov. John Kitzhaber plans a powerful Oregon education board, connecting school funding to performance. *The Oregonian.* Accessed at www.oregonlive.com/politics/index.ssf/2011/02/gov_john_kitzhaber_plans_to_cr.html on September 28, 2012.

Miller, S. (2013, February). Local student works to end child slavery. *Mendo Lake Family Life.* Accessed at www.mendolakefamilylife.com on March 21, 2013.

Modarres, A. (2011). Beyond the digital divide. *National Civic Review.* Accessed at http://group1digitaldivide.pbworks.com/w/file/fetch/51929828/Beyond%20the%20digital%20divide.pdf on February 10, 2013.

Monahan, R. (2011, June 14). New York City high school graduation rate up, but 75% of students not prepared for college. *NY Daily News.* Accessed at http://articles.nydailynews.com/2011-06-14/local/29675551_1_graduation-rate-english-regents-regents-exams on March 19, 2013.

Moore, K. A., & Vandivere, S. (2000). *Stressful family lives: Child and parent well-being.* Washington, DC: Urban Institute Research of Record. Accessed at www.urban.org/publications/309565.html on September 28, 2012.

Muhammad, A. (2009). *Transforming school culture: How to overcome staff division.* Bloomington, IN: Solution Tree Press.

National Center for Education Statistics. (1999). *Highlights from TIMSS: The Third International Mathematics and Science Study—Overview and key findings across grade levels.* Washington, DC: Author. Accessed at http://nces.ed.gov/pubs99/1999081.pdf on January 3, 2013.

National Urban League. (2011, February 21). The great economic divide [Special section]. *Time, 177*(7). Accessed at www.nul.org/sites/default/files/Time_Magazine_NUL_Insert.pdf on September 28, 2012.

Nelsen, J., Lott, L., & Glenn, S. (2002). *Positive discipline in the classroom: Developing mutual respect, cooperation, and responsibility in your classroom* (Rev. 3rd ed.). Roseville, CA: Prima.

Newell, R. J., & Van Ryzin, M. J. (2007). Growing hope as a determinant of school effectiveness. *Phi Delta Kappan, 88*(6), 465–471.

Newell, R. J., & Van Ryzin, M. J. (2009). *Assessing what really matters in schools: Creating hope for the future.* Lanham, MD: Rowman & Littlefield.

November, A. (2011, March 25). *TEDxNYED: Alan November* [Video file]. Accessed at www.youtube.com/watch?v=ebJHzpEy4bE on January 3, 2013.

November, A. (2012). *Students as contributors: The digital learning farm*. Accessed at http://novemberlearning.com/resources/articles/students-as-contributors-the -digital-learning-farm on February 22, 2013.

Orfield, G., Kucsera, J., & Siegel-Hawley, G. (2012). *E pluribus . . . separation: Deepening double segregation for more students*. Los Angeles, CA: The Civil Rights Project. Accessed at http://civilrightsproject.ucla.edu/research/k-12 -education/integration-and-diversity/mlk-national/e-pluribus...separation -deepening-double-segregation-for-more-students on February 18, 2013.

Parrett, W. H. , & Budge, K. M. (2012). *Turning high-poverty schools into high-performing schools*. Alexandria, VA: Association for Supervision and Curriculum Development.

Payne, R. K. (2003). *A framework for understanding poverty* (3rd ed.). Highlands, TX: aha! Process.

Pew Center on the States, Economic Mobility Project. (2011). *Economic mobility and the American dream: Where do we stand in the wake of the great recession?* Washington, DC: Pew Charitable Trusts. Accessed at www.pewstates.org /research/analysis/economic-mobility-and-the-american-dream-where-do-we -stand-in-the-wake-of-the-great-recession-85899378421 on September 28, 2012.

Pink, D. (2009). *Drive: The surprising truth about what motivates us*. New York: Riverhead Books.

Powers, R. (n.d.). *U.S. military enlistment standards: Education*. Accessed at http:// usmilitary.about.com/od/joiningthemilitary/a/enleducation.htm on September 28, 2012.

Public Schools of North Carolina. (2000). *School size and its relationship to achievement and behavior*. Raleigh, NC: Author. Accessed at www.ncpublicschools .org/docs/data/reports/size.pdf on January 3, 2013.

Quint, J. (2008). Lessons from leading models. *Educational Leadership, 65*(8), 64–68.

Rammohan, Y. (Interactive Content Producer), & Ponce, P. (Host). (2011, November 7). High dropout rate for Chicago schools. In M. Field (Producer), *Chicago Tonight: Education* [Television broadcast]. Chicago: WTTW. Accessed at http:// chicagotonight.wttw.com/comment/4823 on September 28, 2012.

Ravitch, D. (2010). *The death and life of the great American school system: How testing and choice are undermining education*. New York: Basic Books.

Reardon, S. F. (2011). The widening academic achievement gap between the rich and the poor: New evidence and possible explanations. In G. J. Duncan & R. J.

Murnane (Eds.), *Whither opportunity? Rising inequality, schools, and children's life chances* (pp. 91–116). New York: Sage. Accessed at www.iga.ucdavis.edu/Research /EJS/conferences/spring-conference-2011/reardon%20SIED%20chapter%20 jan%2031%202011.pdf on January 4, 2013.

Richardson, W., & Mancabelli, R. (2011). *Personal learning networks: Using the power of connections to transform education.* Bloomington, IN: Solutions Tree Press.

RMC Research. (2008). *Achieving graduation: New York benchmark high schools.* Portsmouth, NH: Author. Accessed at http://rmcres.com/documents /Magellan.pdf on January 4, 2013.

Rosenthal, R., & Jacobson, L. (1968). *Pygmalion in the classroom: Teacher expectation and pupils' intellectual development.* New York: Holt, Rinehart & Winston.

Rothstein, R. (2008). Whose problem is poverty? *Education Leadership, 65*(7), 8–13.

Rotter, J. (1975). Some problems and misconceptions related to the construct of internal versus external control of reinforcement. *Journal of Consulting and Clinical Psychology, 43*(1), 56–67.

Samuelson, R. (2010). *Why school "reform" fails.* Accessed at www.thedailybeast.com /newsweek/2010/09/06/school-reform-and-student-motivation.html on September 28, 2012.

Sanders, W., & Rivers, J. (1996). *Cumulative and residual effects of teachers on future student academic achievement.* Knoxville: University of Tennessee Value Added Research and Assessment Center.

Sarason, S. (1971). *The culture of the school and the problem of change.* Boston: Allyn & Bacon.

Schargel, F., & Smink, J. (2001). *Strategies to help solve our school dropout problem.* Larchmont, NY: Eye on Education.

Scheier, L. M., & Botvin, G. J. (1996). Purpose in life, cognitive efficacy, and general deviance as determinants of drug abuse in urban black youth. *Journal of Child and Adolescent Substance Abuse, 5*(1), 1–26

Schmoker, M. (2005). No turning back: The ironclad case for professional learning communities. In R. DuFour, R. Eaker, & R. DuFour (Eds.), *On common ground: The power of professional learning communities* (pp. 135–154). Bloomington, IN: Solution Tree Press.

Seligman, M. E. P. (1972). Learned helplessness. *Annual Review of Medicine, 23,* 407–412.

Seligman, M. E. P. (2007). *The optimistic child: A proven program to safeguard children against depression and build lifelong resilience.* Boston: Houghton Mifflin.

Seligman, M. E. P., & Csikszentmihalyi, M. (2000). Positive psychology: An introduction. *American Psychologist, 55,* 5–14.

Shannon, G. S., & Bylsma, P. (2007). *Nine characteristics of high-performing schools: A research-based resource for schools and districts to assist with improving student learning.* (2nd ed.). Olympia, WA: Office of Superintendent of Public Instruction.

Sharot, T. (2011, June 6). The optimism bias. *Time, 177*(23), 40–45.

Siegel, R. (2004). *Lyndon Johnson's war on poverty.* Accessed at www.npr.org/templates /story/story.php?storyId=1589660 on September 28, 2012.

Snyder, C. R. (1995). Managing for high hope. *R&D Innovator, 4*(6), 6–7.

Snyder, C. R., Harris, C., Anderson, J. R., Holleran, S. A., Irving, L. M., Sigmon, S. T., et al. (1991). The will and the ways: Development and validation of an individual-differences measure of hope. *Journal of Personality and Psychology, 60*(4), 570–585.

Snyder, C. R., Shorey, H. S., Cheavens, J., Pulvers, K. M., Adams, V. H., & Wiklund, C. (2002). Hope and academic success in college. *Journal of Educational Psychology, 94*(4), 820–826.

Steinbeck, J. (1939). *The grapes of wrath.* New York: Viking Press.

Stiggins, R. (2001). *Student-involved classroom assessment* (3rd ed.). Upper Saddle River, NJ: Merrill-Prentice Hall.

Street, P. (2005). *Segregated schools: Educational apartheid in post-civil rights America.* New York: Routledge.

Swanson, C. B., & Hightower, A. M. (2011). *Beyond high school, before baccalaureate: Meaningful alternatives to a four-year degree.* Accessed at www.edweek.org/media /dc11_event_presentation1.pdf on September 28, 2012.

Symonds, W. C., Schwartz, R. B., & Ferguson, R. (2011). *Pathways to prosperity: Meeting the challenge of preparing young Americans for the 21st century.* Accessed at www.gse.harvard.edu/news_events/features/2011/Pathways_to_Prosperity _Feb2011.pdf on February 22, 2013.

Tavernise, S. (2012, February 9). Education gap grows between rich and poor, studies say. *The New York Times,* p. A1. Accessed at www.nytimes.com/2012/02/10 /education/education-gap-grows-between-rich-and-poor-studies-show.html?page wanted=all on February 22, 2013.

Tigges, L. M., Browne, I., & Green, G. P. (1998). Social isolation of the urban poor: Race, class, and neighborhood effects on social resources. *The Sociological Quarterly, 39*(1), 53–77.

Tileston, D. W., & Darling, S. K. (2008). *Why culture counts: Teaching children of poverty.* Bloomington, IN: Solution Tree Press.

Tyack, D., & Cuban, L. (1995). *Tinkering toward utopia: A century of public school reform.* Cambridge, MA: Harvard University Press.

Tyack, D., & Tobin, W. (1994). The "grammar" of schooling: Why has it been so hard to change? *American Educational Research Journal, 31*(3), 453–479.

University of New Hampshire. (2011, September). 1 million more children living in poverty since 2009, new census data released today shows. *Science Newsline Economics and Sociology.* Accessed at www.sciencenewsline.com/articles/2011092300090018.html on March 19, 2013.

U.S. Census. (2010). *Computer and Internet use in the United States: 2010—Table 2B: Presence and type of computer for individuals 3 years and older, by selected characteristics.* Accessed at www.census.gov/hhes/computer/publications/2010.html on February 22, 2013.

U.S. Department of Education, Office of Postsecondary Education. (2008). *A profile of the federal TRIO programs and child care access means parents in school programs.* Washington, DC: Author.

U.S. News & World Report. (2012). *Best high schools rankings 2012.* Accessed at www.usnews.com/education/best-high-schools on February 8, 2012

Vancouver Public Schools. (n.d.a). *Career clusters, pathways and programs of study.* Accessed at http://portalsso.vansd.org/portal/page/portal/VSD_Home_Public/VPS_Parent_and_Families/VPS_Programs/VPS Programs of Study on April 11, 2013.

Vancouver Public Schools. (n.d.b). *Magnet and Career and Technical Education (CTE) opportunities.* Accessed at www.vansd.org/docs/CTE_Magnet_Courses2011_12.pdf on April 11, 2013.

Viadero, D. (2008). Majority of youths found to lack a direction in life. *Education Week, 27*(41), 1, 12.

Von Lunen, J. (2012). Vancouver school found success in "opportunity zone." *The Columbia.* Accessed at www.columbian.com/news/2012/jan/11/vancouver-school-success-opportunity-zone on February 22, 2013.

von Zastrow, C. (2009). *Taking things personally: Principal Paul Chartrand speaks about his school's turnaround.* Accessed at www.learningfirst.org/visionaries/PaulChartrand on September 28, 2012.

Webb, S. (2010, November 12). *Highlighting "bright spots"* [Audio podcast]. Accessed at http://portalsso.vansd.org/portal/page/portal/VSD_Home_Public/Webb_eNEWS_September%202008/WEBB_ENEWS_NOVEMBER_2010 on September 28, 2012.

Williams, T., Kirst, M., Haertel, E., Rosin, M., Perry, M., Webman, B., et al. (2010). *Gaining ground in the middle grades: Why some schools do better.* Mountain View,

CA: EdSource. Accessed at www.edsource.org/assets/files/MGstudy2/MG
_EdSourceNarrSummFnl.pdf on September 28, 2012.

Wise, B. (2012). *Raising the grade: How high school reform can save our youth and our nation.* Washington, DC: Alliance for Excellent Education.

Woodruff, V. (n.d.). *Preparing students for success in college, work & life.* Accessed at www.doe.k12.de.us/infosuites/students_family/rhss/opsed/opsed_1.shtml on September 28, 2012.

Zohar, A., Degani, A., & Vaaknin, E. (2001). Teachers' beliefs about low-achieving students and higher order thinking. *Teaching and Teacher Education, 17*(4), 469–485.

Index

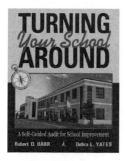

Turning Your School Around
Robert D. Barr and Debra L. Yates
Learn a step-by-step protocol for the self-guided audit that focuses on the most crucial areas of school improvement identified in *The Kids Left Behind*, the nationally recognized work by Robert D. Barr and William H. Parrett.
BKF295

Strengthening the Connection Between School & Home (2nd Edition)
Ricardo LeBlanc-Esparza and Kym LeBlanc-Esparza
Examine the pivotal role family engagement plays in student achievement with this research-based guide. Leaders will find specific strategies to involve families, including 11 ways to create a family-friendly school and advice for connecting with families who are hard to reach.
BKF486

Breaking the Poverty Barrier
Ricardo LeBlanc-Esparza and William S. Roulston
Strong leadership, parent involvement, mentoring, data-based intervention, and high expectations are known factors in student success. This book illustrates the specific strategies and critical steps that transformed a school with shockingly low proficiency into a National Showcase School.
BKF476

Transforming School Culture [Second Edition]
Anthony Muhammad
The second edition of this best-selling resource delivers powerful, new insight into the four types of educators and how to work with each group to create thriving schools. The book also includes Dr. Muhammad's latest research and a new chapter of frequently asked questions.
BKF793

Wait! Your professional development journey doesn't have to end with the last pages of this book.

We realize improving student learning doesn't happen overnight. And your school or district shouldn't be left to puzzle out all the details of this process alone.

No matter where you are on the journey, we're committed to helping you get to the next stage.

Take advantage of everything from **custom workshops** to **keynote presentations** and **interactive web and video conferencing**. We can even help you develop an action plan tailored to fit your specific needs.

Let's get the conversation started.

Call 888.763.9045 today.

 solution-tree.com